5 STEPS TO A >>5

500
AP U.S. History Questions
to Know by Test Day
Third Edition

5 STEPS TO A > 5™

500

AP U.S. History Questions

to Know by Test Day

Third Edition

Scott Demeter

New York Chicago San Francisco Athens London Madrid
Mexico City Milan New Delhi Singapore Sydney Toronto

1 2 3 4 5 6 7 8 9   QFR   24 23 22 21 20 19

ISBN   978-1-260-44195-6
MHID   1-260-44195-4

e-ISBN   978-1-260-44196-3
e-MHID   1-260-44196-2

CONTENTS

ABOUT THE AUTHOR

Scott Demeter teaches and resides in northern New Jersey. His major areas of educational focus include honors and advanced placement programs in American history, world history, U.S. government, and comparative government.

INTRODUCTION

Congratulations! You've taken a big step toward AP success by purchasing *5 Steps to a 5: 500 AP U.S. History Questions to Know by Test Day*. We are here to help you take the next step and score high on your AP exam so you can earn college credits and get into the college or university of your choice!

This book gives you 500 AP-style multiple-choice questions that cover all the most essential course material. Each question has a detailed answer explanation. These questions will give you valuable independent practice to supplement your regular textbook and the groundwork you are already doing in your AP classroom. Furthermore, this new edition incorporates document-based questions to help with the updated components of the exam while maintaining the content questions to make this book useful in preparing for other survey course exams. This and the other books in this series were written by expert AP teachers who know your exam inside out and can identify the crucial exam information, as well as questions that are most likely to appear on the exam.

You might be the kind of student who takes several AP courses and needs to review additional questions several weeks before the exam for a final review. Or you might be the kind of student who puts off preparing until the last weeks before the exam. No matter what your preparation style, you will benefit from reviewing these 500 questions, which closely parallel the content, format, and degree of difficulty of the questions on the actual AP exam. These questions and their answer explanations are the ideal last-minute study tool for those final few weeks before the test.

Remember the old saying "Practice makes perfect." If you practice with all the questions and answers in this book, we are certain you will build the skills and confidence needed to do great on the exam. Good luck!

—Editors of McGraw-Hill Education

5 STEPS TO A 5™

500

AP U.S. History Questions

to Know by Test Day

Third Edition

CHAPTER 1

Pre-Colombian/Native American History

Use the image below and your knowledge of the time period to answer questions 1 to 5.

1. Based on the theory presented on the map, the indigenous people of the Americas would most likely share the closest ancestry with which group?

(A) people of Asian descent

(B) people of European descent

(C) people of African descent

(D) people of Oceanic descent

2. What was the main cause of the exposed land bridge connecting Eurasia to North America?

(A) Extended periods of drought during the last Ice Age lowered ocean levels.

(B) Plate tectonics temporarily led to a rise in the ocean floor within the Bering Sea.

(C) Much of the water in the oceans congealed into vast glacial packs.

(D) Increased snowfall on land during the last Ice Age lowered ocean levels.

3. Which theory best describes the spread of maize as a staple crop through the Native American populations?

(A) Maize was first developed upon the Siberian steppes and carried to the Americas via the land bridge.

(B) Maize was first developed in the region that is now Mexico and spread through the Americas in a slow and uneven process.

(C) The cultivation of maize occurred separately in isolated pockets throughout the two continents.

(D) Maize was developed by the nomadic tribes of North America but was first grown intensively as a staple crop by Native American groups in Central and South America.

4. In Native North American culture along the Eastern Seaboard, the Three Sisters would most accurately refer to

(A) the sustainable agricultural technique of growing maize, beans, and squash

(B) the matrilineal lines upon which most clans were based in this region

(C) the trade and cultural network established between Native Americans living in North America with those in Central and South America

(D) the spiritual belief in three major forces that defined the natural world

5. The early American Indian civilizations of Mexico and Peru were based on which agricultural product?

   (A) wheat
   (B) maize
   (C) cattle
   (D) coffee

Use the image below and your knowledge of the time period to answer questions 6 and 7.

Source: Illinois, Cahokia Mound. Cahokia, Illinois, ca. 1907. Photograph.
https://www.loc.gov/item/97505973/.

6. The Native American Mississippian Valley culture differed from other Native American groups in that it

   (A) existed in mainly seminomadic populations with limited agriculture
   (B) based its social structure on maternal lineage
   (C) had a developed network of trade with other regional tribes
   (D) illustrated a higher level of hierarchical political organization

7. In agricultural terms, how did Native Americans differ from their European counterparts?

(A) Unlike the sedentary European communities, the nomadic lifestyle of the Native Americans limited their ability to develop high-yield strains of vegetation.

(B) Unlike Europeans, Native Americans lacked any efficient means to clear the vast forests to open land for intensive agriculture.

(C) Europeans achieved greater technologies to alter the landscape in a more aggressive manner.

(D) Europeans had a greater diversity in the types of staple crops they used for subsistence.

Use the passage below and your knowledge of the time period to answer questions 8 to 11.

The Great Binding Law (*Constitution of the Iroquois People*) by Gayanashagowa, circa CE 1451

We place you upon those seats . . . beneath the shade of the spreading branches of the Tree of Peace, . . . and all the affairs of the Five Nations shall be transacted at this place. . . A bunch of a certain number of shell strings each two spans in length shall be given to each of the female families in which the Lordship titles are vested. The right of bestowing the title shall be hereditary in the family of the females legally possessing the bunch of shell strings and the strings shall be the token that the females of the family have the proprietary right to the Lordship title for all time to come, subject to certain restrictions hereinafter mentioned.

---

8. Which of the following Native American groups would *not* be associated with the "Five Nations"?

(A) Mohawk

(B) Oneida

(C) Seneca

(D) Powhatan

9. The passage referencing the bestowing of titles of lordship varied from most European cultures of the time in that

    (A) by the fifteenth century much of Europe had moved toward republican forms of government

    (B) European monarchies more commonly were based in male lineage rather than female lineage

    (C) by the fifteenth century most European cultures had abandoned hereditary titles

    (4) European cultures of the time did not create systematic rules for their leaders

10. The preceding passage conflicts with general views of Native American groups of North America in that these groups are most commonly viewed as

    (A) living in dense but isolated pockets throughout the continent

    (B) lacking dense population concentrations or highly developed social life in the modern sense

    (C) independent paternal-based social groups living in small seminomadic populations

    (D) sporadic with inconsistent development between tribes, lacking a common linguistic base

11. The preceding passage illustrates the idea that the Native American clan in North America was primarily based on

    (A) a kinship network

    (B) multiple nuclear families based on paternal lines

    (C) a single religious leader and his followers

    (D) a single chieftain and his warriors with their spouses and children

Use the passage below and your knowledge of the time period to answer questions 12 and 13.

The Saga of Erik the Red, circa thirteenth century English translation by J. Sephton, 1880

Now when spring began, they beheld one morning early, that a fleet of hide-canoes was rowing from the south off the headland; so many were they as if the sea were strewn with pieces of charcoal, and there was also the brandishing of staves as before from each boat. Then they held shields up, and a market was formed between them; and this people in their purchases preferred red cloth; in exchange they had furs to give, and skins quite grey. They wished also to buy swords and lances, but Karlsefni and Snorri forbad it. They offered for the cloth dark hides, and took in exchange a span long of cloth, and bound it round their heads; and so matters went on for a while. But when the stock of cloth began to grow small, then they split it asunder.

---

12. The preceding passage describes early contact between North American Native Americans and

    (A) French fur traders
    (B) English missionaries
    (C) Dutch merchants
    (D) early Norse explorers

13. In reference to the passage, why is L'Anse aux Meadows significant within North American history?

    (A) It marks the first example of pre-Columbian European contact with Native Americans.
    (B) It serves as an example of a highly developed Native American nation state in North America.
    (C) It marks the first example of the cultivation of maize in North America outside of Mexico.
    (D) It illustrates a rare example of a sedentary Native American community.

CHAPTER 2

Early Exploration and the Spanish and French in the Colonies of the New World

Use the document below and your knowledge of the time period to answer questions 14 to 16.

Treaty between Spain and Portugal concluded at Tordesillas June 7, 1494

That, whereas a certain controversy exists between the said lords, their constituents, as to what lands, of all those discovered in the ocean sea up to the present day, the date of this treaty, pertain to each one of the said parts respectively; therefore, for the sake of peace and concord, and for the preservation of the relationship and love of the said King of Portugal for the said King and Queen of Castile, Aragon, etc., it being the pleasure of their Highnesses, they, their said representatives, acting in their name and by virtue of their powers herein described, covenanted and agreed that a boundary or straight line be determined and drawn north and south, from pole to pole, on the said ocean sea, from the Arctic to the Antarctic pole. This boundary or line shall be drawn straight, as aforesaid, at a distance of three hundred and seventy leagues west of the Cape Verde Islands, being calculated by degrees, or by any other manner as may be considered the best and readiest, provided the distance shall be no greater than above said. And all lands, both islands and mainland, found and discovered already, or to be found and discovered hereafter, by the said King of Portugal and by his vessels on this side of the said line and bound determined as above, toward the east, in either north or south latitude, on the eastern side of the said bound provided the said bound is not crossed, shall belong to, and remain in the possession of, and pertain forever to, the said King of Portugal and his successors. And all other lands, both islands and mainland, found or to be found hereafter, discovered or to be discovered hereafter, which have been discovered or shall be discovered by the said King and Queen of Castile, Aragon, etc., and by their vessels, on the western side of the said bound, determined as above, after having passed the said bound toward the west, in either its north or south latitude, shall belong to, and remain in the possession of, and pertain forever to, the said King and Queen of Castile, Leon, etc., and to their successors.

14. The preceding treaty was established by what European leader?
    (A) Ferdinand II of Aragon
    (B) Isabella I of Castile
    (C) Pope Alexander VI
    (D) John II of Portugal

15. In the 1494 Treaty of Tordesillas, the Line of Demarcation was established, granting
    (A) all of the land north of the meridian not already claimed by Christian nations to the Spanish
    (B) all of the land east of the meridian not already claimed by Christian nations to the Spanish
    (C) Portugal the right to establish a colonial empire in South America
    (D) all of the land west of the meridian not already claimed by Christian nations to the Spanish

16. The impact of this treaty can be primarily seen in the contemporary societies of South America through
    (A) Spanish being the dominant language with the exception of Brazil
    (B) Catholicism being widely practiced in Brazil, while the remainder of the continent is primarily Protestant
    (C) the indigenous populations of Brazil remaining more intact than in neighboring South American countries
    (D) the existence of military juntas within South American nations

Use the passage below and your knowledge of the time period to answer questions 17 to 19.

Hernán Cortés: From Second Letter to Charles V (1520)

In these chapels are the images of idols, although, as I have before said, many of them are also found on the outside; the principal ones, in which the people have greatest faith and confidence, I precipitated from their pedestals, and cast them down the steps of the temple, purifying the chapels in which they had stood, as they were all polluted with human blood, shed ill the sacrifices. In the place of these I put images of Our Lady and the Saints, which excited not a little feeling in Montezuma who said that if the idols were ill-treated, these would be angry and the people would perish with famine. I said . . . he must learn there is but one God, the universal Lord of all.

17. Based on the passage, what role did the Catholic Church play in Spain's rule of its colonial possessions in North America?

(A) The pope indirectly ruled the colonies through the Spanish monarchy, requiring papal approval for all policies in the colonies.

(B) Responsibilities to the Catholic Church dominated expansion policies into the northern territories.

(C) The papacy provided the majority of funding for Spanish exploration.

(D) The Spanish missions reported to the pope rather than the Spanish monarchy.

18. Based on the passage and your knowledge of the time period, in what way did early Spanish colonization differ from that of the early French efforts during the 1600s?

(A) Unlike the French, the Spanish made religious conversion a major focus of settlement.

(B) Unlike the Spanish, the French focused on establishing larger permanent communities in their colonies.

(C) The French focused less on the accumulation of wealth and more on territorial expansion than the Spanish.

(D) Unlike the Spanish, the French based much of their colonial economy on the fur trade.

19. Based on the passage and your knowledge of the time period, which of the following statements best describes the reason the Dutch settlers in North America practiced greater religious tolerance?

(A) They were following the policy of tolerance practiced by the French and British in their New World possessions.

(B) Religious tolerance was a method to entice more settlers to their North American colonies.

(C) The Dutch believed religious tolerance would maintain order within their New World possessions.

(D) The major religion of the Dutch called for religious tolerance.

Use the passage below and your knowledge of the time period to answer questions 20 to 22.

Brief Account of the Devastation of the Indies by Bartolomé de Las Casas, 1542

After the wars and the killings had ended, when usually there survived only some boys, some women, and children, these survivors were distributed among the Christians to be slaves. The *repartimiento* or distribution was made according to the rank and importance of the Christian to whom the Indians were allocated, one of them being given thirty, another forty, still another, one or two hundred, and besides the rank of the Christian there was also to be considered in what favor he stood with the tyrant they called Governor. The pretext was that these allocated Indians were to be instructed in the articles of the Christian Faith. As if those Christians who were as a rule foolish and cruel and greedy and vicious could be caretakers of souls! And the care they took was to send the men to the mines to dig for gold, which is intolerable labor, and to send the women into the fields of the big ranches to hoe and till the land, work suitable for strong men. Nor to either the men or the women did they give any food except herbs and legumes, things of little substance.

---

20. The Spanish colonial system defined in the passage of forcing Native Americans to work for individual Spaniards in the Americas was known as

(A) peonage

(B) indentured servitude

(C) encomienda

(D) ejido

21. The Spanish system of forced labor of the Native Americans described in the passage most accurately had its origins in which European event?

(A) the Hundred Years' War

(B) the War of the Spanish Succession

(C) the Anglo–Spanish War

(D) the Reconquista

22. Which of the following theories best explains why the system of labor described in the passage was not successfully employed in the English colonies of North America?

(A) English Protestantism forbade forced labor on religious grounds.

(B) Population densities of indigenous peoples were too little for the system to be effectively utilized.

(C) The English settlers preferred to use trade and land treaties in their dealings with indigenous populations.

(D) The English did not possess the military strength to subjugate the indigenous populations.

Use the image below and your knowledge of the time period to answer questions 23 and 24.

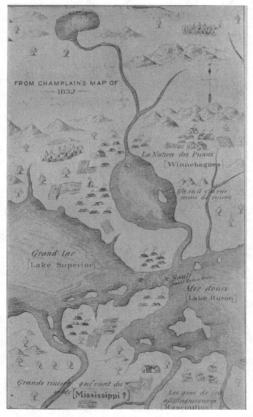

Source: From Champlain's map of 1632. History of Brulé's discoveries and explorations, 1610–1626, by Consul Willshire Butterfield, 1898. LC General Collections.

23. Samuel de Champlain is most associated with

(A) establishing Quebec, France's first permanent settlement in North America

(B) exploring the Great Lakes and upper Mississippi River

(C) exploring the Saint Lawrence River

(D) exploring the lower Mississippi River

24. Based on the map and your knowledge of history, which major resource was acquired by the French in this region?

(A) fur

(B) gold

(C) silver

(D) coal

CHAPTER 3

Early English Colonies

Use the passage below and your knowledge of the time period to answer questions 25 and 26.

> **"Reasons for Raising a Fund to Settle America On the Value of Colonies to England"**
> **by Richard Hakluyt, January 5, 1607**
>
> REASONS OR MOTIVES for the raising of a PUBLIC STOCK to be employed for the peopling and discovering of such countries as may be found most convenient for the supply of those defects which this Realm of England most requires:
> —Where colonies are founded for a public-weal, they may continue in better obedience and become more industrious than where private men are absolute backers of a voyage. Men of better behavior and quality will engage themselves in a public service, which carries more reputation with it, than a private, which is for the most part ignominious in the end, because it is presumed to aim at a profit and is subject to rivalry, fraud, and envy, and when it is at the greatest height of fortune can hardly be tolerated because of the jealousy of the state.

25. The author of this passage, Richard Hakluyt, is arguing that England pursue specifically which type of colony?

   (A) royal colonies
   (B) proprietary colonies
   (C) religious colonies
   (D) joint stock colonies

26. Which statement is the most accurate concerning the North American colonies but also illustrates a rejection of Hakluyt's assertions?

(A) Most of the colonies were able to become profitable within the first years of their creation.

(B) Most of the colonies started as independent colonies but later received charters.

(C) Most of the colonies started as corporate and proprietary but became royal colonies by the mid-eighteenth century.

(D) Most of the colonies started as proprietary colonies but became independent by purchasing their charters.

Use the passage below and your knowledge of the time period to answer questions 27 to 30.

John Winthrop's "City upon a Hill," 1630

Now the only way to avoid this shipwreck, and to provide for our posterity, is to follow the counsel of Micah, to do justly, to love mercy, to walk humbly with our God. For this end, we must be knit together, in this work, as one man. We must entertain each other in brotherly affection. We must be willing to abridge ourselves of our superfluities, for the supply of other's necessities. We must uphold a familiar commerce together in all meekness, gentleness, patience and liberality. We must delight in each other; make other's conditions our own; rejoice together, mourn together, labor and suffer together, always having before our eyes our commission and community in the work, as members of the same body . . . The Lord will be our God, and delight to dwell among us, as his own people, and will command a blessing upon us in all our ways. . . . ; when he shall make us a praise and glory that men shall say of succeeding plantations, "the Lord make it like that of New England." For we must consider that we shall be as a *city upon a hill*. The eyes of all people are upon us.

---

27. The notion of a city upon a hill within the passage is best defined as

(A) a model for an ideal Christian society and rightful living for the rest of Europe

(B) a high elevation settlement to avoid the troubles of disease that the Virginia colony experienced

(C) a utilitarian workers utopia based on the notions of Jeremy Bentham

(D) a model society for the purpose of freedom of religion and religious practice

28. While the passage describes the goals of Puritans in migrating to the colonies, what was the major reason for Catholics migrating to the Americas from England during the 1600s?

(A) The return of a Catholic sovereign to the English monarchy granted them greater rights to establish colonies.

(B) The papacy called upon English Catholics to migrate as a protest to Anglican rule.

(C) Catholic nations in Europe granted them lands within the southern region of the New World.

(D) English Catholics wanted to escape the persecution they faced under Anglican rule.

29. How does Roger Williams's view of "liberty of conscience" illustrate a rejection of the idealism noted in the passage?

(A) It states all people have freedom of speech.

(B) It notes men could avoid military service on religious grounds.

(C) It argues religious freedom requires a separation of church and state.

(D) It argues the press should be free to report honestly about political and religious figures.

30. How did the Toleration Act of 1649 differ from the vision of religion from John Winthrop's sermon?

(A) Its focus was to maintain order in Boston after the passage of the Coercive Acts.

(B) It called for religious protections for Jewish people and other non-Christians.

(C) Its focus was to protected Catholic rights from Protestant persecution.

(D) It extended voting rights to non-Protestants in New England.

Use the passage below and your knowledge of the time period to answer questions 31 to 34.

Letter from London Merchants Urging Repeal of the Stamp Act—January 17, 1766

That the petitioners have been long concerned in carrying on the trade between this country and the British colonies on the continent of North America; and that they have annually exported very large quantities of British manufacturers, consisting of woolen goods of all kinds, cottons, linens, hardware, shoes, household furniture, and almost without exception of every other species of goods manufactured in these kingdoms, besides other articles imported from abroad, chiefly purchased with our manufacturers and with the produce of our colonies. By all which, many thousand manufacturers, seamen and laborers have been employed, to the very great and increasing benefit of this nation; and that, in return for these exports, the petitioners have received from the colonies rice, indigo, tobacco, naval stores, oil, whale fins, furs and, lately potash, with other commodities, besides remittances by bills of exchange and bullion obtained by the colonists in payment for articles of the produce not required for the British market and therefore exported to other places.

From the nature of this trade, consisting of British manufacturers exported and of the imported of raw materials from America, many of them used in our manufactures and all of them tending to lessen our dependence on neighboring states, it must be deemed of the highest importance in the commercial system of this nation;

31. Based on the passage, what was the major function of the colonies?

   (A) They produced manufactured goods for the mother country.
   (B) They operated as independent economic units that required little support from the mother country.
   (C) They produced raw materials for the mother country.
   (D) The created a tax surplus for the mother country's treasury which funded further territorial gain.

32. Based on the passage "Letter from London Merchants," what economic system is specifically being described?

   (A) stochastic
   (B) mercantilism
   (C) qualitative
   (D) laissez-faire

33. Based on the passage and your knowledge of history, how did the Southern Colonies fit into the economic system being described?

   (A) The economy was equally mixed among farming, trade, and small manufacturing.
   (B) The economy was dominated by skilled labor in port towns.
   (C) Tobacco, rice, and indigo served as the major export crops.
   (D) The growth of upland cotton dominated the economy.

34. Which seventeenth-century act would most directly enforce the trade system described in the passage?

(A) the creation of the Dominion of New England

(B) The Declaratory Act

(C) the Act of Supremacy

(D) the Navigation Acts

Use the passage below and your knowledge of the time period to answer questions 35 to 38.

The Interesting Narrative of the Life of Olaudah Equiano, Or Gustavus Vassa, The African Written By Himself, 1789

But I came at length to a country, the inhabitants of which differed from us in all those particulars. I was very much struck with this difference . . . They cooked also in iron pots, and had European cutlasses and cross bows, which were unknown to us. . . . The first object which saluted my eyes when I arrived on the coast was the sea, and a slave ship, which was then riding at anchor, and waiting for its cargo. These filled me with astonishment, which was soon converted into terror when I was carried on board. I was immediately handled and tossed up to see if I were sound by some of the crew; and I was now persuaded that I had gotten into a world of bad spirits, and that they were going to kill me. Their complexions too differing so much from ours, their long hair, and the language they spoke, (which was very different from any I had ever heard) united to confirm me in this belief. . . . When I looked round the ship too and saw a large furnace or copper boiling, and a multitude of black people of every description chained together, every one of their countenances expressing dejection and sorrow, I no longer doubted of my fate; and, quite overpowered with horror and anguish, I fell motionless on the deck and fainted. . . . I now saw myself deprived of all chance of returning to my native country. . . . I was soon put down under the decks, and there I received such a salutation in my nostrils as I had never experienced in my life: so that, with the loathsomeness of the stench, and crying together, I became so sick and low that I was not able to eat, nor had I the least desire to taste anything. . . . I would have jumped over the side, but I could not; and, besides, the crew used to watch us very closely who were not chained down to the decks, lest we should leap into the water: and I have seen some of these poor African prisoners most severely cut for attempting to do so, and hourly whipped for not eating.

35. The author of the passage describes the start of the Middle Passage, which refers to

(A) the passage of African people across the Atlantic to the Americas

(B) the forced passage of Cherokee Indians west

(C) the movement of African Americans out of the southern United States to northern cities

(D) the passage of Irish Catholics to the United States

36. In relation to this passage, what is the African Diaspora?

(A) the strict slave codes put into place to maintain order on plantations

(B) the passage of slaves from West Africa to the Americas

(C) the use of Africans in mines and on plantations as forced labor

(D) the dispersal of Africans throughout the Americas under the system of slavery

37. Which of the following statements does *not* accurately describe slavery in the North American colonies?

(A) The slaves contributed to the growth of the Atlantic economy as shipbuilders and dock workers in the middle colonies.

(B) Slaves in Georgia and South Carolina's coastal region primarily worked on large plantations in dangerous and brutal conditions.

(C) In Virginia, slaves made up a minority of the population and had varied jobs.

(D) Strict slave laws prevented slave revolts through the 1700s.

38. American colonists began to use African slaves primarily because

(A) the European population was too limited to provide the needed labor

(B) the papacy created an edict calling for the use of African slaves in Catholic-controlled lands

(C) the Native Americans were decimated by European disease, while the Africans developed immunity

(D) the African slaves were more accustomed to agriculture than the Native Americans

Use the map below and your knowledge of the period to answer questions 39 to 41.

Source: Gavin, H. (1767) A map of Virginia and Maryland. [Edinburgh?: Publisher not identified] [Map] Retrieved from the Library of Congress, https://www.loc.gov/item/2013587749/.

39. In reference to the map, the Piedmont referred to

(A) foothills of the mountains in western Virginia

(B) the area in eastern Virginia along the major rivers

(C) wide open plains in western Virginia

(D) coastal highlands in the southern part of Virginia

40. Bacon's Rebellion is most associated with which early colony?

(A) Virginia

(B) Maryland

(C) North Carolina

(D) Pennsylvania

41. Which of the following changes was a direct result of Bacon's Rebellion?

(A) Southern colonies began to farm tobacco as a staple export.

(B) A balance of power no longer existed between Native Americans and colonists in New England.

(C) Southern labor shifted from African slaves and began to rely more on indentured servants.

(D) Southern labor moved away from indentured servants and began to rely more on African slaves.

Use the document below and your knowledge of the time period to answer questions 42 to 45.

A Declaration of the State of the Colony and Affaires in Virginia (1622)

This spacious and fruitful Country of Virginia, is (as is generally known to all) naturally rich, and exceedingly well watered, very temperate, and healthful to the Inhabitants, abounding with as many naturall blessings . . . as any Country in the world is known to afford.

In the three last yeares of 1619, 1620, and 1621, there hath been provided and sent for VIRGINIA forty two Sail of ships, three thousand five hundred and seventy men and women for Plantation, with requisite provisions, besides store of Cattle, and in those ships have been about twelve hundred Mariners employed . . . In which space have been granted fifty Patents to particular persons, for Plantation in VIRGINIA, who with their Associates have undertaken therein to transport great multitudes of people and cattle thither . . .

The Letters written from the Governor and Treasurer in VIRGINIA in the beginning of March last, (which came hither in April) gave assurance of ouercomming and bringing to perfection in this year, the Iron-works, Glasse-works, Salt-works, the plentifull sowing of all sorts of English grain with the Plough, having now cleared good quantity of ground; setting of store of Indian Corne or Maize, sufficient for ourselves, and for trade with the Natives; restraint of the quantity of Tobacco, and amendment of it in the quality, learned by time and experience; . . . and for the erecting of a fair inn in James-City (Jamestown) for the better entertainment of newcomers, whereto and to other public works, every old planter there offered freely and liberally to contribute . . .

---

42. The second passage of the excerpt discusses the headright system, which served the purpose of

    (A) opening up more land for tobacco cultivation
    (B) ensuring the separation between slaves and indentured servants
    (C) keeping non-Protestants from taking part in colonial government
    (D) encouraging increased migration to the Virginia Colony

43. In what way did the Jamestown Colony and the Massachusetts Bay Colony differ greatly?

    (A) Unlike Jamestown, Massachusetts Bay was established as a joint stock company.
    (B) Jamestown became a royal colony, while Massachusetts remained a proprietary colony.
    (C) Unlike Jamestown, Massachusetts Bay maintained peaceful relations with the Native Americans within the region.
    (D) Massachusetts Bay did not suffer from the same hardships as Jamestown during its first years.

44. Which of the following statements is *not* true of the House of Burgesses in colonial Virginia?

    (A) It consisted initially of 22 representatives.
    (B) All laws passed by the body could be vetoed by the governor.
    (C) Only landowning males could vote for representatives.
    (D) It was responsible for electing the governor.

45. In reference to the second paragraph and your knowledge of history, the majority of colonists who migrated to Maryland and Virginia during the seventeenth century would be best described as

    (A) wealthy planters
    (B) indentured servants
    (C) bankers and financiers
    (D) African slaves

Use the passage below and your knowledge of the time period to answer questions 46 to 48.

William Penn, Some Account of the Province of Pennsylvania (1681).

These persons that Providence seems to have most fitted for plantations are,

1st. Industrious husbandmen and day laborers, that are hardly able (with extreme labor) to maintain their families and portion their children.

2dly. Laborious handicrafts, especially carpenters, masons, smiths, weavers, tailors, tanners, shoemakers, shipwrights, etc., where they may be spared or are low in the world. And as they shall want no encouragement, so their labor is worth more there than here, and there provision cheaper.

3dly. A plantation seems a fit place for those ingenious spirits that being low in the world, are much clogged and oppressed about a livelihood. For the means of subsisting being easy there, they may have time and opportunity to gratify their inclinations, and thereby improve science and help nurseries of people.

4thly. A fourth sort of men to whom a plantation would be proper, takes in those that are younger brothers of small inheritances; yet because they would live in sight of their kindred in some proportion to their quality, and can't do it without a labor that looks like farming, their condition is too strait for them; and if married, their children are often too numerous for the estate, and are frequently bred up to no trades, but are a kind of hangers on or retainers to the elder brothers' table and charity; which is a mischief, as in itself to be lamented, so here to be remedied. For land they have for next to nothing, which with moderate labor produces plenty of all things necessary for life, and such an increase as by traffic may supply them with all conveniences.

---

46. Based on the origin of this passage, what was the primary reason for creating this document?

(A) limit movement to Pennsylvania by setting stringent requirements

(B) attract a variety of laborers of all skill levels and incomes to move to the colony

(C) discourage those of means from moving to Pennsylvania to allow for a more egalitarian government

(D) establish a society that strictly reflected Quaker ideals

47. The 4th point directly addressed which practice in England at the time?

(A) The older male heirs of the aristocracy inherited most of the wealth, leaving younger heirs less prosperous.

(B) English land titles could not be inherited by Quakers.

(C) Because of the return of the house of Stuart, many families lost their land titles.

(D) English law limited family size to better control overpopulation.

48. Which of the following statements is not true about the colony of Pennsylvania?

(A) It increased its population through heavy advertising by paid agents.

(B) Because of Quaker beliefs, it strongly supported upholding land treaties with the Native Americans.

(C) It did not require taxes to fund a state-held church.

(D) It allowed Catholics and Jews to vote and hold public office.

Use the document and knowledge of the time period to answer questions 49 to 51.

Albany Plan of Union 1754

It is proposed that humble application be made for an act of Parliament of Great Britain, by virtue of which one general government may be formed in America, including all the said colonies, within and under which government each colony may retain its present constitution, except in the particulars wherein a change may be directed by the said act, as hereafter follows.

1. That the said general government be administered by a President-General, to be appointed and supported by the crown; and a Grand Council, to be chosen by the representatives of the people of the several Colonies met in their respective assemblies. . . . in the following proportion, that is to say,

Massachusetts Bay	7
New Hampshire	2
Connecticut	5
Rhode Island	2
New York	4
New Jersey	3
Pennsylvania	6
Maryland	4
Virginia	7
North Carolina	4
South Carolina	4
Total	48

7. That the Grand Council have power to choose their speaker; and shall neither be dissolved, prorogued, nor continued sitting longer than six weeks at one time, without their own consent or the special command of the crown.

10. That the President-General, with the advice of the Grand Council, hold or direct all Indian treaties, in which the general interest of the Colonies may be concerned; and make peace or declare war with Indian nations.

11. That they make such laws as they judge necessary for regulating all Indian trade.

12. That they make all purchases from Indians, for the crown, of lands not now within the bounds of particular Colonies, or that shall not be within their bounds when some of them are reduced to more convenient dimensions.

14. That they make laws for regulating and governing such new settlements, till the crown shall think fit to form them into particular governments.

15. That they raise and pay soldiers and build forts for the defense of any of the Colonies, and equip vessels of force to guard the coasts and protect the trade on the ocean, lakes, or great rivers; but they shall not impress men in any Colony, without the consent of the Legislature.

16. That for these purposes they have power to make laws, and lay and levy such general duties, imposts, or taxes, as to them shall appear most equal and just (considering the ability and other circumstances of the inhabitants in the several Colonies), and such as may be collected with the least inconvenience to the people; rather discouraging luxury, than loading industry with unnecessary burdens.

25. That the particular military as well as civil establishments in each Colony remain in their present state, the general constitution notwithstanding; and that on sudden emergencies any Colony may defend itself, and lay the accounts of expense thence arising before the President-General and General Council, who may allow and order payment of the same, as far as they judge such accounts just and reasonable.

49. The described government body above is most similar to which of the following in terms of representation?

(A) the Senate

(B) the House of Representatives

(C) the Articles of Confederation

(D) the House of Burgesses

50. Based on the apportionment of representation noted in the first clause, which assertion would be the most valid?

(A) The newer colonies had the largest number of apportioned seats.

(B) Most of the colonial population was concentrated in the southern colonies.

(C) The two oldest colonies also had the largest number of apportioned seats.

(D) The population of each colony directly correlated to is overall size.

51. The purpose of raising a colonial military would most likely be done for protection against which group?

(A) the French

(B) the Spanish

(C) the Iroquois Confederacy

(D) the British Royal Army

Use the passage below and your knowledge of the time period to answer questions 52 to 54.

A Letter to William Pitt, 1762

Sir,

I can address you in no terms more proper than those at are sometimes made use from the throne, *the eyes of all Europe are upon you*; I say *of all Europe*, because the resolutions of the British Parliament, in which you have so extensive an influence, in great measure decide the fate of the public, whether Great Britain shall bend, or endeavor to break the neck of France.

There seems, Sir, to be no medium; she has offered to submit to the former; your friends insist upon the later; they insist that there is no safety for our American interests should France be allowed to keep a foot of ground on the continent. . . .

When our present dispute with France began, we had not in our eye a single objective, but the ascertainment of the bounds of Canada . . . All that we then wanted was to secure our back settlements. Security and protection against the encroachments of the French was the ultimatum of our' designs. Not a whisper transpired about Canada, and far less about Guadeloupe or Martinico.

Some very disagreeable incidents, such as the defeat of Braddock, and the taking of our forts in America, changed the aspect of the war greatly to our prejudice. I am far from wanting to revive the remembrance of disagreeable events; but I am certain, that the shameful disputes that reigned over all the British interests' in America confirmed the obstinacy and increased the intolerance of the French.

52. Based on the origin of the document, this letter is most likely describing which conflict directly?

   (A) King William's War
   (B) Queen Anne's War
   (C) King George's War
   (D) the French and Indian War

53. Based on the document and your knowledge of history, what was the initial objective of the conflict?

   (A) protecting the British Colonies of North America
   (B) removing French competition within the sugar trade
   (C) capturing the colonies of Guadeloupe or Martinico
   (D) capturing the colony of Canada

54. Based on the document and your knowledge of history, what is the ultimate objective of Great Britain in North America?

   (A) the regaining of forts lost to the French during the first part of the conflict
   (B) the complete removal of France from North America
   (C) a speedy resolution of fighting and peace agreement with the French
   (D) a normalization of trade with France after the conflicts resolution

CHAPTER 4

The Era of Discontent and War for Independence

Use the document and your knowledge of the time period to answer questions 55 to 57.

The Royal Proclamation
By King George, October 7, 1763

And whereas it is just and reasonable, and essential to our Interest, and the Security of our Colonies, that the several Nations or Tribes of Indians with whom We are connected, and who live under our Protection, should not be molested or disturbed in the Possession of such Parts of Our Dominions and Territories as, not having been ceded to or purchased by Us, are reserved to them, or any of them, as their Hunting Grounds.

And We do further . . . reserve under our Sovereignty, Protection, and Dominion, for the use of the said Indians, all the Lands and Territories not included within the Limits of Our said Three new Governments . . . . And We do hereby strictly forbid, on Pain of our Displeasure, all our loving Subjects from making any Purchases or Settlements whatever, or taking Possession of any of the Lands above reserved.

We do further strictly enjoin and require all Persons whatever who have either willfully or inadvertently seated themselves upon any Lands within the Countries above described . . . forthwith to remove themselves from such Settlements.

55. The Proclamation of 1763 was most associated with the end of which of the following conflicts?

(A) American War for Independence

(B) Queen Anne's War

(C) the French and Indian War

(D) King George's War

56. The tensions created by the Proclamation of 1763 are most similar to the tensions caused by what later British actions toward the North American colonists?

(A) the Quartering Act

(B) the Quebec Act

(C) the Townshend Acts

(D) the Currency Act

57. Based on the second paragraph, the Proclamation of 1763 was similar to the later Northwest Ordinance of 1787 in that they both

(A) limited expansion into the Ohio River Valley

(B) attempted to offer protections for Native American land claims

(C) were put in place to limit the emergence of manufacturing

(D) contained provisions limiting slavery

Use the document and your knowledge of the time period to answer questions 58 to 60.

The Objections to the taxation consider'd by Soame Jenyns, 1765

The right of the Legislature of Great-Britain to impose taxes on her American Colonies, and the expedicocy of exerting that right in the present conjuncture, are propositions so indisputably clear, that I should never have thought it necessary to have undertaken their defense, had not many arguments been lately flung out, both in papers and conversation, which with insolence equal to their absurdity deny them both. As these are usually mixt up with several patriotic and favorite words such as Liberty, Property, Englishmen, etc. . . .

I am well aware, that I shall hear Locke . . . quoted to prove that every Englishman, whether he has a right to vote for a representative, or not, is still represented in the British Parliament; in which opinion they all agree . . . . If the towns of Manchester and Birmingham sending no representatives to parliament, are notwithstanding there represented, why are not the cities of Albany and Boston equally represented in that assembly? Are they not alike British subjects? Are they not Englishmen? Or are they only Englishmen when they solicit for protection, but not Englishmen when taxes are required to enable this country to protect them?

58. The notion of "virtual representation" alluded to in this passage is best defined as which of the following?

(A) The British government represents all citizens, regardless of their actual representation in Parliament.

(B) Although slaves lack the right to vote, they need to be considered when conducting an official government census.

(C) Paper currency has value as long as it is backed by precious metal.

(D) Only those males who own land can rightly participate in government and vote.

59. Based on the origin of the document, Soame Jenyns would most likely be criticizing the American colonists for

(A) their rejection of the Townshend Acts

(B) their protests of the Coercive Acts

(C) their rejection of the Stamp Act

(D) their failure to enforce the Navigation Acts

60. The assertion that "The right of the Legislature of Great-Britain to impose taxes on her American Colonies . . . so indisputably clear" best reflects the assertion made in which of the following British actions?

(A) the Sugar Act

(B) the Declaratory Act

(C) the Stamp Act

(D) the Townshend Acts

Use the document and your knowledge of the period to answer questions 61 and 62.

Examination before the Committee of the Whole of the House of Commons, 13 February 1766

Parliament Member: What is your name, and place of abode?

Benjamin Franklin: Franklin, of Philadelphia . . .

Parliament Member: What was the temper of America towards Great-Britain before the year 1763?

Benjamin Franklin: The best in the world. They submitted willingly to the government of the Crown, and paid, in all their courts, obedience to acts of parliament . . .

Parliament Member: And what is their temper now?

Benjamin Franklin: Oh, very much altered.

Benjamin Parliament Member: Did you ever hear the authority of parliament to make laws for America questioned till lately?

Benjamin Franklin: The authority of parliament was allowed to be valid in all laws, except such as should lay internal taxes. It was never disputed in laying duties to regulate commerce.

Parliament Member: What is your opinion of a future tax, imposed on the same principle with that of the stamp-act; how would the Americans receive it?

Benjamin Franklin: Just as they do this. They would not pay it.

Parliament Member: Have not you heard of the resolutions of this House, and of the House of Lords, asserting the right of parliament relating to America, including a power to tax the people there?

Franklin: Yes, I have heard of such resolutions.

Parliament Member: What will be the opinion of the Americans on those resolutions?

Benjamin Franklin: They will think them unconstitutional and unjust.

Parliament Member: Was it an opinion in America before 1763, that the parliament had no right to lay taxes and duties there?

Benjamin Franklin: I never heard any objection to the right of laying duties to regulate commerce; but a right to lay internal taxes was never supposed to be in parliament, as we are not represented there.

Parliament Member: If the act is not repealed, what do you think will be the consequences?

Benjamin Franklin: A total loss of the respect and affection the people of America bear to this country, and of all the commerce that depends on that respect and affection.

Parliament Member: How can the commerce be affected?

Benjamin Franklin: You will find, that if the act is not repealed, they will take very little of your manufactures in a short time.

61. When Benjamin Franklin states, "they will take very little of your manufactures in a short time," he is describing the colonial practice of

(A) virtual representation

(B) salutary neglect

(C) nonimportation

(D) impressment

62. Based on the passage discussing internal taxes, what would Benjamin Franklin see as the major difference between the earlier Sugar Act and the Stamp Act?

(A) Because he was the Post Master General at the time, the Stamp Act would affect him more directly.

(B) Sugar was distinctly a luxury item and unneeded in the colonies.

(C) The Stamp Act was placed directly upon goods in the colonies, while the Sugar Act was on goods shipped into the colonies.

(D) The colonists had representation in Parliament with the Sugar Act, but had lost representation prior to the passage of the Stamp Act.

Use the passage and your knowledge of the time period to answer questions 63 and 64.

Speech by John Adams at the Boston Massacre Trial, 1770

The next witness that knows anything, was, James Bailey . . ., he saw some round the Sentry, heaving pieces of ice, large and hard enough to hurt any man, as big as your fist: one question is whether the Sentinel was attacked or not. If you want evidence of an attack upon him there is enough of it, here is a witness an inhabitant of the town, surely no friend to the soldiers . . . he says he saw twenty or thirty round the Sentry, pelting with cakes of ice, as big as one's fist; certainly cakes of ice of this size may kill a man, if they happen to hit some part of the head. So that, here was an attack on the Sentinel, the consequence of which he had reason to dread, and it was prudent in him to call for the Main-Guard: he retreated as far as he could, he attempted to get into the Custom-house, but could not; then he called to the Guard, and he had a good right to call for their assistance . . .

This witness certainly is not prejudiced in favor of the soldiers, he swears, he saw a man come up to Montgomery with a club, and knock him down before he fired, and that he not only fell himself, but his gun flew out of his hand, and as soon as he rose he took it up and fired. If he was knocked down on his station, had he not reason to think his life in danger, or did it not raise his passions and put him off his guard; so that it cannot be more than manslaughter . . .

Bailey "Saw the Mulatto seven or eight minutes before the firing, at the head of twenty or thirty sailors in Corn-hill, and he had a large cordwood stick." So that this Attucks . . . appears to have undertaken to be the hero of the night; and to lead this army with banners, to form them in the first . . . march them up to King-street, with their clubs . . . up to the Main-guard, in order to make the attack. If this was not an unlawful assembly, there never was one in the world. . . . when the soldiers pushed the people off, this man with his party cried, do not be afraid of them, they dare not fire, kill them! kill them! knock them over! And he tried to knock their brains out.

It is plain the soldiers did not leave their station, but cried to the people, standoff: now to have this reinforcement coming down under the command of a stout Mulatto fellow, whose very looks, was enough to terrify any person, what had not the soldiers then to fear? He had hardiness enough to fall in upon them, and with one hand took hold of a bayonet, and with the other knocked the man down: This was the behavior of Attucks; to whose mad behavior, in all probability, the dreadful carnage of that night, is chiefly to be ascribed.

63. Which reason would most likely explain why John Adams represented the British soldiers following the Boston Massacre?

   (A) Adams hoped to use Crispus Attuck's race to tighten black codes in Boston.

   (B) Adams was still an outspoken Loyalist and disagreed with the emerging Patriot movement.

   (C) Adams felt all citizens had a right to trial and the necessity of the rule of law.

   (D) Adams hoped his actions would gain a pardon for his brother, Samuel Adams.

64. Why does Adams argue that the British Officer Montgomery was not guilty of murder when he fired his rifle?

   (A) Adams argued soldiers had the right to kill in the line of duty.

   (B) The rifle only discharged after Montgomery was knocked to the ground after being clubbed.

   (C) Lethal force was justified because it was an unlawful assembly.

   (D) Montgomery was threatened verbally, so he was justified under self-defense.

Use the document and your knowledge of the time period to answer questions 65 to 67.

The Declaration of Independence
July 4, 1776

When in the Course of human events, it becomes necessary for one people to dissolve the political bands which have connected them with another, and to assume among the powers of the earth, the separate and equal station to which the Laws of Nature and of Nature's God entitle them, a decent respect to the opinions of mankind requires that they should declare the causes which impel them to the separation.

> We hold these truths to be self-evident, that all men are created equal, that they are endowed by their Creator with certain unalienable Rights that among these are Life, Liberty and the pursuit of Happiness. . . . The history of the present King of Great Britain is a history of repeated injuries and usurpations, all having in direct object the establishment of an absolute Tyranny over these States. To prove this, let Facts be submitted to a candid world.
>
> He has dissolved Representative Houses repeatedly, for opposing with manly firmness his invasions on the rights of the people.
>
> He has combined with others to subject us to a jurisdiction foreign to our constitution, and unacknowledged by our laws; giving his Assent to their Acts of pretended Legislation:
>
> For quartering large bodies of armed troops among us:
>
> For cutting off our Trade with all parts of the world:
>
> For imposing Taxes on us without our Consent:

65. Which of the following issues was *not* addressed in the Declaration of Independence?

(A) the disbanding of colonial governments

(B) the principle that all men deserve access to equal wealth

(C) the idea of taxation without representation

(D) the trade restrictions being placed on the colonies

66. What movement most directly influenced the writing of the Declaration of Independence?

(A) scholasticism

(B) humanism

(C) transcendentalism

(D) the Enlightenment

67. The Declaration of Independence is most similar to Thomas Paine's *Common Sense* in that both

(A) utilized colloquial and common terminology, making it accessible to commoners

(B) strongly denounced the institution of slavery within their list of stated grievances

(C) primarily focused their cases for independence in grievances against the British Parliament

(D) primarily focused their cases for independence in grievances against the British king

Use the map and your knowledge of the time period to answer questions 68 to 73.

Battles of the American War for Independence

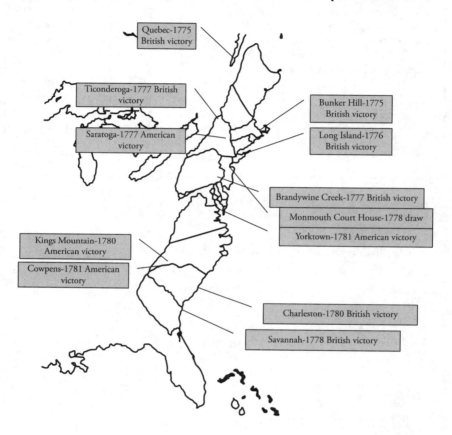

68. Based on the map, after 1778, the British military adopted a strategy of

(A) using Native American allies to regain control of the West and then march east to the Atlantic

(B) adopting a defensive strategy and winning through attrition

(C) ending the revolution by cutting off New England from the rest of the colonies

(D) capturing key southern ports with the aid of loyalist militias, and then advancing northward

69. General Charles Cornwallis was forced to surrender at Yorktown mainly because
    (A) the British failed to capture key southern ports such as Charleston and Savannah
    (B) the Spanish agreed to reinforce Washington's army at Cowpens
    (C) the French navy won control of the Chesapeake Bay
    (D) the Americans successfully recaptured New York City

70. Which Revolutionary War battle is considered the turning point in favor of the American colonists?
    (A) Brandywine
    (B) Saratoga
    (C) Long Island
    (D) Monmouth

71. Which of the following battles did *not* include the presence of George Washington?
    (A) Saratoga
    (B) Brandywine
    (C) Monmouth Court House
    (D) Trenton

72. Which of the following was *not* an advantage of the British during the American Revolution?
    (A) They had a superior navy.
    (B) They had more Native American allies.
    (C) They successfully utilized loyalist support.
    (D) They had a greater treasury.

73. Which of the following statements best describes the role African Americans played in the American Revolution?
    (A) The colonists actively enlisted black slaves to build up the Continental Army's strength.
    (B) The British army adopted a policy of enlisting runaway slaves and offered emancipation to gain support.
    (C) After the war, Britain returned most of the slaves who attempted to seek refuge in Canada.
    (D) African Americans did not play a significant role during the American Revolution.

Use the document and your knowledge of the time period to answer questions 74 and 75.

The Paris Peace Treaty of September 30, 1783

Article 1:

His Britannic Majesty acknowledges the said United States, viz., New Hampshire, Massachusetts Bay, Rhode Island and Providence Plantations, Connecticut, New York, New Jersey, Pennsylvania, Maryland, Virginia, North Carolina, South Carolina and Georgia, to be free sovereign and independent states, that he treats with them as such, and for himself, his heirs, and successors, relinquishes all claims to the government, propriety, and territorial rights of the same and every part thereof.

Article 2:

And that all disputes which might arise in future on the subject of the boundaries of the said United States may be prevented, it is hereby agreed and declared, that the following are and shall be their boundaries . . . thence through the said lake to the most northwestern most point thereof, and from thence on a due west course to the river Mississippi; thence by a line to be drawn along the middle of the said river Mississippi until it shall intersect the northernmost part of the thirty-first degree of north latitude . . .

Article 6:

That there shall be no future confiscations made nor any prosecutions commenced against any person or persons for, or by reason of, the part which he or they may have taken in the present war, and that no person shall on that account suffer any future loss or damage, either in his person, liberty, or property; and that those who may be in confinement on such charges at the time of the ratification of the treaty in America shall be immediately set at liberty, and the prosecutions so commenced be discontinued.

Article 7:

There shall be a firm and perpetual peace between his Britannic Majesty and the said states, and between the subjects of the one and the citizens of the other, wherefore all hostilities both by sea and land shall from henceforth cease. All prisoners on both sides shall be set at liberty, and his Britannic Majesty shall with all convenient speed, and without causing any destruction, or carrying away any Negroes or other property of the American inhabitants, withdraw all his armies, garrisons, and fleets from the said United States, and from every post, place, and harbor within the same; leaving in all fortifications, the American artillery that may be therein. . . .

Article 8:

The navigation of the river Mississippi, from its source to the ocean, shall forever remain free and open to the subjects of Great Britain and the citizens of the United States.

74. Which of the following terms was *not* part of the 1783 Treaty of Paris?

(A) Britain agreed to remove troops from U.S. territory.

(B) The importation of slaves was banned.

(C) The borders of the United States were established.

(D) The United States agreed not to persecute loyalists remaining in the country.

75. Which of the following described the overall impact of the conclusion of American War for Independence on the Native Americans?

(A) They participated in the peace talks, directly leading to the finalized Treaty of Paris.

(B) Earlier land protections granted by the British government were extended to the new American government.

(C) They faced harsh treatment and lost further land under the independent United States.

(D) Only tribes that sided with the British were punished by the new government.

CHAPTER 5

The Constitution and Early U.S. Government

Use the document and your knowledge of the period to answer questions 76 to 79.

George Washington to Henry Knox, Mount Vernon, Virginia, February 3, 1787.

My dear Sir,

I feel myself exceedingly obliged to you for the full, & friendly communications in your letters . . . and shall . . . . be extremely anxious to know the issue of the movements of the forces that were assembling, the one to support, the other to oppose the constitutional rights of Massachusetts. – The moment is, indeed, important! – If government shrinks, or is unable to enforce its laws; fresh maneuvers will be displayed by the insurgents – anarchy & confusion must prevail – and everything will be turned topsy-turvey in that State; where it is not probable the mischiefs will terminate.

In your letter of the 14th, you express a wish to know my intention respecting the Convention, proposed to be held at Philadelphia, in May next. In confidence I inform you, that it is not, at this time, my purpose to attend it.

The legality of this Convention I do not mean to discuss, nor how problematical the issue of it may be. That powers are wanting, none can deny. Through what medium they are to be derived, will, like other matters, engage public attention. That which takes the shortest course to obtain them, will, in my opinion, under present circumstances, be found best. Otherwise, like a house on fire, whilst the most regular mode of extinguishing it is contending for, the building is reduced to ashes. My opinion of the energetic wants of the federal government are well known, publicly & privately, I have declared it; and however constitutionally it may be for Congress to point out the defects of the federal system, I am strongly inclined to believe that it would not be found the most efficacious channel for the recommendation, more especially the alterations, to flow, for reasons too obvious to enumerate. The System on which you seem disposed to build a national government . . . is certainly more energetic, and I dare say, in every point of view is more desirable than the present one; which, from experience; we find is not only slow, debilitated, and liable to be thwarted by every breath, but is defective in that secrecy, which for the accomplishment of many of the most important national purposes, is indispensably necessary; and besides, having the Legislative, Executive & Judiciary departments concentered, is exceptionable. But at the same time I give this opinion, I believe that the political machine will yet be much tumbled & tossed, and possibly be wrecked altogether, before such a system as you have defined, will be adopted. – The darling Sovereignties of the States individually, – The Governors elected & elect. The Legislators . . . whose political consequence will be lessened, if not annihilated, would give their weight of opposition to such a revolution.

76. Based on the document, what unrest is being described by Washington in Massachusetts?

(A) Gabriel Prosser's Rebellion

(B) Bacon's Rebellion

(C) Shays' Rebellion

(D) the Whiskey Rebellion

77. Based on the passage, which of the following best describes Washington's views of the proposed Philadelphia Convention?

(A) While he supports the notion of a stronger federal government, he is concerned about its legalities and the divisions it will create.

(B) He finds the proposed convention too revolutionary and strongly disagrees with the notion of a stronger central government.

(C) He strongly supports the convention and the notion of a strong central government despite states' rights groups' opposition.

(D) He plans to attend it with his state's delegation, but has not made up his mind on the type of reforms to government he supports.

78. Which of the following people would best serve as an example of a supporter of the notion of "darling Sovereignties of the States"?

(A) Alexander Hamilton

(B) John Jay

(C) James Madison

(D) George Mason

79. While Washington notes his concerns about the strength of the Articles of Confederation, which of the following powers was vested within that government?

    (A) the power to regulate interstate trade

    (B) the power to tax

    (C) the power to declare war

    (D) the power to regulate foreign trade

80. Which of the following would *not* be similarities between the Articles of Confederation and the Southern Confederacy during the American Civil War?

    (A) The states retained most of the political power in both.

    (B) Both governments had limited power to raise an army.

    (C) Both had the ability to raise revenue from the states through direct taxes.

    (D) Both called for a weak central government.

Use the passage and your knowledge of the time period to answer questions 81 to 83.

Federal v. Consolidated Government
Brutus, no. 1 October 18th, 1787

The first question that presents itself on the subject is, whether a confederated government be the best for the United States or not? Or in other words, whether the thirteen United States should be reduced to one great republic, governed by one legislature, and under the direction of one executive and judicial; or whether they should continue thirteen confederated republics, under the direction and controul of a supreme federal head for certain defined national purposes only?

This enquiry is important, because, although the government reported by the convention does not go to a perfect and entire consolidation, yet it approaches so near to it, that it must, if executed, certainly and infallibly terminate in it.

This [new] government is to possess absolute and uncontrollable powers, legislative, executive and judicial, with respect to every object to which it extends, for by the last clause of section eighth, article first, it is declared, that the Congress shall have power "to make all laws which shall be necessary and proper for carrying into execution the foregoing powers, and all other powers vested by this Constitution in the government of the United States, or in any department or office thereof."

81. The author of this passage would most likely support the views of which of the following?

    (A) Federalists
    (B) Anti-Federalists
    (C) Loyalists
    (D) Constitutionalists

82. Which of the following beliefs would *not* be held by the author of the passage?

    (A) The "necessary and proper" clause gave the central government too much power.
    (B) The government should be able to hold a standing army in times of peace.
    (C) Power was best vested in the hands of state governments.
    (D) The executive branch threatened states' rights.

83. Which of the following framers of the Constitution would most likely disagree with the sentiments of this passage?

    (A) Patrick Henry
    (B) Samuel Adams
    (C) George Mason
    (D) Alexander Hamilton

Use the passage and your knowledge of the time period to answer questions 84 to 86.

Notes on the Debates in the Federal Convention by James Madison, 1787

Mr. Pinkney moved "that the National Legislature should have authority to negative all Laws which they should judge to be improper." He urged that such a universality of the power was indispensably necessary to render it effectual; that the States must be kept in due subordination to the nation; that if the States were left to act of themselves in any case, it would be impossible to defend the national prerogatives . . .

Mr. Madison . . . In a word, to recur to the illustrations borrowed from the planetary System, this prerogative of the General Govt. is the great pervading principle that must control the centrifugal tendency of the States; which, without it, will continually fly out of their proper orbits and destroy the order & harmony of the political system . . .

Mr. Mason, argued strongly for an election of the larger branch by the people. It was to be the grand depository of the democratic principle of the Government. . . . It ought to know and sympathize with every part of the community. . . . He admitted that we had been too democratic but was afraid we should incautiously run into the opposite extreme. We ought to attend to the rights of every class of the people. . . . Every selfish motive therefore, every family attachment, ought to recommend such a system of policy as would provide no less carefully for the rights and happiness of the lowest than of the highest orders of Citizens.

84. Mr. Pinkney's statement would raise which of the following concerns amongst the Anti-Federalists?
   (A) The "necessary and proper" clause gave the central government too much power.
   (B) The government should be able to hold a standing army in times of peace.
   (C) A Bill of Rights was necessary.
   (D) Power was best vested in the hands of state governments.

85. Mr. Mason's statement would illustrate which of the Anti-Federalist beliefs?
   (A) The common people should have the ability to participate directly in government.
   (B) The federal government would oppress the powers of the state governments.
   (C) The common people lack the education to participate in government.
   (D) A Bill of Rights was necessary to protect individual rights from the central government.

86. Which of the following framers of the Constitution would most likely view a Bill of Rights as a threat to individual liberties?
   (A) Patrick Henry
   (B) George Mason
   (C) James Madison
   (D) Alexander Hamilton

Use the document and your knowledge of the time period to answer questions 87 to 90.

The Virginia Plan and New Jersey Plan, 1787

Virginia Plan, 1787

1. Resolved, that the Articles of Confederation ought to be so corrected and enlarged as to accomplish the objects proposed by their institution, namely common Defense, Security of Liberty and general welfare.
2. Resolved therefore, that the rights of Suffrage in the National Legislature ought to be proportioned to the Quotas of contribution, or to the number of free inhabitants, as the one or the other rule may seem best in different cases.
3. Resolved, that the National Legislature ought to consist of two branches.
4. Resolved, that the Members of the first Branch of the National Legislature ought to be elected by the people of the several States . . .
5. Resolved, that the members of the second branch of the National Legislature ought to be elected by those of the first, out of a proper number of persons nominated by the individual Legislatures. . . .
6. Resolved, that each Branch ought to possess the right of originating Acts, that the National Legislature ought to be empowered to enjoy, the Legislative rights vested in Congress by the Confederation, and moreover to Legislate in all cases to which the Separate States are incompetent; or in which the harmony of the United States may be interrupted, by the exercise of individual Legislation . . .
7. Resolved, that a National Executive be instituted; to be chosen by the National Legislature . . . and that beside a general authority to execute the National laws, it ought to enjoy the Executive rights vested in Congress by the Confederation.
8. Resolved, that the Executive and a convenient number of the National Judiciary, ought to compose a Council of revision, with authority to examine every act of the National Legislature before it shall operate, and every act of a particular Legislature before a negative thereon shall be final . . .

New Jersey Plan, 1787

1. Resolved, that the Articles of Confederation ought to be so revised, corrected, and enlarged as to render the federal Constitution adequate to the exigencies of Government, and the preservation of the Union.
2. Resolved, that in addition to the Powers vested in the United States in Congress by the present existing Articles of Confederation, they be authorized to . . . pass Acts for the regulation of trade and commerce, as well with foreign Nations . . .

3. Resolved, that whenever requisitions shall be necessary, instead of the rule for making requisition mentioned in the Articles of Confederation, the United States in Congress be authorized to make such requisitions in proportion to the whole number of white and other free citizens and Inhabitants of every age, sex and condition, including those bound to servitude for a term of years, and three fifths of all other persons not comprehended in the foregoing description—(except Indians not paying Taxes) . . .

4. Resolved, that the United States in Congress be authorized to elect a federal Executive . . . besides their general authority to execute the federal Acts, ought to appoint all federal officers not otherwise provided for, and to direct all military operations; provided that none of the persons composing the federal Executive shall on any occasion take command of any troops so as personally to conduct any enterprise as General or in any other capacity.

5. Resolved, that a federal Judiciary be established, to consist of a supreme Tribunal, the Judges of which to be appointed by the Executive . . . That the Judiciary so established shall have authority to hear and determine in the first instance on all impeachments of federal officers, and by way of appeal in the dernier resort in all cases touching the rights of Ambassadors, in all cases of captures from an enemy, in all cases of piracies and felonies on the high Seas, in all cases in which foreigners may be interested in the construction of any treaty or treaties, or which may arise on any of the Acts for regulation of trade . . .

87. The New Jersey plan differed from the Virginia Plan in that

(A) the Virginia Plan called for a bicameral legislative branch, while the New Jersey Plan called for a unicameral legislative branch

(B) The New Jersey Plan called for the creation of a judicial branch, while the Virginia Plan did not

(C) the Virginia Plan called for the creation of the executive branch, while the New Jersey plan did not

(D) the Virginia Plan sought to maintain most of the Articles of Confederation, while the New Jersey Plan directly rejected it

88. The New Jersey Plan would most likely be supported by

(A) states with large populations

(B) states with small populations

(C) states that were mostly agricultural

(D) states in the North

89. Article 3 of the New Jersey Plan states, "three fifths of all other persons not comprehended in the foregoing description." Which of the following statements best describes the overall impact of the Three-Fifths Compromise?

(A) The institution of slavery became officially recognized under the Constitution.

(B) The compromise gave the Southern states a clear majority in the House of Representatives.

(C) The compromise provided a clear method for amending the Constitution.

(D) The compromise secured the Northern states' support for the Constitution.

90. Article 8 of the Virginia Plan alludes to judicial review which is best defined as

(A) the Supreme Court's power to strike down laws that are unconstitutional

(B) the requirement that the Senate approve all Supreme Court nominations

(C) the president's right to appoint judges to the Supreme Court

(D) the establishment of lower federal circuit courts

Use the document and your knowledge of the time period to answer questions 91 to 94.

Report on the Subject of Manufactures
by Alexander Hamilton
December 5th, 1791

The Secretary of the Treasury in obedience to the order of ye House of Representatives, of the 15th day of January 1790, has applied his attention, at as early a period as his other duties would permit, to the subject of Manufactures; and particularly to the means of promoting such as will tend to render the United States, independent on foreign nations, for military and other essential supplies. And he there [upon] respectfully submits the following Report.

The expediency of encouraging manufactures in the United States, which was not long since deemed very questionable, appears at this time to be pretty generally admitted. The embarrassments, which have obstructed the progress of our external trade, have led to serious reflections on the necessity of enlarging the sphere of our domestic commerce: the restrictive regulations, which in foreign markets abridge the vent of the increasing surplus of our Agricultural produce, serve to beget an earnest desire, that a more extensive demand for that surplus may be created at home . . . which are or may be experienced, as well as an accession of resources, favorable to national independence and safety.

There still are, nevertheless, respectable patrons of opinions, unfriendly to the encouragement of manufactures. The following are, substantially, the arguments, by which these opinions are defended.

"In every country (say those who entertain them) Agriculture is the most beneficial and productive object of human industry. This position, generally, if not universally true, applies with peculiar emphasis to the United States, on account of their immense tracts of fertile territory, uninhabited and unimproved . . .

"To endeavor by the extraordinary patronage of Government, to accelerate the growth of manufactures, is in fact, to endeavor, by force and art, to transfer the natural current of industry, from a more, to a less beneficial channel . . . This under the quick sighted guidance of private interest, will, if left to itself, infallibly find its own way to the most profitable employment: and 'tis by such employment, that the public prosperity will be most effectually promoted. To leave industry to itself, therefore, is, in almost every case, the soundest as well as the simplest policy.

91. Alexander Hamilton's "Report on Manufacturing" was similar to the "American System" issued by Henry Clay in the following ways *except*

(A) both plans made use of tariffs to help promote the growth of manufacturing

(B) both plans saw the importance of developing an internal economy

(C) both saw economic growth between an expansion of agriculture and manufacturing

(D) the Democratic-Republicans championed both plans for the United States' development

92. Which of the following groups would most likely support the policies of Alexander Hamilton?

(A) states that independently paid off their debt from the Revolution

(B) western farmers

(C) entrepreneurs in manufacturing

(D) strict constitutionalists

93. Hamilton's statement that, "To leave industry to itself, therefore, is, in almost every case, the soundest as well as the simplest policy," best illustrates the ideology of:

(A) mercantilism

(B) capitalism

(C) physiocracy

(D) Malthusianism

94. Alexander Hamilton's debt plan consolidated the nation's Revolutionary War debts into one debt to be paid off by

(A) American merchants

(B) the individual states

(C) the national government

(D) foreign investors

Use the following passage and your knowledge of the period to answer questions 95 and 96.

Washington's Farewell Address by George Washington, 1796

The great rule of conduct for us in regard to foreign nations is in extending our commercial relations, to have with them as little political connection as possible. So far as we have already formed engagements, let them be fulfilled with perfect good faith. Here let us stop.

Europe has a set of primary interests which to us have none; or a very remote relation.

In contemplating the causes which may disturb our Union, it occurs as matter of serious concern that any ground should have been furnished for characterizing parties by geographical discriminations, Northern and Southern, Atlantic and Western; whence designing men may endeavor to excite a belief that there is a real difference of local interests and views. One of the expedients of party to acquire influence within particular districts is to misrepresent the opinions and aims of other districts. You cannot shield yourselves too much against the jealousies . . . which spring from these misrepresentations; they tend to render alien to each other those who ought to be bound together by fraternal affection.

I have already intimated to you the danger of parties in the State, with particular reference to the founding of them on geographical discriminations. Let me now take a more comprehensive view, and warn you in the most solemn manner against the baneful effects of the spirit of party generally . . .

It serves always to distract the public councils and enfeeble the public administration. It agitates the community with ill-founded jealousies and false alarms, kindles the animosity of one part against another, foments occasionally riot and insurrection.

The great rule of conduct for us in regard to foreign nations is in extending our commercial relations, to have with them as little political connection as possible. So far as we have already formed engagements, let them be fulfilled with perfect good faith. Here let us stop . . . Hence, therefore, it must be unwise in us to implicate ourselves by artificial ties in the ordinary vicissitudes of her politics, or the ordinary combinations and collisions of her friendships or enmities.

Our detached and distant situation invites and enables us to pursue a different course. If we remain one people under an efficient government, the period is not far off when we may defy material injury from external annoyance; when we may take such an attitude as will cause the neutrality we may at any time resolve upon to be scrupulously respected; when belligerent nations, under the impossibility of making acquisitions upon us, will not lightly hazard the giving us provocation; when we may choose peace or war, as our interest, guided by justice, shall counsel.

95. When George Washington states, "In regard to foreign nations is in extending our commercial relations, to have with them as little political connection as possible," he is echoing which earlier action of policy during his presidency?

(A) the supremacy of the federal government as illustrated by the suppression of the Whiskey Rebellion

(B) his earlier support for Alexander Hamilton's financial plan for the United States

(C) his Declaration of Neutrality in response to the French Revolution

(D) his rejection of the development of political parties

96. Which of the following people served as an example of an individual who sought to interfere with Washington's declaration of United States neutrality during the French Revolution?

(A) Edmond-Charles Genêt

(B) Charles Talleyrand

(C) Ferdinand Maximilian

(D) Georges Clemenceau

Use the image below and your knowledge of the time period to answer questions 97 to 99.

Property protected—à la Françoise

Source: Property protected—à la Françoise. America, 1798. [London: Pubd. by S.W. Fores, June 1] [Photograph] Retrieved from the Library of Congress, https://www.loc.gov/item/93509853/.

97. Based on the origin of the image above, it is most likely depicting which of the following events?

(A) the Alien and Sedition Acts

(B) Jay's Treaty

(C) the XYZ Affair

(D) the Treaty of Alliance

98. Based on the origin of the image, it most likely is depicting what perspective?

(A) the viewpoint of the Democratic-Republicans

(B) the viewpoint of Great Britain

(C) the viewpoint of France

(D) the viewpoint of Spain

99. Which action taken by the U.S. government was a direct response to the events depicted in the image?

(A) the Whiskey Tax

(B) the Declaration of Neutrality

(C) the Non-Intercourse Act

(D) the Alien and Sedition Acts

Use the document and your knowledge of the time period to answer questions 100 and 101.

Transcript of *Marbury v. Madison* (1803)

By the constitution of the United States, the President is invested with certain important political powers, in the exercise of which he is to use his own discretion, and is accountable only to his country in his political character, and to his own conscience. To aid him in the performance of these duties, he is authorized to appoint certain officers, who act by his authority and in conformity with his orders. . . .

The constitution vests the whole judicial power of the United States in one Supreme Court, and such inferior courts as congress shall, from time to time, ordain and establish. This power is expressly extended to all cases arising under the laws of the United States; and, consequently, in some form, may be exercised over the present case; because the right claimed is given by a law of the United States . . .

In the distribution of this power it is declared that "the Supreme Court shall have original jurisdiction in all cases affecting ambassadors, other public ministers and consuls, and those in which a state shall be a party. In all other cases, the Supreme Court shall have appellate jurisdiction . . ."

Certainly all those who have framed written constitutions contemplate them as forming the fundamental and paramount law of the nation, and consequently, the theory of every such government must be, that an act of the legislature, repugnant to the constitution, is void.

---

100. The notion that, "an act of the legislature, repugnant to the constitution, is void." helped establish the precedent for

(A) judicial review

(B) lower federal courts

(C) executive privilege

(D) the position of the attorney general

101. The *Marbury v. Madison* decision strengthened the power of the

    (A) executive branch

    (B) judicial branch

    (C) judicial and executive branches

    (D) legislative and judicial branches

Use the image and your knowledge of the time period to answer questions 102 and 103.

The Prairie Dog sickened at the sting of the HORNET or a Diplomatic puppet exhibiting his deceptions

Source: James Akin. "The PRAIRIE DOG Sickened at the Sting of the HORNET or a Diplomatic Puppet exhibiting his Deceptions," Newburyport, Massachusetts. c. 1806.

102. Based on its origin and purpose, the cartoon above is most likely mocking which of the following events?

    (A) the election of Thomas Jefferson

    (B) the Louisiana Purchase

    (C) the beginning of the War of 1812

    (D) the passage of Jefferson's embargo

103. The sentiments depicted in the cartoon would most directly reflect the views of

(A) the Jeffersonian Democratic-Republicans

(B) the Federalists

(C) western farmers

(D) the French government

Use the image and your knowledge of the time period to answer questions 104 and 105.

Source: Cruikshank, G. (1813) British valour and Yankee boasting or, Shannon versus Chesapeake / G. Cruikshank fect. United States, 1813. September 1st. [Photograph] Retrieved from the Library of Congress, https://www.loc.gov/item/99471628/.

104. The image above most directly reflects which factor leading to the War of 1812?

(A) the act impressment during the Chesapeake Incident

(B) Native American attacks in the western frontier

(C) the disruption of trade by caused by the British Orders of Counsel

(D) attacks by the Barbary pirates

105. Based on the image, what commentary is being made about the American sailors?

(A) They are well organized and proud.

(B) They are disorganized and cowardly.

(C) They are valiant, yet overpowered.

(D) They are overwhelming the better-trained British forces.

Use the passage below and your knowledge of the time period to answer questions 106 to 108.

Tecumseh to Governor Harrison at Vincennes August 20th, 1810

I would not then come to Governor Harrison to ask him to tear the treaty and to obliterate the landmark. But I should say to him: Sir, you have liberty to return to your own country. The Being within, communing with past ages, tells me that . . . until lately there was no white man on this continent; that it then all belonged to red men, children of the same parents, placed on it by the Great Spirit that made them, to keep it, to traverse it, to enjoy its productions, and to fill it with the same race—once a happy race, since made miserable by the white people, who are never contented, but always encroaching. The way—and the only way—to check and to stop this evil is for all the red men to unite in claiming a common equal right in the land, as it was at first, and should be yet. For it never was divided, but belongs to all for the use of each. That no part has a right to sell, even to each other, much less to strangers, those who want all, and will not do with less. The white people have no right to take the land from the Indian, because they had it first. It is theirs. They may sell, but all must join. Any sale not made by all is not valid. The late sale is bad. It was made by a part only. Part do not know how to sell. It requires all to make a bargain for all. All red men have equal rights to the unoccupied land. The right of occupancy is as good in one place as in another. There cannot be two occupations in the same place. The first excludes all others. It is not so in hunting or traveling; for there the same ground will serve many, as they may follow each other all day. But the camp is stationary, and that is occupancy. It belongs to the first who sits down on his blanket or skins which he has thrown upon the ground; and till he leaves it no other has a right . . .

---

106. Based on the passage, why does Tecumseh argue that the land sale being described is invalid?

(A) He states the natives that sold the land were tricked by white settlers during the land deal.

(B) He believes the land was sold too cheaply and did not reflect its actual value.

(C) He feels that all of the natives must agree to the land sale because more than one group used the land.

(D) He feels that since the natives had developed the land with permanent settlements, it could no longer be sold.

107. Based on the passage, Tecumseh's views would contrast with other Native Americans such as Handsome Lake in that, unlike Tecumseh, Handsome Lake would support which policy?

(A) full assimilation into American society

(B) the development of sedentary agriculture

(C) ending land treaties with the U.S. government

(D) total rejection of white society

108. Which of the following objectives was *not* a goal of Tecumseh's confederacy noted in his speech?

(A) creating a broad alliance to stop settlers

(B) working for the common defense of the confederacy

(C) establishing a new settlement west of the Mississippi River

(D) stopping future treaties that ceded land

Use the passage and your knowledge of the time period to answer questions 109 to 111.

James Madison's War Message to Congress, June 1, 1812

To the Senate and House of Representatives of the United States:

I communicate to Congress certain documents, being a continuation of those heretofore laid before them on the subject of our affairs with Great Britain.

Without going back beyond the renewal in 1803 of the war in which Great Britain is engaged, and omitting unrepaired wrongs of inferior magnitude, the conduct of her Government presents a series of acts hostile to the United States as an independent and neutral nation. British cruisers have been in the continued practice of violating the American flag on the great highway of nations, and of seizing and carrying off persons sailing under it. . . . British jurisdiction is thus extended to neutral vessels in a situation where no laws can operate but the law of nations and the laws of the country to which the vessels belong. . . .

. . . under the pretext of searching for these (British subjects), thousands of American citizens, under the safeguard of public law and of their national flag, have been torn from their country and from everything dear to them; have been dragged on board ships of war of a foreign nation . . . to risk their lives in the battles of their oppressors. . . .

British cruisers have been in the practice also of violating the rights and the peace of our coasts. They hover over and harass our entering and departing commerce . . . and have wantonly spilt American blood. . . .

. . . our commerce has been plundered in every sea, the great staples of our country have been cut off from their legitimate markets, and a destructive blow aimed at our agricultural and maritime interests. . . .

. . . Great Britain . . . formally avowed (declared) a determination to persist in them (insults to American maritime rights) against the United States until the markets of her enemy (Britain's enemy, France) should be laid open to British products, thus asserting an obligation on a neutral power (the U.S.) to require one belligerent (combatant in a war) to encourage by its internal regulations the trade of another belligerent

In reviewing the conduct of Great Britain toward the United States our attention is necessarily drawn to the warfare just renewed by the savages (Native Americans) on one of our extensive frontiers - a warfare which is known to spare neither age nor sex and to be distinguished by features peculiarly shocking to humanity. It is difficult to account for . . . their hostility . . . without recollecting the authenticated examples of such interpositions (British intrigues with the Indians). . . .

We behold, in fine, on the side of Great Britain, a state of war against the United States, and on the side of the United States a state of peace toward Great Britain.

Whether the United States shall continue passive (not to take any action) . . . or, opposing force to force in defense of their national rights, shall commit a just cause into the hands of the Almighty Disposer of Events . . . is a solemn question which the Constitution wisely confides to the legislative department of the Government. In recommending it to their early deliberations I am happy in the assurance that the decision will be worthy the enlightened and patriotic councils of a virtuous, a free, and a powerful nation.

. . . the communications last made to Congress on the subject of our relations with France will have shown that since the revocation of her decrees, as they violated the neutral rights of the United States, her Government has authorized illegal captures by its privateers and public ships, and that other outrages have been practiced on our vessels and our citizens. . . . I abstain (refrain) at this time from recommending to the consideration of Congress definitive measures with respect to that nation (France), in the expectation that the result of . . . discussions between our minister . . . at Paris and the French Government will speedily enable Congress to decide with greater advantage on the course due to the rights, the interests, and the honor of our country.

109. Based on the passage, which of the following causes of the War of 1812 was *not* discussed?

   (A) Britain's support of Native American uprisings

   (B) British impressments of American sailors

   (C) a desire to take Spanish-held lands in North America

   (D) Britain's disruption of United States' trade and commerce

110. Which group of people would most reject Madison's statement and support the Hartford Convention?

(A) New England merchants

(B) Southern plantation owners

(C) western frontiersmen

(D) Democratic-Republicans

111. Which of the following statements does *not* describe a direct result of the War of 1812?

(A) British impressments of American ships increased.

(B) The United States gained further fishing rights along the eastern Canadian coast.

(C) The border between Canada and the United States was restored to the prewar locations.

(D) American domestic manufacturing increased.

CHAPTER 6

The Era of Good Feelings to the Age of Jackson

Use the document and your knowledge of the time period to answer questions 112 to 114.

Transcript of *McCulloch v. Maryland* (1819)

Chief Justice Marshall delivered the opinion of the Court.

The result is a conviction that the States have no power, by taxation or otherwise, to retard, impede, burden, or in any manner control, the operations of the constitutional laws enacted by Congress to carry into execution the powers vested in the general government . . .

This opinion does not deprive the States of any resources which they originally possessed . . . But this is a tax on the operations of the bank, and is, consequently, a tax on the operation of an instrument employed by the government of the Union to carry its powers into execution. Such a tax must be unconstitutional.

---

112. Which of the following was a major result of the *McCulloch v. Maryland* decision?

(A) It established the federal government's right to regulate interstate commerce.

(B) It stated that the national bank was illegal.

(C) It prevented states from interfering with business contracts

(D) It enforced the principle that the federal government has authority over state governments.

113. What event led to the *McCulloch v. Maryland* case?

(A) Maryland attempted to nullify tariffs imposed by the federal government.

(B) Maryland attempted to stop the appointment of a federal judge.

(C) Maryland attempted to impose a tax on the national bank.

(D) Maryland tried to regulate interstate commerce.

114. Unlike *McCulloch v. Maryland,* which of the following Supreme Court decisions directly dealt with Native American territorial rights?

(A) *Worcester v. Georgia*

(B) *Dartmouth College v. Woodward*

(C) *Marbury v. Madison*

(D) *Gibbons v. Ogden*

Use the document and your knowledge of the time period to answer questions 115 and 116.

Missouri Compromise (1820)

An Act to authorize the people of the Missouri territory to form a constitution and state government, and for the admission of such state into the Union on an equal footing with the original states, and to prohibit slavery in certain territories.

Be it enacted by the Senate and House of Representatives of the United States of America, in Congress assembled, That the inhabitants of that portion of the Missouri territory included within the boundaries herein after designated, be, and they are hereby, authorized to form for themselves a constitution and state government, and to assume such name as they shall deem proper; and the said state, when formed, shall be admitted into the Union, upon an equal footing with the original states, in all respects whatsoever . . .

SEC. 7. And be it further enacted, That in case a constitution and state government shall be formed for the people of the said territory of Missouri, the said convention or representatives, as soon thereafter as may be, shall cause a true and attested copy of such constitution or frame of state government, as shall be formed or provided, to be transmitted to Congress.

SEC. 8. And be it further enacted. That in all that territory ceded by France to the United States, under the name of Louisiana, which lies north of thirty-six degrees and thirty minutes north latitude, not included within the limits of the state, contemplated by this act, slavery and involuntary servitude, otherwise than in the punishment of crimes, whereof the parties shall have been duly convicted, shall be, and is hereby, forever prohibited: Provided always, That any person escaping into the same, from whom labour or service is lawfully claimed, in any state or territory of the United States, such fugitive may be lawfully reclaimed and conveyed to the person claiming his or her labour or service as aforesaid.

115. Which of the following statements about the Missouri Compromise is *not* true?

(A) Maine was admitted into the Union as a free state.

(B) Missouri joined the Union as a slave state.

(C) Slavery was allowed in the Old Northwest Territory.

(D) Slavery was outlawed north of latitude 36°30′ north.

116. Which of the following was a direct result of the Missouri Compromise?

(A) The balance of free and slave states ended.

(B) Slavery was allowed only in states south of Missouri's northern border.

(C) Kentucky outlawed slavery.

(D) The state of Maine was created.

Use the document and your knowledge of the time period to answer questions 117 to 119.

Epistle of Condolence from a Slave-Lord to a Cotton-Lord
Thomas Moore (1833)

Alas! My dear friend, what a state of affairs!
How unjustly we both are despoil'd of our rights!
Not a pound of black flesh shall I leave to my heirs,
Nor must *you* any more work to death little whites.
Both forced to submit to that general controller
Of Kings, Lords, and cotton-mills – Public Opinion;
Nor more shall *you* beat with a big billy-roller,
Nor *I* with the cart-whip assert my dominion.
Whereas, were we suffered to do as we please
With our Blacks and our Whites, as of yore we were let,
We might range them alternate, like harpsichord keys,
And between us thump out a good piebald duet.

---

117. The author of this passage is attempting to make which argument through satire?

(A) Southern slave owners mistreat slaves, while factory owners take care of their employees.

(B) Northern factories labor conditions are much worse than the conditions on Southern plantations.

(C) Both Northern factories and Southern plantations exploit their workers for personal gain.

(D) Organized labor is addressing both the plight of factory and agricultural workers.

118. What does the author argue will stop abuses he describes in his work?

(A) the creation of strong unions to represent both skilled and non-skilled labor

(B) stricter federal regulations on textile production in both the North and the South

(C) improved compulsory education which includes classes in music and the arts

(D) public opinion and action calling on the end of these practices

119. Industrialism emerged in the Northern states prior to the Civil War as a result of all of the following conditions *except*

(A) availability of water power from streams and rivers

(B) availability of capital

(C) a shortage of labor

(D) poor agricultural conditions

Use the chart and your knowledge of the time period to answer questions 120 to 122.

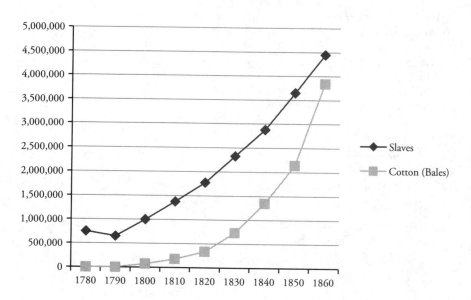

Cotton Production and Slavery from the Late Eighteenth Century to 1860

120. Which of the following best describes the practice of slavery from the end of the American Revolution to 1793?

    (A) The number of slaves was gradually decreasing.

    (B) All Northern states abolished the practice of slavery.

    (C) Most slaves worked on cotton plantations.

    (D) The federal government did not formally acknowledge the practice of slavery.

121. Based on the chart, at the start of the Civil War, roughly how many slaves were in the United States?

    (A) 2.8 million

    (B) 1.3 million

    (C) 3.8 million

    (D) 4.4 million

122. A limitation of this chart would be the following:

    (A) It does not note the amount of cotton being produced each decade.

    (B) It does not clarify the increase of slaves by decade.

    (C) It does not account for non-cotton-related factors and slavery.

    (D) It does not illustrate the growth of slavery versus cotton production.

Use the document and your knowledge of the time period to answer questions 123 and 124.

"Reports on the Strike," *Boston Transcript* (1834)

"We learn that extraordinary excitement was occasioned at Lowell, last week, by an announcement that the wages paid in some of the departments would be reduced 15 percent on the 1st of March. The reduction principally affected the female operatives, and they held several meetings, or caucuses, at which a young woman presided, who took an active part in persuading her associates to give notice that they should quit the mills, and to induce them to 'make a run' on the Lowell Bank and the Savings Bank, which they did. On Friday morning, the young woman referred to was dismissed, by the Agent . . . and on leaving the office . . . waved her calash in the air, as a signal to the others, who were watching from the windows, when they immediately 'struck' and assembled about her, in despite of the overseers.

"The number soon increased to nearly 800. A procession was formed, and they marched about the town, to the amusement of a mob of idlers and boys, and we are sorry to add, not altogether to the credit of Yankee girls. . . . We are told that one of the leaders mounted a stump and made a flaming Mary Wollstonecraft speech on the rights of women and the iniquities of the 'monied aristocracy,' which produced a powerful effect on her auditors, and they determined to 'have their way if they died for it.'"

123. In relation to the passage, "we are sorry to add, not altogether to the credit of Yankee girls," which of the following statements best defines the cult of domesticity?

- (A) Women should exemplify the notions of virtue in fulfilling their duties to the family.
- (B) Slave women needed to be taught how to fulfill their duties as mothers.
- (C) Education should include a heavy focus on manners and conduct.
- (D) Religious education was an important part of public schooling to avoid domestic cults.

124. The first national labor union in the United States was the

- (A) International Workers Union
- (B) Knights of Labor
- (C) National Trades Union
- (D) National Labor Union

Use the document and your knowledge of the time period to answer questions 125 to 128.

Monroe Doctrine by James Monroe, 1823

At the proposal of the Russian Imperial Government, made through the minister of the Emperor residing here, a full power and instructions have been transmitted to the minister of the United States at St. Petersburg to arrange by amicable negotiation the respective rights and interests of the two nations on the northwest coast of this continent. . . . [T]he occasion has been judged proper for asserting, as a principle . . . that the American continents . . . are henceforth not to be considered as subjects for future colonization by any European powers. . . .

Of events in that quarter of the globe . . . we have always been anxious and interested spectators. The citizens of the United States cherish sentiments the most friendly in favor of the liberty and happiness of their fellowmen on that side of the Atlantic. In the wars of the European powers . . . we have never taken any part. . . . It is only when our rights are invaded or seriously menaced that we resent injuries or make preparation for our defense. . . . The political system of the allied powers is essentially different in this respect from that of America. . . . We owe it, therefore, to . . . the amicable relations existing between the United States and those powers to declare that we should consider any attempt on their part to extend their system to any portion of this hemisphere as dangerous to our peace and safety. With the existing colonies or dependencies of any European power we have not interfered and shall not interfere.

> It is impossible that the allied powers should extend their political system to any portion of either continent . . . nor can anyone believe that our southern brethren . . . would adopt it of their own accord. It is equally impossible . . . we should behold such interposition in any form with indifference. If we look to the comparative strength and resources of Spain and those new Governments, and their distance . . . it must be obvious that she can never subdue them. It is still the true policy of the United States to leave the parties to themselves, in the hope that other powers will pursue the same course.

125. Which of the following was *not* a provision of the initial Monroe Doctrine?

(A) The United States would use military intervention in the Western Hemisphere if needed.

(B) The Americas were politically different from the nations of Europe.

(C) The Western Hemisphere was closed to colonization.

(D) The United States would not intervene in European wars and conflicts.

126. Which of the following did *not* lead to the creation of the Monroe Doctrine?

(A) France's desire to reassert itself in the Western Hemisphere

(B) Russia's ambitions in the Pacific Northwest

(C) England's interest in annexing Texas

(D) the emergence of independent Latin American states

127. In the passage, the negotiations at St. Petersburg were in regard to what area of land?

(A) Florida

(B) the Hawaiian Islands

(C) the Oregon Territory

(D) Alaska

128. The Monroe Doctrine asserts which of the following observations?

(A) The United States will serve as the chief arbitrator in the Western Hemisphere.

(B) The systems of government in Europe are decidedly different from those in the Western Hemisphere.

(C) The United States had the right to assist in the liberation of other European colonies in the region.

(D) The Latin American nations are unstable and require protection from the United States.

Use the document and your knowledge of the time period to answer questions 129 to 132.

> ## The American System, Henry Clay, speech to the Senate (1832)
>
> Eight years ago, it was my painful duty to present to the other house of Congress an unexaggerated picture of the general distress pervading the whole land. We must all yet remember some of its frightful features. We all know that the people were then oppressed and borne down by an enormous load of debt; that the value of property was at the lowest point of depression; that ruinous sales and sacrifices were everywhere . . .
>
> This transformation of the condition of the country from gloom and distress to brightness and prosperity has been mainly the work of American legislation, fostering American industry, instead of allowing it to be controlled by foreign legislation, cherishing foreign industry. The foes of the American System, in 1824, with great boldness and confidence, predicted . . . The ruin of the public revenue, and the creation of a necessity to resort to direct taxation . . . the destruction of our navigation . . . the desolation of commercial cities . . . and the augmentation of the price of objects of consumption, and further decline in that of the articles of our exports. Every prediction which they made has failed-utterly failed . . .
>
> And I now say, preserve the protective system in full vigor, give us the proceeds of the public domain for internal improvements, or, if you please, partly for that object, and partly for the removal of the free blacks, with their own consent, from the United States . . .

129. The economic theory referred to as the American System can best be described in the following manner.

    (A) The United States consisted of regions that were complementary to economic development.
    (B) The United States should maintain its agricultural heritage instead of pursuing manufacturing.
    (C) The United States should focus on internal trade and isolation.
    (D) The United States should pursue a policy of free trade, avoiding protective tariffs.

130. In terms of public improvements, which construction project connected New York City to the Great Lakes?

    (A) Erie Canal
    (B) Baltimore & Ohio Railroad
    (C) Cumberland Road
    (D) National Highway

131. The statement that "for the removal of the free blacks, with their own consent, from the United States" relates to the goals of the American Colonization Society during the early part of the nineteenth century in that the society supported

(A) expanding the U.S. influence in the Pacific

(B) returning free blacks to Africa

(C) ending slavery and emancipating all non-free people

(D) gaining territory in Africa

132. The American System was a major factor of the Era of Good Feelings, which is most associated with which presidency?

(A) Thomas Jefferson

(B) James K. Polk

(C) Andrew Jackson

(D) James Monroe

Use the chart and your knowledge of the time period to answer questions 133 to 135.

U.S. Presidential Election 1824

Candidate	Electoral Vote	Popular Vote	States Won
Andrew Jackson	99	43.1%	Al, Ill, In, La, Md, Ms, NC, NJ, Pa, SC, Tn
John Quincy Adams	84	30.5%	Ct, Ma, Me, NH, NY, RI, Vt
William Crawford	41	13.1%	De, Ga, Va
Henry Clay	37	13.2%	Ky, Mo, Oh
	131 = Electoral Majority		

133. Which of the following statements best describes the result of the 1824 presidential election?

(A) John Quincy Adams won the popular vote.

(B) No candidate won the majority of electoral votes.

(C) Andrew Jackson won the majority of electoral votes.

(D) The election was decided by the Senate.

134. Based on the chart, John Quincy Adams had his strongest support in which region?

(A) New England

(B) the Mid-Atlantic

(C) the South

(D) the Western states

135. Based on the chart, Andrew Jackson and Henry Clay seemed to share the most similar popularity in which region?

(A) New England

(B) the Mid-Atlantic

(C) the South

(D) western states

Use the document and your knowledge of the time period to answer questions 136 to 139.

How Equality Suggests to the Americans the Idea of the Indefinite Perfectibility of Man Democracy in America, Book II: Chapter VIII Alexis de Tocqueville: (1835)

The English laws concerning the transmission of property were abolished in almost all the States at the time of the Revolution. The law of entail was so modified as not to interrupt the free circulation of property. The first generation having passed away, estates began to be parcelled out, and the change became more and more rapid with the progress of time. At this moment, after a lapse of a little more than sixty years, the aspect of society is totally altered; the families of the great landed proprietors are almost all commingled with the general mass.

Equality suggests to the human mind several ideas which would not have originated from any other source, and it modifies almost all those previously entertained. I take as an example the idea of human perfectibility, because it is one of the principal notions that the intellect can conceive, and because it constitutes of itself a great philosophical theory, which is everywhere to be traced by its consequences in the conduct of human affairs.

Although man has many points of resemblance with the brutes, one trait is peculiar to himself,—he improves: they are incapable of improvement. Mankind could not fail to discover this difference from the beginning. The idea of perfectibility is therefore as old as the world; equality did not give birth to it, but has imparted to it a new character.

When the citizens of a community are classed according to rank, profession, or birth, and when all men are constrained to follow the career which chance has opened before them, everyone thinks that the utmost limits of human power are to be discerned in proximity to himself, and no one seeks any longer to resist the inevitable law of his destiny. Not, indeed, that an aristocratic people absolutely deny man's faculty of self-improvement, but they do not hold it to be indefinite; they can conceive amelioration, but not change: they imagine that the future condition of society may be better, but not essentially different; and, whilst they admit that humanity has made progress, and may still have some to make, they assign to it beforehand certain impassable limits.

Thus, they do not presume that they have arrived at the supreme good or at absolute truth, (what people or what man was ever wild enough to imagine it?) but they cherish a persuasion that they have pretty nearly reached that degree of greatness and knowledge which our imperfect nature admits of; and, as nothing moves about them, they are willing to fancy that everything is in its fit place. Then it is that the legislator affects to lay down eternal laws; that kings and nations will raise none but imperishable monuments; and that the present generation undertakes to spare generations to come the care of regulating their destinies . . .

I accost an American sailor, and inquire why the ships of his country are built so as to last but for a short time; he answers without hesitation, that the art of navigation is every day making such rapid progress, that the finest vessel would become almost useless if it lasted beyond a few years. In these words, which fell accidentally, and on a particular subject, from an uninstructed man, I recognize the general and systematic idea upon which a great people direct all their concerns.

Aristocratic nations are naturally too apt to narrow the scope of human perfectibility; democratic nations, to expand it beyond reason.

136. According to Alexis de Tocqueville, what happens to a society when it is divided into social classes?

(A) It creates clear and organized social order.

(B) It promotes self-improvement in one's defined area.

(C) It limits individual and social progress.

(D) It leads to disorder and revolution.

137. What was Alexis de Tocqueville's opinion of the "scope of human perfectibility" in aristocratic verses democratic societies?

(A) Both aristocratic and democratic societies naturally narrow improvement and growth.

(B) Aristocratic societies naturally narrow improvement and growth, while democratic societies encourage it.

(C) Democratic and aristocratic societies play a limited role, as it is up to an individual to find improvement regardless of social class.

(D) Class division is inevitable in both democratic and aristocratic societies, so human perfectibility can never be achieved.

138. Which of the following was an observation of Alexis de Tocqueville concerning American society?

(A) the perpetual gap between the rich and poor

(B) the continued notion of European aristocracy

(C) the ability of newcomers to own land

(D) the separation of wealthy land owners versus small, poorer farmers

139. Based on the passage, which statement would best serve as a counter argument to Alexis de Tocqueville's "scope of human perfectibility" during this time period in the United States?

(A) Tradespeople had limited hope of social improvement during the first part of the nineteenth century.

(B) African Americans, especially those in slavery, had nearly no access to improvement in social standing.

(C) The United States has an established class of wealthy landowners as well as poor and landless farmers.

(D) The United States suffered from regional divisions such as the agricultural South versus the industrial North.

Use the passage and your knowledge of the time period to answer questions 140 to 145.

Veto Message by Andrew Jackson, 1832

A bank of the United States is in many respects convenient for the Government and useful to the people. Entertaining this opinion, and deeply impressed with the belief that some of the powers and privileges possessed by the existing bank are unauthorized by the Constitution, subversive of the rights of the States, and dangerous to the liberties of the people, I felt it my duty at an early period of my Administration to call the attention of Congress to the practicability of organizing an institution combining all its advantages and obviating these objections. I sincerely regret that in the act before me I can perceive none of those modifications of the bank charter which are necessary, in my opinion, to make it compatible with justice, with sound policy, or with the Constitution of our country.

. . . Of the twenty-eight millions of private stock in the corporation, $8,405,500 were held by foreigners, mostly of Great Britain. The amount of stock held in the nine Western and Southwestern States is $140,200, and in the four Southern States is $5,623,100, and in the Middle and Eastern States . . . $13,522,000. The profits of the bank in 1831 . . . were about $3,455,598; . . . in the nine western States . . . $1,640,048; in the four Southern States . . . $352,507, and in the Middle and Eastern States . . . $1,463,041. As little stock is held in the West, it is obvious that the debt of the people in that section to the bank is principally a debt to the Eastern and foreign stockholders; that the interest they pay . . . is carried into the Eastern States and . . . Europe, and that it is a burden upon their industry and a drain of their currency, which no country can bear. . . . When by a tax on resident stockholders the stock of this bank is made worth 10 or 15 per cent more to foreigners than to residents, most of it will inevitably leave the country.

140. Which of the following statements best describes Andrew Jackson's reason for issuing the veto?

   (A) It mainly benefited Northern and Eastern bankers.
   (B) It symbolized Southern power and strength.
   (C) It protected the nation's democratic government.
   (D) It was needed to protect U.S. currency.

141. According to the passage, which foreign nation received the highest level of benefit from the policy he was vetoing?

   (A) France
   (B) Great Britain
   (C) Spain
   (D) Russia

142. Which of the following was *not* a result of the policy of Andrew Jackson noted in the passage?

   (A) creation of state "pet" banks
   (B) creation of the Whig Party
   (C) the Specie Circular
   (D) Philadelphia becoming the center of American banking

143. This veto marked the end of a policy first introduced by which of the following people?

   (A) Alexander Hamilton
   (B) Benjamin Franklin
   (C) Thomas Jefferson
   (D) James Madison

144. In relation to the passage, what was the Specie Circular?

    (A) a state institution chosen to hold funds from the national bank

    (B) a bill that authorized the use of military force to uphold federal law

    (C) an executive order requiring that government land be paid for in gold or silver

    (D) the basing of currency on both a gold and a silver standard

145. Which of the following is *not* considered part of Andrew Jackson's legacy?

    (A) creation of a two-party political system

    (B) the modern media-driven election campaign

    (C) reduction of influence in the executive branch over the branches of the federal government

    (D) ending of the second national bank

Use the passage and your knowledge of the time period to answer questions 146 to 148.

South Carolina Ordinance of Nullification, November 24, 1832

An ordinance to nullify certain acts of the Congress of the United States, purporting to be laws laying duties and imposts on the importation of foreign commodities.

Whereas the Congress of the United States by various acts, purporting to be acts laying duties and imposts on foreign imports, but in reality intended for the protection of domestic manufactures and the giving of bounties to classes and individuals engaged in particular employments, at the expense and to the injury and oppression of other classes and individuals, and by wholly exempting from taxation certain foreign commodities, such as are not produced or manufactured in the United States, to afford a pretext for imposing higher and excessive duties on articles similar to those intended to be protected, bath exceeded its just powers under the constitution, which confers on it no authority to afford such protection, and bath violated the true meaning and intent of the constitution, which provides for equality in imposing the burdens of taxation upon the several States and portions of the confederacy: And whereas the said Congress, exceeding its just power to impose taxes and collect revenue for the purpose of effecting and accomplishing the specific objects and purposes which the constitution of the United States authorizes it to effect and accomplish, hath raised and collected unnecessary revenue for objects unauthorized by the constitution.

We, therefore, the people of the State of South Carolina, in convention assembled, do declare and ordain and it is hereby declared and ordained, that the several acts and parts of acts of the Congress of the United States, purporting to be laws for the imposing of duties and imposts on the importation of foreign commodities, and now having actual operation and effect within the United States . . . are unauthorized by the constitution of the United States, and violate the true meaning and intent thereof and are null, void, and no law, nor binding upon this State...

And we, the people of South Carolina, to the end that it may be fully understood by the government of the United States, and the people of the co-States, that we are determined to maintain this our ordinance and declaration, at every hazard, do further declare that we will not submit to the application of force on the part of the federal government, to reduce this State to obedience . . .

146. Which theme is most accurately shared in both Thomas Jefferson and James Madison's Kentucky and Virginia Resolutions and the 1832 Ordinance of Nullification?

   (A) They both asserted the states' rights over federal law and authority.
   (B) They both specifically focus on the notion of import tariffs.
   (C) They both predominantly target the Democratic-Republican Party.
   (D) They both directly lead to a military response by the federal government.

147. The tariffs being protested resemble a continuation of the American System in that they were

   (A) passed to punish British funding of Native Americans
   (B) designed to protect Northern manufacturing
   (C) designed to protect Southern cotton production
   (D) utilized primarily to pay down the national debt

148. In relation to the passage, which of the following best defines the Force Bill?

   (A) It allowed federal circuit courts to appoint federal supervisors of elections.
   (B) It forced censure upon representatives from states that did not comply with federal law.
   (C) It allowed the president to use military force to get South Carolina to comply to federal laws.
   (D) It forced states that did not comply with federal law to hold new elections.

Use the image below and your knowledge of the time period to answer questions 149 and 150.

Source: King Andrew the First, http://hdl.loc.gov/loc.pnp/cph.3a05351.

149. Based on the image, which action of Andrew Jackson's presidency is *not* being directly addressed?

(A) his use of the veto

(B) his increase of executive authority

(C) his treatment of Native Americans

(D) his ending of the second national bank

150. Based on the image, which of the following groups would *not* be a supporter of the Whig Party, who opposed Andrew Jackson?

(A) supporters of term limits

(B) supporters of the national bank

(C) states' rights activists

(D) supporters of a powerful executive branch

CHAPTER 7

Antebellum Reform Movements

Use the document and your knowledge of the time period to answer questions 151 and 152.

Reminiscences of Levi Coffin, The Reputed President of the Underground Railroad (1880)

. . . Soon after we located at Newport, I found that we were on a line of the Underground Railroad. Fugitives often passed through that place, and generally stopped among the colored people. . . . I learned that the fugitive slaves who took refuge with these people were often pursued and captured, the colored people not being very skillful in concealing them, or shrewd in making arrangements to forward them to Canada . . . I was willing to receive and aid as many fugitives as were disposed to come to my house. I knew that my wife's feelings and sympathies regarding this matter were the same as mine, and that she was willing to do her part. . . .

In the winter of 1826–27, fugitives began to come to our house, and as it became more widely known on different routes that the slaves fleeing from bondage would find a welcome and shelter at our house, and be forwarded safely on their journey, the number increased. Friends in the neighborhood, who had formerly stood aloof form the work, fearful of the penalty of the law, were encouraged to engage in it when they saw the fearless manner in which I acted, and the success that attended my efforts. . . .

. . . the Underground Railroad business increased as time advanced, and it was attended with heavy expenses, which I could not have borne had not my affairs been prosperous. I found it necessary to keep a team and a wagon always at command, to convey the fugitive slaves on their journey. Sometimes, when we had large companies, one or two other teams and wagons were required. These journeys had to be made at night, often through deep mud and bad roads, and along by ways that were seldom traveled. Every precaution to evade pursuit had to be used, as the hunters were often on the track, and sometimes ahead of the slaves. . . .

I soon became extensively known to the friends of the slaves, at different points on the Ohio River, where fugitives generally crossed, and to those northward of us on the various routes leading to Canada. . . . Three principal lines from the South converged at my house: one from Cincinnati, one from Madison, and one from Jeffersonville, Indiana. The roads were always in running order, the connections were good, the conductors active and zealous, and there was no lack of passengers. Seldom a week passed without our receiving passengers by the mysterious road. . . .

151. Based on the passage, why did so many slaves pass through Levi Coffin's station on the Underground Railroad?

(A) Multiple roots to Canada passed through his location.

(B) None of his neighbors supported his activities in helping runaway slaves.

(C) Levi Coffin openly advertised his support for the Underground Railroad.

(D) Fugitive slave hunters were not active in the area where Coffin lived.

152. In addition to Levi Coffin, which of the following people also gained fame as a conductor on the Underground Railroad?

(A) Frederick Douglas

(B) Dorothea Dix

(C) Harriet Tubman

(D) John Brown

Use the excerpt and your knowledge of the time period to answer questions 153 to 155.

A Lecture Read at the Masonic Temple, Boston
Ralph Waldo Emerson, January, 1842

The first thing we have to say respecting what are called new views here in New England, at the present time, is, that they are not new, but the very oldest of thoughts cast into the mold of these new times. The light is always identical in its composition, but it falls on a great variety of objects, and by so falling is first revealed to us, not in its own form, for it is formless, but in theirs; in like manner, thought only appears in the objects it classifies. What is popularly called Transcendentalism among us is Idealism; Idealism as it appears in 1842. As thinkers, mankind have ever divided into two sects, Materialists and Idealists; the first class founding on experience, the second on consciousness; the first class beginning to think from the data of the senses, the second class perceive that the senses are not final, and say, the senses give us representations of things, but what are the things themselves, they cannot tell. The materialist insists on facts, on history, on the force of circumstances, and the animal wants of man; the idealist on the power of Thought and of Will, on inspiration, on miracle, on individual culture. These two modes of thinking are both natural, but the idealist contends that his way of thinking is in higher nature . . .

---

153. The passage best illustrates which nineteenth-century movement?

(A) idealism

(B) social Gospel

(C) social Darwinism

(D) transcendentalism

154. Which characteristics would *not* be associated with the nineteenth-century movement noted in the passage?

(A) a greater level of emotional understanding

(B) the movement of learning beyond empiricism

(C) a complete and total rejection of religion

(D) moving away from materialism and traditionalism

155. Which of the following people would *not* be considered a part of the nineteenth-century movement described in the passage?

(A) Nathaniel Hawthorne

(B) Henry David Thoreau

(C) Margaret Fuller

(D) Frederick Henry Hedge

Use the document and your knowledge of the time period to answer questions 156 to 159.

The Declaration of Sentiments
Elizabeth Cady Stanton (1848)

When, in the course of human events, it becomes necessary for one portion of the family of man to assume among the people of the earth a position different from that which they have hitherto occupied, but one to which the laws of nature and of nature's God entitle them, a decent respect to the opinions of mankind requires that they should declare the causes that impel them to such a course.

We hold these truths to be self-evident: that all men and women are created equal; that they are endowed by their Creator with certain inalienable rights; that among these are life, liberty, and the pursuit of happiness; that to secure these rights governments are instituted, deriving their just powers from the consent of the governed . . . The history of mankind is a history of repeated injuries and usurpations on the part of man toward woman, having in direct object the establishment of an absolute tyranny over her. To prove this, let facts be submitted to a candid world.

He has never permitted her to exercise her inalienable right to the elective franchise.

He has compelled her to submit to laws, in the formation of which she had no voice.

He has withheld from her rights which are given to the most ignorant and degraded men—both natives and foreigners . . .

He has made her, if married, in the eye of the law, civilly dead.

He has taken from her all right in property, even to the wages she earns.

He has made her, morally, an irresponsible being, as she can commit many crimes with impunity, provided they be done in the presence of her husband. In the covenant of marriage, she is compelled to promise obedience to her husband, he becoming, to all intents and purposes, her master—the law giving him power to deprive her of her liberty, and to administer chastisement . . .

He has usurped the prerogative of Jehovah himself, claiming it as his right to assign for her a sphere of action, when that belongs to her conscience and to her God.

After depriving her of all rights as a married woman, if single, and the owner of property, he has taxed her to support a government which recognizes her only when her property can be made profitable to it.

He has monopolized nearly all the profitable employments, and from those she is permitted to follow, she receives but a scanty remuneration. He closes against her all the avenues to wealth and distinction which he considers most honorable to himself. As a teacher of theology, medicine, or law, she is not known.

He has denied her the facilities for obtaining a thorough education, all colleges being closed against her . . .

156. The origin of the document is from Lucretia Mott and Elizabeth Cady Stanton at the first U.S. convention on the rights of women held at which location?

    (A) Seneca Falls, New York

    (B) Niagara Falls, New York

    (C) Washington, D.C.

    (D) Boston, Massachusetts

157. In reference to the statement, "He has monopolized nearly all the profitable employments, and from those she is permitted to follow," which field was *not* traditionally open to women for employment during the early nineteenth century?

    (A) nursing

    (B) textile work

    (C) teaching

    (D) secretarial work

158. Mary Lyon is most associated with addressing which of the noted grievances described in the passage for women?

(A) access to suffrage

(B) property ownership

(C) access to higher education

(D) ability to sit on juries

159. The passage "He has usurped the prerogative of Jehovah himself, claiming it as his right to assign for her a sphere of action" relates to the term *domestic feminism* during the first half of the nineteenth century, as is defined as

(A) women gaining greater access to local politics and regional elections

(B) women being awarded primary custody of their children

(C) women adopting a more assertive role in the home

(D) women gaining broader rights in the area of property ownership

Use the document and your knowledge of the time period to answer questions 160 to 163.

Defense of His Positions
William Lloyd Garrison (1854)

Let me define my positions, and at the same time challenge anyone to show wherein they are untenable.

I am a believer in that portion of the Declaration of American Independence in which it is set forth, as among self-evident truths, "that all men are created equal; that they are endowed by their Creator with certain inalienable rights; that among these are life, liberty, and the pursuit of happiness." Hence, I am an abolitionist. Hence, I cannot but regard oppression in every form, and most of all, that which turns a man into a thing, with indignation and abhorrence. Not to cherish these feelings would be recreancy to principle. They who desire me to be dumb on the subject of slavery, unless I will open my mouth in its defense, ask me to give the lie to my professions, to degrade my manhood, and to stain my soul . . .

The abolitionism which I advocate is as absolute as the law of God, and as unyielding as his throne. It admits of no compromise. Every slave is a stolen man; every slaveholder is a man stealer. By no precedent, no example, no law, no compact, no purchase, no bequest, no inheritance, no combination of circumstances, is slaveholding right or justifiable. While a slave remains in his fetters, the land must have no rest. Whatever sanctions his doom must be pronounced accursed. The law that makes him a chattel is to be trampled underfoot; the compact that is formed at his expense, and cemented with his blood, is null and void; the church that consents to his enslavement is horribly atheistical; the religion that receives to its communion the enslaver is the embodiment of all criminality.

160. Based on the passage, which belief would most be associated with William Lloyd Garrison?

(A) federal regulation of slavery

(B) strict constitutional interpretation

(C) returning freed slaves to Africa

(D) abolition of slavery

161. Garrison's argument is similar to the "Declaration of Sentiments" in that both

(A) predominantly focus on the abolition of slavery

(B) cite the Declaration of Independence as a foundation for their argument

(C) ignore the women's suffrage movement

(D) avoid religious support in their arguments

162. Many Northern workers would reject the goals of Garrison's movement because

(A) African Americans lacked education

(B) they feared competition for jobs

(C) the Constitution clearly supported slavery

(D) Southern cotton production was needed to keep the factories running

163. Which of the following best defines a division within the movement supported by Garrison in the passage?

(A) the role that women should be allowed to play

(B) whether freed slaves should be given constructional protections

(C) whether slavery was protected by the U.S. Constitution

(D) how the Southern economy was to be maintained if slavery was ended

Use the image and your knowledge of the time period to answer questions 164 and 165.

Source: Macbrair, and Archibald. "Tree of Temperance."
www.loc.gov/pictures/item/2003689278/.

164. In relation to the image, the main focus of the temperance movement was to

(A) promote equality between races

(B) promote equality between genders

(C) limit the influx of immigrants

(D) prohibit the consumption of alcohol

165. The social movement illustrated in the image would eventually help lead to the passage of which amendment to the U.S. Constitution?

(A) the 12th Amendment

(B) the 18th Amendment

(C) the 19th Amendment

(D) the 13th Amendment

Use the document and your knowledge of the time period to answer questions 166 to 168.

"Twelfth Annual Report to the Secretary of the Massachusetts State Board of Education" 1846

Education, then, beyond all other devices of human origin, is the great equalizer of the conditions of men—the balance—wheel of the social machinery. I do not here mean that it so elevates the moral nature as to make men disdain and abhor the oppression of their fellow men. . . . I mean that it gives each man the independence and the means, by which he can resist the selfishness of other men.

It does better than to disarm the poor of their hostility towards the rich; it prevents being poor. . . . Education prevents both the revenge and the madness. On the other hand, a fellow feeling for one's class or caste is the common instinct of hearts not wholly sunk in selfish regards for person, or for family. The spread of education, by enlarging the cultivated class or caste, will open a wider area over which the social feelings will expand.

---

166. Based on the origin and purpose of this document, it was most likely created by which of the following reformers?

(A) Horace Mann

(B) John Dewey

(C) Dorothea Dix

(D) Jane Addams

167. Which of the following views of public education would most likely *not* be supported by the author?

(A) Schools should be publicly funded.

(B) Elementary education should be offered to affluent males only.

(C) Students should be taught citizenship and self-discipline.

(D) Education should be nonsectarian.

168. Which of the following was a main goal of the educational reform movement of the early 1800s?

(A) providing vocational training

(B) creating responsible new citizens

(C) creating coeducational schools

(D) ending public funding of schools

Use the image and your knowledge of the time period to answer questions 169 to 171.

Source: Cole Thomas. The Oxbow (The Connecticut River near Northampton 1836), 1835.

169. The image above is an example of the Hudson River School art movement of the mid-nineteenth century, which addressed all of the following themes *except*

(A) the depiction of pastoral settings

(B) notions of realism and the common man

(C) the peaceful coexistence of humans and nature

(D) the ideas of American exploration and settlement

170. Which of the following would *not* be considered a major theme of the Hudson River School of art?

(A) realistic, detailed, and idealized portrayal of nature

(B) pastoral settings

(C) the notions of discovery, exploration, and settlement

(D) modernization and improvements of industrialization

171. The themes found in James Fennimore Cooper's literary works were similar to those of the Hudson River School in that they both

(A) were based heavily on European influence

(B) described the conflict between nature and progress

(C) focused mainly on industrialization and urbanization

(D) rejected the notion of the pioneer spirit

Use the image below and your knowledge of the time period to answer questions 172 and 173.

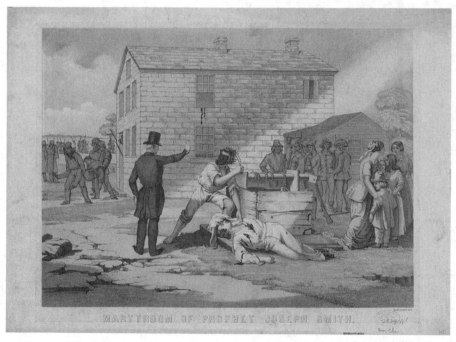

Source: Martyrdom of Prophet Joseph Smith. Jan. 19. Photograph. Retrieved from the Library of Congress, www.loc.gov/item/2003688098/.

172. Joseph Smith is associated with the establishment of which movement in the United States?

(A) the Church of Latter-Day Saints

(B) the Shakers

(C) New Harmony

(D) Seventh-Day Adventists

173. Joseph Smith was considered to be part of which movement of the early nineteenth century?

(A) the First Great Awakening

(B) the Second Great Awakening

(C) transcendentalism

(D) abolitionism

Use the image as well as your knowledge of the time period to answer questions 174 to 178.

Source: N. Currier. The Propagation Society. More free than welcome, ca. 1855. Photograph. https://www.loc.gov/item/2003656589/.

Pope: "My friend we have concluded to take charge of your spiritual welfare, and your temporal estate, so that you need not be troubled with the care of them in future; we will say your prayers and spend your money, while you live, and bury you in the Potters Field, when you die. Kneel then! and kiss our big toe in token of submission."

Young American Boy: "You can neither coax, nor frighten our boys, Sir! we can take care of our own worldly affairs, and are determined to "Know nothing" but this book, to guide us in spiritual things."

Second bishop: "Only let us get a good foot hold on the soil, and we'll burn up those Books and elevate this Country to the Same degree of happiness and prosperity, to which we have brought Italy, Spain, Ireland and many other lands."

174. Which theme is *not* represented in the cartoon above?

(A) American fears of the spread of Catholicism

(B) anti-immigrant sentiments held in the United States during the mid-nineteenth century

(C) American nationalism and identity

(D) American rejection of traditional religious values

175. As referenced in the cartoon, between the 1820s and 1850s, the largest population of immigrants to the United States originated from what country?

(A) Russia

(B) Spain

(C) Ireland

(D) Italy

176. As noted by the young American boy, which of the following political parties based its entire platform on the issue of immigration?

(A) Whigs

(B) Republicans

(C) Free-Soilers

(D) Know-Nothings

177. During the nineteenth century, settlement patterns of new immigrants were mostly based on

(A) the U.S. port they migrated to first

(B) areas where populations of their native communities had already been established

(C) regions where the government offered the best land grants

(D) regions where employment was most readily available

178. Which group would most likely support the message created by the image?

(A) Northern factory workers

(B) Northern factory owners

(C) Southern plantation owners

(D) pro-slave groups

Use the image and your knowledge of the time period to answer questions 179 to 180.

Source: Commodore Matthew Perry's "Black Ship" c. 1860.

179. Based on its origin, the image above most likely depicts the opening of U.S. trade with which nation?

(A) Korea

(B) Japan

(C) China

(D) India

180. The administration of which president is credited with opening trade with the nation depicted in the image?

(A) James Polk

(B) Millard Fillmore

(C) Franklin Pierce

(D) James Buchanan

CHAPTER 8

Antebellum Cultural Movements and Manifest Destiny

Use the document and your knowledge of the time period to answer questions 181 to 187.

> ### Letter from the Alamo
> ### by William Travis, 1836
> #### Fellow citizens & compatriots
>
> I am besieged, by a thousand or more of the Mexicans under Santa Anna I have sustained a continual Bombardment & cannonade for 24 hours & have not lost a man. The enemy has demanded a surrender at discretion, otherwise, the garrison are to be put to the sword, if the fort is taken I have answered the demand with a cannon shot, & our flag still waves proudly from the walls I shall never surrender or retreat. Then, I call on you in the name of Liberty, of patriotism & everything dear to the American character, to come to our aid, with all dispatch. The enemy is receiving reinforcements daily & will no doubt increase to three or four thousand in four or five days. If this call is neglected, I am determined to sustain myself as long as possible & die like a soldier who never forgets what is due to his own honor & that of his country VICTORY OR DEATH.

181. What argument does William Travis make to attempt to gain support?

    (A) He invokes American patriotism and notions of liberty.

    (B) He utilizes the notion of America's Manifest Destiny and expansion.

    (C) He invokes anti-Catholic sentiments held by Americans during the time period.

    (D) He addresses the sentiments of abolitionist groups.

182. In response to the events of the Alamo and the Texas independence movement, the United States

(A) officially remained neutral

(B) sent troops to support the Americans fighting in Texas

(C) offered to purchase the land in Texas

(D) plotted to overthrow the government of Santa Anna

183. The Battle of the Alamo was significant because

(A) it was an overwhelming victory by Americans seeking independence

(B) Americans obtained much-needed supplies in their fight for independence

(C) it launched James Bowie to national prominence, later allowing him to win a Senate seat

(D) it served as a rallying cry to recruit more support for the Texas independence movement

184. Which of the following defenders of the Alamo was also a former congressman?

(A) James Bowie

(B) George Brown

(C) David Crockett

(D) Andrew Jackson Harrison

185. Which of the following was *not* a factor that led to the Battle of the Alamo in the War for Texas Independence?

(A) The Mexican government outlawed the practice of slavery.

(B) The Mexican government closed the border to further U.S. immigration.

(C) The U.S. government directly funded American settlers to rebel to help U.S. westward expansion.

(D) The Mexican government imposed higher taxes on American imports.

186. Which battle resulted in Texas gaining independence from Mexico?

(A) the Alamo

(B) San Jacinto

(C) Goliad

(D) Guadalupe Hidalgo

187. Which of the following treaties ended the fighting during the Texan independence movement?

(A) Treaties of Velasco

(B) Treaty of San Juan

(C) Treaty of the Wilmot

(D) Treaty of San Jacinto

Use the document and your knowledge of the time period to answer questions 188 to 192.

"Annexation" 1845

It is now time for the opposition to the Annexation of Texas to cease . . . in regard to Texas, enough has now been given to party. It is time for the common duty of Patriotism to the Country to succeed. . . .

Texas is now ours. Already . . . her Convention has undoubtedly ratified the acceptance . . . and made the requisite changes in her already republican form of constitution to adapt it to its future federal relations. Her star and her stripe may already be said to have taken their place in the glorious blazon of our common nationality. . . .

Why, were other reasoning wanting, in favor of now elevating this question of the reception of Texas into the Union, out of the lower region of our past party dissensions, up to its proper level of a high and broad nationality, it surely is to be found, found abundantly, in the manner in which other nations have undertaken to intrude themselves into it, between us and the proper parties to the case, in a spirit of hostile interference against us, for the avowed object of thwarting our policy and hampering our power, limiting our greatness and checking the fulfillment of our manifest destiny to overspread the continent allotted by Providence for the free development of our yearly multiplying millions . . . This we have seen done by England, our old rival and enemy; and by France, strangely coupled with her against us, under the influence of the Anglicism strongly tinging the policy of her present prime minister . . .

---

188. Who is generally credited with being one of the first people to popularize the phrase Manifest Destiny?

(A) James Monroe

(B) John Quincy Adams

(C) Andrew Jackson

(D) John L. O'Sullivan

189. In relation to the passage, Manifest Destiny would be best defined as

(A) the idea that Mexico and Canada would inevitably seek to join the United States

(B) the belief that the westward expansion of the United States over North America was justified and inevitable

(C) the rejection of the establishment of future European colonies in the Western Hemisphere

(D) the concept that individual states had the right to choose whether slavery would be permitted within their boundaries

190. Which of the following ideas would *not* be considered a justification for Manifest Destiny?

(A) the merit of American democratic institutions

(B) the need to develop America's infrastructure

(C) belief in a divine mandate to expand

(D) the goal of furthering the Monroe Doctrine

191. Which of the following was *not* a cause of delaying the annexation of Texas?

(A) resistance to the creation of another Southern state

(B) abolitionists' opposition to creating another slave state

(C) British trade and defensive treaties with Texas

(D) lack of support from the Whig Party in the Senate

192. Which would *not* be a political and regional difference caused by Manifest Destiny during the 1840s?

(A) Expansion would limit development the U.S. eastern infrastructure.

(B) Some worried that westward expansion would increase political representation of Native Americans.

(C) Northern states feared they would lose political influence with the creation of western states.

(D) Abolitionists feared the creation of new slave states.

Use the document and your knowledge of the time period to answer questions 193 to 196.

Message to Congress
James Polk (December 2, 1845)

Near a quarter of a century ago the principle was distinctly announced to the world, in the annual message of one of my predecessors, that:

The American continents, by the free and independent condition which they have assumed and maintain, are henceforth not to be considered as subjects for future colonization by any European powers. This principle will apply with greatly increased force should any European power attempt to establish any new colony in North America. In the existing circumstances of the world the present is deemed a proper occasion to reiterate and reaffirm the principle . . . and to state my cordial concurrence in its wisdom and sound policy. The reassertion of this principle, especially in reference to North America, is at this day but the promulgation of a policy which no European power should cherish the disposition to resist. Existing rights of every European nation should be respected, but it is due alike to our safety and our interests that the efficient protection of our laws should be extended over our whole territorial limits, and that it should be distinctly announced to the world as our settled policy that no future European colony or dominion shall with our consent be planted or established on any part of the North American continent.

---

193. Based on the passage, James K. Polk cited which U.S. policy to justify Manifest Destiny?

(A) Monroe Doctrine

(B) Washington's pledge of neutrality

(C) Missouri Compromise

(D) Preemption Act

194. Polk's message marks a continuation of which theme of the initial Monroe Doctrine?

(A) The United States would seek neutrality in European affairs.

(B) The United States rejected future attempts of colonization within the Western Hemisphere.

(C) The Western Hemisphere's political systems were unique from those found in Europe.

(D) The United States had a right to expand its boarders across all of North America.

195. In relation to the passage, the slogan "Fifty-Four Forty or Fight!" dealt with which disputed U.S. border with another nation?

(A) Maine and British-held Canada

(B) Oregon and British-held Canada

(C) Alaska and British-held Canada

(D) Texas and Mexico

196. Which of the following was *not* a reason Britain considered annexing Texas prior to its annexation by the United States?

(A) Annexation would curb future U.S. westward expansion.

(B) Annexation would reduce the dependence on U.S. cotton.

(C) Annexation of Texas would ease problems caused by population growth in England.

(D) Expansion would weaken the U.S. authority under the Monroe Doctrine.

Use the image and your knowledge of the time period to answer questions 197 to 199.

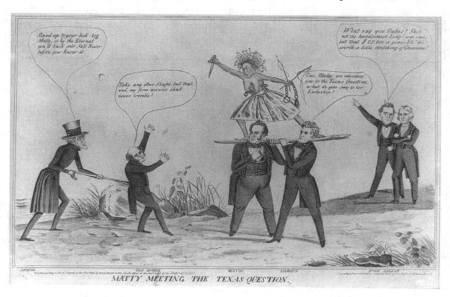

Source: H. Bucholzer. Matty meeting the Texas Question, 1844. Photograph. http://www.loc.gov/pictures/item/2008661437/.

Calhoun: "Come, Matty, we introduce you to the Texas Question, what do you say to her Ladyship?"

Van Buren: "Take any other shape but that and my firm nerves shall never tremble!"

Andrew Jackson: "Stand up to your lick-log Matty or by the Eternal you'll back into Salt River before you know it."

Polk: "What say you Dallas? She's not the handsomest Lady I ever saw but that $25,000 a year—Eh! it's worth a little stretching of Conscience!"

197. Based on the image, which of the following was the central issue of the presidential election of 1844?

(A) the anti-Masons movement

(B) the end of Jacksonian Politics

(C) the passage of women's suffrage

(D) westward expansion and Texas annexation

198. In relation to the cartoon, who is the individual being referred to as Matty?

(A) Martin Van Buren

(B) Henry Clay

(C) James Polk

(D) James Birney

199. Based on the cartoon, which of the following statements best describes the main reason Southerners supported the annexation of Texas?

(A) They wanted a safer route across the country.

(B) They wanted new seaports to help trade with Asia.

(C) They wanted better access to trade with Mexico.

(D) They wanted more territory and land where slavery had been established.

Use the image and your knowledge of the time period to answer questions 200 to 202.

Source: C. J. Pollard. At the Battle of Palo Alto, the Americans greatly distinguished themselves . . ., c. 1846. Print. http://www.loc.gov/pictures/item/2003690751/.
Text: At the Battle of Palo Alto, the Americans greatly distinguished themselves, as well for their bravery, as their humanity toward their unfortunate adversaries.

200. In the image, what is the contrast made between the U.S. soldiers and those of the Mexican Army?

(A) The U.S. soldiers are depicted a cruel, while the Mexican soldiers are depicted as weak.

(B) The U.S. soldiers are drawn as unorganized and disinterested, while the Mexican soldiers are drawn as desperate.

(C) The U.S. soldiers are depicted as brave and honorable, while the Mexican soldiers are depicted as disorganized and beast-like.

(D) The U.S. soldiers are drawn as blood-thirsty and violent, while the Mexican soldiers are illustrated and honorable and brave.

201. The Mexican–American War ended with the signing of what treaty?

(A) Treaty of Guadalupe Hidalgo
(B) Treaty of San Juan
(C) Treaty of San Jacinto
(D) Treaty of Ghent

202. Which of the following people actively opposed the Mexican–American War?

(A) John Calhoun
(B) Daniel Webster
(C) Zachary Taylor
(D) Stephen Kearney

Use the map and your knowledge of the time period to answer question 203.

Source: Disturnell, J. (1847) Mapa de los Estados Unidos de Méjico: segun lo organizado y definido por las varias actas del congreso de dicha república y construido por las mejores autoridades. New York: J. Disturnell. [Map] Retrieved from the Library of Congress, https://www.loc.gov/item/2004627240/.

203. In reference to the map, which land action gave the United States possession of the southern part of Arizona and New Mexico, west of the Rio Grande and south of the Gila River?

(A) Gadsden Purchase
(B) Treaty of Guadalupe Hidalgo
(C) Hay–Herrán Treaty
(D) Webster–Ashburton Treaty

Use the document and your knowledge of the time period to answer questions 204 to 208.

Compromise of 1850

It being desirable, for the peace . . . of the Union of these States, to settle . . . amicably all existing questions . . . arising out [of] . . . slavery upon a fair . . . and just basis: therefore,

1. Resolved, That California . . . to be admitted as one of the States of this Union, without the imposition by Congress of any restriction in respect to the exclusion or introduction of slavery . . .

2. Resolved, That as slavery does not exist by law, and is not likely to be introduced into any of the territory acquired by the United States from the republic of Mexico . . . and that appropriate territorial governments ought to be established by Congress in all of the said territory . . . without the adoption of any restriction or condition on the subject of slavery.

3. Resolved, That the western boundary of the State of Texas ought to be fixed on the Rio del Norte, commencing one marine league from its mouth, and running up that river to the southern line of New Mexico; thence with that line eastwardly, and so continuing in the same direction to the line as established between the United States and Spain, excluding any portion of New Mexico, whether lying on the east or west of that river.

4. Resolved, That it be proposed to the State of Texas, that the United States will provide for the payment of all that portion of the legitimate and bona fide public debt of that State contracted prior to its annexation to the United States, and for which the duties on foreign imports were pledged by the said State to its creditors, . . . in consideration of the said duties so pledged having been no longer applicable to that object after the said annexation, but having thenceforward become payable to the United States; and upon the condition, also, that the said State of Texas shall, by some solemn and authentic act of her legislature or of a convention, relinquish to the United States any claim which it has to any part of New Mexico.

5. Resolved, That it is inexpedient to abolish slavery in the District of Columbia whilst that institution continues to exist in the State of Maryland, without the consent of that State, without the consent of the people of the District, and without just compensation to the owners of slaves within the District.

6. But, resolved, That it is expedient to prohibit, within the District, the slave trade in slaves brought into it from States or places beyond the limits of the District, either to be sold therein as merchandise, or to be transported to other markets without the District of Columbia.

7. Resolved, That more effectual provision ought to be made by law, according to the requirement of the constitution, for the restitution and delivery of persons bound to service or labor in any State, who may escape into any other State or Territory in the Union. And,

8. Resolved, That Congress has no power to promote or obstruct the trade in slaves between the slaveholding States; but that the admission or exclusion of slaves brought from one into another of them, depends exclusively upon their own particular laws.

204. Which of the following actions was *not* considered part of the Compromise of 1850?

(A) California was admitted into the Union as a free state.

(B) Citizens of New Mexico and Utah were granted popular sovereignty.

(C) Texas's borders were extended to Santa Fe.

(D) The Fugitive Slave Act was created.

205. How does the document define popular sovereignty?

(A) Slavery would be decided by the Missouri Compromise.

(B) Inhabitants of territories becoming states would decide on the issue of slavery.

(C) The practice of slavery was to be outlawed in all U.S. states.

(D) The issue of slavery would be decided through a national ballot.

206. Which of the following statements was *not* an argument against the Fugitive Slave Act?

(A) The law made it easy for freedmen to be kidnapped.

(B) Accused fugitive slaves lacked the rights of due process.

(C) The law violated the Dred Scott decision.

(D) The practice further institutionalized the practice of slavery.

207. In relation to the Fugitive Slave Act noted in the passage, which of the following provisions was *not* considered part of personal liberty laws during the mid-nineteenth century?

(A) forbidding the use of state jails to imprison alleged fugitives

(B) interfering with state officials to stop them from enforcing the strict law against fugitives

(C) citing the state's right of nullification

(D) forcing bounty hunters to provide proof that captives were fugitives

208. Which senator is credited with creating the Compromise of 1850?

(A) Stephen Douglas

(B) Henry Clay

(C) Millard Fillmore

(D) Thomas Benton

CHAPTER 9

The Mid-Nineteenth Century and the Causes of the Civil War

Use the document and your knowledge of history to answer questions 209 to 211.

Uncle Tom's Cabin: Anti-Slavery Agitation From the Daily Dispatch, VA (1852)

"There seems to be no end to the expedients which the fanatics of the North are determined to resort to, to disturb the peace of the country, and produce, if they possibly can the dissolution of the Union. Having failed in this generation, they are bending their efforts to poison the minds of those who are to come, while they are yet too young to be conscious of the dangerous doctrines to which they are to be committed. A more hateful execrable plot against the happiness and safety of millions of human beings—against the government itself—against society, and the hopes of man—was never conceived by human heart nor carried on by human intelligence . . . But the immediate effect we can well enough imagine. It will operate heavily upon the colored class of the South, both slave and free—it will cause laws to be enacted and enforced which will cut up their few remaining privileges by the roots—it will not advance emancipation one iota.

We subjoin the following remarks of the New York Herald: ANTI-SLAVERY AGITATION—Abolition meetings are being held all over the North. The most violent language is used against all who differ in opinion with the agitators. Every man who does not agree with them is sent directly to the bottomless pit the moment he dies, like Judge Woodbury and Judge Story. In fact, they will hardly wait for a man's death to send him to the devil—they want him despatched to pandemonium "right away." As another sign of the times, the fact is very remarkable that the work of Mrs. Beecher Stowe, "Uncle Tom's Cabin," selling a thousand copies per day, cannot half supply the demand for this species of work—antislavery literature , , ,

The Northern States will soon be inundated by a flood of abolition novels, and the effect upon the opinions, the politics, the peace and happiness of the country, is beyond calculation. The Union itself will become again periled by this tremendous revival of anti-slavery sentiment, and the toil and up-hill work that resulted in the Compromise measures will go for nothing, and the battle of the Union and the Constitution will have to be fought again."

209. Based on the passage, which of the following statements about *Uncle Tom's Cabin* is the most accurate?

   (A) It was written in response to John Brown's raid at Harpers Ferry.

   (B) It illustrated the political beliefs of the Know-Nothing Party.

   (C) It motivated others to write articles and novels refuting the book's assertions.

   (D) It was ill-received in both the North and South.

210. The assertions, "the toil and up-hill work that resulted in the Compromise measures will go for nothing," is most likely a reference to which of the following?

   (A) the Missouri Compromise

   (B) the Three-Fifths Compromise

   (C) the Compromise of 1850

   (D) the Great Compromise

211. How does the author feel *Uncle Tom's Cabin* will impact slaves living in the Southern states?

   (A) While they may receive some improved treatment, slavery will not be abolished.

   (B) They will lose even more freedoms to counteract tensions caused by the work.

   (C) More slaves will become literate in order to attempt to read the work.

   (D) The work will most likely have no impact on slaves living in the south.

Use the document and your knowledge of the time period to answer questions 212 to 216.

An Act to Organize the Territories of Nebraska and Kansas. (1854)

Be it enacted by the Senate and House of Representatives of the United States of America in Congress assembled . . .

the said Territory or any portion of the same, shall be received into the Union with without slavery, as their constitution may prescribe at the time of the admission: Provided, That nothing in this act contained shall be construed to inhibit the government of the United States from dividing said Territory into two or more Territories . . .

That the Constitution, and all laws of the United States which are not locally inapplicable, shall have the same force and effect within the said Territory of Kansas as elsewhere within the United States, except the eighth section of the act preparatory to the admission of Missouri into the Union, approved March sixth, eighteen hundred and twenty, which, being inconsistent with the principle of non-intervention by Congress with slavery in the States and Territories, as recognized by the legislation of eighteen hundred and fifty, commonly called the Compromise Measures, is hereby declared inoperative and void; it being the true intent and meaning of this act not to legislate slavery into any Territory or State, nor to exclude it therefrom, but to leave the people thereof perfectly free to form and regulate their domestic institutions in their own way, subject only to the Constitution of the United States: *Provided,* That nothing herein contained shall be construed to revive or put in force any law or regulation which may have existed prior to the act of sixth of March, eighteen hundred and twenty, either protecting, establishing, prohibiting, or abolishing slavery . . .

212. Based on the passage, the Kansas–Nebraska Act directly rejects which prior piece of legislation?

(A) the Compromise of 1850

(B) the Fugitive Slave Act

(C) the Missouri Compromise

(D) popular sovereignty

213. Which of the following was *not* true of the Kansas–Nebraska Act?

(A) It was overturned by the Dred Scott decision.

(B) It allowed for popular sovereignty within the region.

(C) It allowed for the creation of a transcontinental railroad.

(D) It was an attempt to gain Southern support for Stephen Douglas.

214. Which of the following reasons best explains why the Act would be unpopular amongst Northern states?

(A) It created a transcontinental railroad in the South.

(B) It could increase the number of slave states.

(C) The Northern states disapproved of Stephen Douglas seeking Southern support.

(D) It weakened the influence of Northern business interests.

215. How would the Free-Soil Party most likely react to the stated act?

(A) They would oppose it because it allowed for the expansion of slavery into western territories.

(B) They would support it because expansion of territories would provide cheaper land sales in the West.

(C) They would support it because it advocated the notion of popular sovereignty in western territories.

(D) They would oppose it because the addition of western states would diminish the political power of eastern states.

216. Which event would be considered the most direct consequence of the Kansas–Nebraska Act?

(A) Nat Turner's Rebellion
(B) Bleeding Kansas
(C) Bleeding Sumner
(D) John Brown's raid on Harpers Ferry

Use the graphic and your knowledge of the time period to answer questions 217 to 220.

Immigrants Entering the United States 1820 through 1862

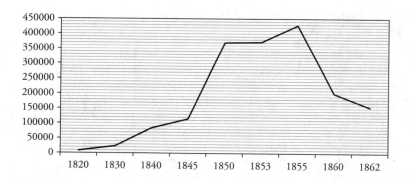

217. Based on the chart, which period illustrated the greatest increase in immigration?

(A) the early 1840s
(B) the late 1850s
(C) the late 1840s
(D) the early 1860s

218. Which historic event most likely led to the large jump in immigration depicted in the graph?

(A) the conclusion of the Mexican–American War
(B) the Free-Soiler movement
(C) the German March Revolution
(D) the Irish Potato Famine

219. During the early 1800s, immigration in the United States was unrestricted primarily because

(A) such restrictions were deemed unconstitutional

(B) labor unions called for new immigrant labor

(C) the industrial economy was creating new jobs

(D) Southern plantations needed additional workers

220. Which of the following factors most logically would explain the decrease in immigration in the 1860s?

(A) The federal government passed strict immigration laws.

(B) Industrialism in Europe led to increased demand for workers.

(C) The emancipation of slaves in the United States decreased the number of available jobs.

(D) The tensions caused by the American Civil War disrupted the flow on immigration.

Use the document and your knowledge of the time period to answer questions 221 to 224.

Dred Scott, Plaintiff In Error, v. John F. A. Sandford 1857

I.1.   . . . He himself, in making out his case, states that he is of African descent, was born a slave, and claims that he and his family became entitled to be freed by being taken by their owner to reside in a territory where slavery is prohibited by act of Congress—and that, in addition to this claim, he himself became entitled to freedom being taken to . . . the State of Illinois—and being free when he was brought back to Missouri, he was by the laws of that State a citizen.

I.2.   If, therefore, the facts he states do not give him or his family a right to freedom, the plaintiff is still a slave, and not entitled in sue as a "citizen."

IV.3.   Every citizen has a right to take with him into the Territory any article of property which the Constitution of the United States recognizes as property.

IV. 4.   The Constitution of the United States recognises slaves as property, and pledges the Federal Government to protect it. And Congress cannot exercise any more authority over property of that description than it may constitutionally exercise over property of any other kind.

IV.5.   The act of Congress, therefore, prohibiting a citizen of the United States from taking with him his slaves when he removes to the Territory in question to reside, is an exercise of authority over private property which is not warranted by the Constitution.

221. Based on the court case, Dred Scott sued for his freedom, arguing that

(A) the institution of slavery was immoral and unjust

(B) he had been forced into slavery through illegal means

(C) he had been a resident of a state where slavery was illegal

(D) slavery was a violation of constitutional rights

222. The Dred Scott decision ruled that

(A) accused fugitive slaves had a right to trial by jury

(B) only Congress had the right to prohibit slavery

(C) the federal ban on the importation of slaves was unconstitutional

(D) African Americans were not citizens and did not have legal protection

223. The Dred Scott decision upheld the institution of slavery based on which constitutional amendment?

(A) Fifth Amendment

(B) Sixth Amendment

(C) Seventh Amendment

(D) Fourteenth Amendment

224. How was the Freeport Doctrine a response to the court's decision?

(A) It argued that the Kansas–Nebraska Act was unconstitutional under the Dred Scott decision.

(B) It argued that the Dred Scott decision did not void the notion of popular sovereignty.

(C) It stated that slavery could be prevented by states passing laws unfriendly toward the practice.

(D) It stated that Dred Scott decision upheld the Kansas–Nebraska Act.

Use the two documents and your knowledge of the time period to answer questions 225 to 227.

JOHN BROWN: Our Harpers Ferry and Charlestown News.

Cincinnati, Ohio, *Enquirer* [Democratic] (December 3, 1859)

. . . But what a great wrong has been inflicted on Virginia by her brethren of the North that compels her to resort to such extreme measures for her safety. She has done nothing to merit such treatment.

She is now as she was in the days of the Revolution, at the adoption of the Constitution, and has done nothing since to demand worse treatment from the people of the free States than she merited at these periods from those with whom she was laboring for the liberties of the people and the establishment of a National Government. She was slave then; she is no more so now. And the people of the free States have entered into a compact with her not to interfere in her internal domestic affairs, and if any of her slave property escapes, to interpose no obstacle to its return. Why, then, should her peace be threatened, the lives and property of her citizens jeopardized by citizens of the free States?

We rejoice that old BROWN has been hung. He was not only a murderer of innocent persons, but he attempted one of the greatest crimes against society—the stirring up of a servile and civil war. He has paid the penalty for his crimes, and we hope his fate may be a warning to all who might have felt inclined to imitate his aggressive conduct.

Gazette Pittsburgh, Pennsylvania, [Republican] (December 3, 1859)

The immolation of John Brown was, in short, in accordance with the philosophy of slavery—*a necessity*. He had dared to act on the conviction of his life, and these settled principles of his were the only ones which such a man could entertain. He was too brave to have thought differently from what he did, and the same noble impulses which inculcated a love of Freedom and Right, impelled him constantly and irresistibly to the practical development of his theory. He has failed, according to the popular mode of calculating failure and success; but that his life and tragic death must of necessity constitute a failure, is a point too broad and high to be disposed of in this summary manner. We cannot but disapprove his mad and folly-stricken act, but the unselfishness of the deed; his moderation, when victorious, over the town which he captured; his Spartan courage in defending himself and his fellows, and his sublime contempt of death while overborne and made the manacled tenant of a prison; his stern integrity in scorning the technicalities of the law, and his manliness *in all things*, will not be quickly forgotten; but rather a contemplation of this heroic old man's character will irresistibly compel thinking men to ask themselves whether it is John Brown, of Ossawatomie, or the system of slavery which has failed in this conflict.

The execution of the old man at Charlestown yesterday, was a plain admission on the part of Slavery that they dare not spare a brave man's life . . . History will do justice to the institution of Slavery and its uncompromising foe alike . . .

225. How does the Democratic paper defend the institution of slavery in Virginia in the face of the North's criticism?

(A) It states that it has remained consistent over time, and it is the North that is inciting division.

(B) It argues that immigration has led to radical views on the Constitution and the institution of slavery.

(C) It argues that popular sovereignty has allowed the people of Virginia to decide the issue of slavery.

(D) It argues that while the North and South disagree on slavery, it feels John Brown's actions were independent of their disagreement.

226. How do the two viewpoints presented illustrate that sectional differences were becoming irreconcilable by 1859?

(A) Both viewpoints discuss how the vast economic differences between the two regions led to the event.

(B) Both viewpoints blame the event on a region as a whole rather than on the individuals specifically involved.

(C) Both viewpoints call for direct military action against the opposing region.

(D) Both viewpoints call for economic boycotts of the opposing region.

227. Which of the following best describes the goal of John Brown's raid of Harpers Ferry?

(A) raiding the military arsenal to supply later slave uprisings

(B) liberating the slaves being held there

(C) taking the pro-slavery governor hostage to bargain for the release of slaves within the state

(D) preventing pro-slavery groups from influencing popular sovereignty in western territories

Use the image and your knowledge of the time period to answer questions 228 to 230.

LITTLE BO-PEEP AND HER FOOLISH SHEEP.

Source: Goater, J. H. & Strong, T. W. (1861) Strong's dime caricatures. No. 2, Little Bo-Peep and her foolish sheep. Alabama Georgia Kansas Louisiana Mississippi South Carolina Virginia, 1861. N.Y.: Published by Thomas W. Strong. [Photograph] Retrieved from the Library of Congress, https://www.loc.gov/item/2008661617/.
Little Bo Peep: Sic 'em Buck! sic 'em! I wish poor old Hickory was alive. He'd bring 'em back in no time.
Wolves: If we can only get them separated from the flock, we can pick their bones at our leisure.

228. Based on the image, Hickory would most likely represent

    (A) the strength of the presidency under Andrew Jackson

    (B) the abilities of the U.S. Navy with the USS *Constitution*

    (C) the Era of Good Feelings

    (D) the end of the New England lumber trade

229. The wolves emerging from the forest most likely symbolize

(A) Northern abolitionists descending upon Southern states

(B) freed former states leading uprisings in the South

(C) European powers waiting to take advantage of the United States during the succession crisis

(D) immigrants looking to take advantage of lax U.S. immigration policies

230. Based on the cartoon, which of the following most accurately summarizes James Buchanan's legacy as president?

(A) a great unifier of the Democratic Party, though faced with insurmountable challenges

(B) a weak leader that had limited ability to preserve the Union

(C) a sympathizer of abolitionism who pandered needlessly to the pro-slavery South

(D) an accomplished leader in fiscal matters, but weak in diplomacy between the states

CHAPTER 10

The Civil War

Use the chart and your knowledge of the time period to answer questions 231 to 234.

Overview of the Union and the Confederate States of America

	Union	Confederate States
President	Abraham Lincoln	Jefferson Davis
Treasury	$207,000,000	$47,000,000
Free population	21,700,000	5,600,000
Slave population	400,000	3,500,000
Soldiers	2,100,000	1,064,000
Military colleges	1	7
Factories	110,100	20,600
Corn and wheat production (bushels)	698,000,000	314,000,000
Railroads (in miles)	21,788	8,838

* According to the 1860 census

231. Based on the chart, which of the following was a Union advantage over the Confederacy during the Civil War?

(A) The Union had more experienced generals.

(B) The Union had a better-funded treasury.

(C) The Union could fight mainly a defensive war.

(D) The Union had greater support from its citizens.

232. Which of the following was an advantage the South had in the Civil War?

    (A) the size of the Southern population

    (B) development of the Southern infrastructure

    (C) a unified and strong central government

    (D) experienced military leadership

233. Which of the following would *not* be a contrast in the experience and leadership of Abraham Lincoln and Jefferson Davis during the Civil War?

    (A) Davis had more political experience than Lincoln.

    (B) Davis had more military experience than Lincoln.

    (C) Jefferson successfully used skilled advisors compared to Lincoln.

    (D) Lincoln had a better understanding of public opinion than Davis.

234. Which of the following statements was *not* true of the Confederacy during the Civil War?

    (A) It lacked sufficient textile factories for troop uniforms.

    (B) It had few rifle factories.

    (C) It suffered from food shortages.

    (D) The number of slave uprisings increased.

Use the map and your knowledge of the period to answer questions 235 to 240.

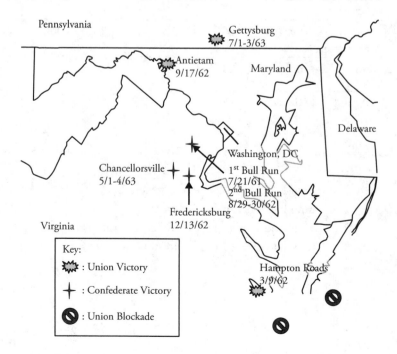

235. Based on the map, which of the following Civil War battles occurred first?

(A) Battle of Fredericksburg

(B) Battle of Chancellorsville

(C) First Battle of Bull Run

(D) Battle of Antietam

236. The USS *Merrimac* and the USS *Monitor* are most associated with which battle?

(A) First Bull Run

(B) Chancellorsville

(C) Hampton Roads

(D) Fredericksburg

237. Which of the following was *not* a reason the North needed to maintain control of the Border States during the Civil War?

(A) The Border States would have allowed for the spread of slavery if they became part of the Confederacy.

(B) The Border States such as Maryland kept the Confederacy from surrounding Union capitol.

(C) The Border States contained factories that would have aided Confederate manufacturing capabilities.

(D) The Border States created a buffer zone between the Confederate and Union states.

238. What was the primary strategy of the Confederacy during the early part of the Civil War is illustrated in the map?

(A) capturing key shipping ports in New England

(B) attacking the North through the Mississippi River

(C) creating a naval blockade along the northern Atlantic coast

(D) waging a war of attrition against the Union

239. Which battle on the map marks a deviation from this strategy?

(A) Battle of Chancellorsville

(B) Battle of Antietam

(C) Battle of Second Bull Run

(D) Battle of First Bull Run

240. Of the following battles on the map, which was considered a major turning point in the Civil War?

(A) Battle of Antietam

(B) Battle of Fredericksburg

(C) Battle of Gettysburg

(D) Battle of Hampton Roads

Use the image and your knowledge of the time period to answer questions 241 to 243.

Source: Elliott, J. B. (1861) Scott's great snake. Entered according to Act of Congress in the year. [S.l] [Map] Retrieved from the Library of Congress, https://www.loc.gov/item/99447020/.

241. The image above represents which strategy during the Civil War?

(A) the March to the Sea

(B) the Anaconda Plan

(C) the War of Attrition

(D) the suspension of habeas corpus

242. Based on the image, which most logically defines the focus of the plan depicted?

(A) using a solely a naval blockade to lay siege on the Confederacy

(B) defeating the Confederacy by capturing Texas and fighting eastward

(C) using Union forces to encircle Washington, D.C., and Richmond

(D) dividing the Confederacy in half through both blockades and military force

243. Which of the following battles is considered to be a major turning point in the strategy depicted in the image, as well as the Civil War in the West?

(A) Battle of Cold Harbor

(B) Battle of Gettysburg

(C) Battle of Vicksburg

(D) Battle of Hampton Roads

Use the document and your knowledge of the time period to answer questions 244 to 246.

The Emancipation Proclamation
by Abraham Lincoln, 1863

Now, therefore I, Abraham Lincoln, President of the United States, by virtue of the power in me vested as Commander-in-Chief, of the Army and Navy of the United States in time of actual armed rebellion against the authority and government of the United States, and as a fit and necessary war measure for suppressing said rebellion, do, on this first day of January, in the year of our Lord one thousand eight hundred and sixty-three, and in accordance with my purpose so to do publicly proclaimed for the full period of one hundred days, from the day first above mentioned, order and designate as the States and parts of States wherein the people thereof respectively, are this day in rebellion against the United States, the following, to wit:

Arkansas, Texas, Louisiana, (except the Parishes of St. Bernard, Plaquemines, Jefferson, St. John, St. Charles, St. James Ascension, Assumption, Terrebonne, Lafourche, St. Mary, St. Martin, and Orleans, including the City of New Orleans) Mississippi, Alabama, Florida, Georgia, South Carolina, North Carolina, and Virginia, (except the forty-eight counties designated as West Virginia, and also the counties of Berkley, Accomac, Northampton, Elizabeth City, York, Princess Ann, and Norfolk, including the cities of Norfolk and Portsmouth[)], and which excepted parts, are for the present, left precisely as if this proclamation were not issued.

And by virtue of the power, and for the purpose aforesaid, I do order and declare that all persons held as slaves within said designated States, and parts of States, are, and henceforward shall be free; and that the Executive government of the United States, including the military and naval authorities thereof, will recognize and maintain the freedom of said persons.

244. Which of the following statements best describes the impact of the Emancipation Proclamation?

(A) All slaves were freed in both the North and the South.

(B) The slaves of the Confederacy were freed.

(C) All slaves who joined the Union Army would be freed.

(D) Slaves were freed in the North.

245. In regard to the Emancipation Proclamation, what was a major significance of the 1864 presidential election?

(A) The Copperheads began to support Lincoln.

(B) Northern voters showed their approval of Lincoln's stand against slavery.

(C) Northern voters showed their disapproval of Lincoln's war leadership.

(D) Northern voters rejected Lincoln's stand on slavery.

246. Which of the following statements is most accurate concerning African Americans during the Civil War?

(A) African Americans were readily conscripted into combat duty early on both sides.

(B) At the war's start, the North quickly created numerous African-American combat units.

(C) African Americans were not allowed to serve on either side's navy.

(D) The Emancipation Proclamation increased African-American enlistments in the North.

Use the image and your knowledge of the time period to answer questions 247 to 249.

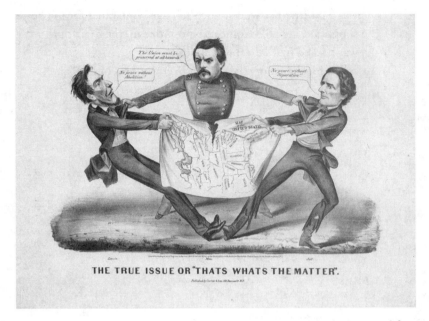

THE TRUE ISSUE OR "THATS WHATS THE MATTER".

Source: The true issue or "that's whats the matter."" [Print]. (1864). Retrieved from
https://ark.digitalcommonwealth.org/ark:/50959/9880w945c.
McClellan: "The Union must be preserved at all hazards!"
Lincoln: "No peace without abolition."
Davis: "No peace without Separation!!"

247. What is the central argument being made by this cartoon?

(A) The Republican Party's plan is best to bring about the end of the Civil War.

(B) The failed Peninsular Campaign led to greater division within the country.

(C) The Democratic Party was best suited to keep the union together.

(D) The best solution to the Civil War was dividing the nation in half.

248. In George McClellan's race for the presidency, he stated he would

(A) call for a total Union victory

(B) reinstitute slavery in the border states

(C) call for negotiations ending the war

(D) suspend habeas corpus in rebellious regions

249. During the election of 1864, McClellan may have been considered "Copperhead" because

(A) he was a Northerner who seemed to have sympathies for the South

(B) he supported the police officers who broke up the draft riots

(C) he was backed by Radical Republicans

(D) he called for the Copperhead Plan over the Anaconda Plan

CHAPTER 11

Post–Civil War and Reconstruction

Use the documents and your knowledge of your time period to answer questions 250 to 255.

Amendment XIII

Section 1.

Neither slavery nor involuntary servitude, except as a punishment for crime whereof the party shall have been duly convicted, shall exist within the United States, or any place subject to their jurisdiction.

Section 2.

Congress shall have power to enforce this article by appropriate legislation.

Amendment XIV

Section 1.

All persons born or naturalized in the United States, and subject to the jurisdiction thereof, are citizens of the United States and of the state wherein they reside. No state shall make or enforce any law which shall abridge the privileges or immunities of citizens of the United States; nor shall any state deprive any person of life, liberty, or property, without due process of law; nor deny to any person within its jurisdiction the equal protection of the laws.

Section 2.

. . . But when the right to vote at any election for the choice of electors for President and Vice President of the United States, Representatives in Congress, the executive and judicial officers of a state, or the members of the legislature thereof, is denied to any of the male inhabitants of such state, being twenty-one years of age, and citizens of the United States, or in any way abridged, except for participation in rebellion, or other crime, the basis of representation therein shall be reduced in the proportion which the number of such male citizens shall bear to the whole number of male citizens twenty-one years of age in such state.

Amendment XV

Section 1.

The right of citizens of the United States to vote shall not be denied or abridged by the United States or by any state on account of race, color, or previous condition of servitude.

250. The practice of slavery was officially ended in the United States with the

    (A) passage of the Twelfth Amendment
    (B) passage of the Fifteenth Amendment
    (C) passage of the Thirteenth Amendment
    (D) passage of the Fourteenth Amendment

251. The Fourteenth Amendment officially undid which Supreme Court ruling?

    (A) *Worcester v. Georgia*
    (B) *Dartmouth College v. Woodward*
    (C) *Marbury v. Madison*
    (D) *Dred Scott v. Sandford*

252. Which government action extended suffrage to African-American males during Reconstruction?

    (A) passage of the Thirteenth Amendment
    (B) passage of the Fourteenth Amendment
    (C) passage of the Fifteenth Amendment
    (D) passage of the Sixteenth Amendment

253. Based on the Thirteenth Amendment, which of the following would be considered a valid case for involuntary servitude?

(A) unresolved debt

(B) punishment for a crime

(C) the draft

(D) states with gradual emancipation statutes

254. Article 2 of the Fourteenth Amendment would most negatively impact which group?

(A) women

(B) white males

(C) African-American males

(D) nonwhites born in the United States

255. Which action had to be ratified by former Confederate states as part of the Radical Republican plan for reconstruction?

(A) the Thirteenth Amendment

(B) the Fourteenth Amendment

(C) the Fifteenth Amendment

(D) the Wade–Davis Bill

Use the documents and your knowledge of the time period to answer questions 256 to 260.

Proclamation of Amnesty and Reconstruction

Abraham Lincoln (December 8, 1863)

I, Abraham Lincoln, President of the United States, do proclaim, declare, and make known to all persons who have, directly or by implication, participated in the existing rebellion, except as hereinafter excepted, that a full pardon is hereby granted to them and each of them, with restoration of all rights of property, except as to slaves, and in property cases where rights of third parties shall have intervened, and upon the condition that every such person shall take and subscribe an oath, and thenceforward keep and maintain said oath inviolate; and which oath shall be registered for permanent preservation . . .

And I do further proclaim, declare, and make known that whenever, in any of the States . . . a number of persons, not less than one tenth in number of the votes cast in such state at the presidential election of . . . one thousand eight hundred and sixty, each having taken the oath aforesaid, and not having since violated it, and being a qualified voter by the election law of the state existing immediately before the so-called act of secession, and excluding all others, shall reestablish a state government which shall be republican, and in nowise contravening said oath, such shall be recognized as the true government of the state, and the state shall receive thereunder the benefits of the constitutional provision . . .

And I do further proclaim, declare, and make known that any provision which may be adopted by such state government in relation to the freed people of such state, which shall recognize and declare their permanent freedom, provide for their education, and which may yet be consistent as a temporary arrangement with their present condition as a laboring, landless, and homeless class, will not be objected to by the National Executive.

Wade–Davis Bill (1864)

A Bill to guarantee to certain States whose Governments have been usurped or overthrown a Republican Form of Government

SEC. 2. And be it further enacted, That so soon as the military resistance to the United States shall have been suppressed in any such state . . . the provisional governor shall direct the marshal of the United . . . to enroll all white male citizens of the United States . . . to take the oath to support the constitution of the United States, and in his enrolment to designate those who take and those who refuse to take that oath . . . and if the persons taking that oath shall amount to a majority of the persons enrolled in the state, he shall . . . invite the loyal people of the state to elect delegates to a convention charged to declare the will of the people of the state relative to the reestablishment of a state government . . .

SEC. 12. And be it further enacted, that all persons held to involuntary servitude or labor in the states aforesaid are hereby emancipated and discharged therefrom, and they and their posterity shall be forever free.

256. Based on the documents, why was President Lincoln's plan for Reconstruction opposed by some Radical Republicans?

(A) They felt it was too harsh on Southerners.

(B) They felt it was too lenient on the South.

(C) They believed it was too generous to the freedmen.

(D) They believed it would be impractical to carry out.

257. Which executive power did Lincoln cite in justifying his plan for Reconstruction?

(A) commander and chief of the United States

(B) the power of the pardon

(C) the power of chief executive

(D) the power of chief diplomat

258. The Wade–Davis Bill stated that Southern states could reenter the Union after

(A) they ratified the Thirteenth Amendment

(B) half the voters took a loyalty pledge

(C) 10 percent of voters took a loyalty pledge

(D) they ratified the Fourteenth Amendment

259. Both Lincoln's Plan and the Wade–Davis Bill include which provision?

(A) a pardon of to all individuals who fought for or served in the Confederate government

(B) an open guarantee of reinstatement into the Union

(C) the emancipation and guaranteed freedom of former slaves

(D) an immediate withdraw of Union troops from occupied states

260. Which was *not* a similarity in the Reconstruction plan of President Lincoln and to that of President Johnson?

(A) They both called for land to be redistributed to former slaves.

(B) They both supported the 10 Percent Plan.

(C) Both allowed for pardons of former Confederates.

(D) Both offered simplified plans for states to reenter the Union.

Use the image and your knowledge of the time period to answer question 261.

Source: Waud, Alfred R. (1868) The Freedmen's Bureau. Retrieved from the Library of Congress, http://hdl.loc.gov/loc.pnp/cph.3c05555.

261. Based on the image, what was the main purpose of the Freedman's Bureau?

(A) segregate Southern white and black populations

(B) provide aid to freed people and help them make the adjustment to freedom

(C) suppress Southern rebellions following the Civil War

(D) redistribute land to former slaves

Use the image and your knowledge of the time period to answer questions 262 to 265.

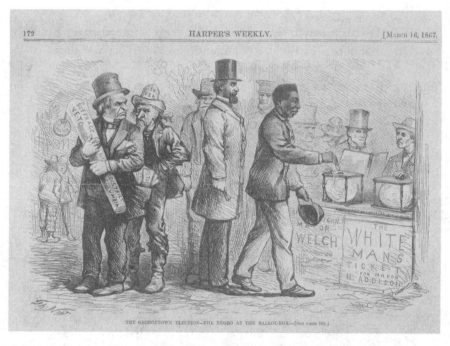

Source: Nast, Thomas (1867). The Georgetown elections - the Negro at the ballot-box. Retrieved from the Library of Congress, http://hdl.loc.gov/loc.pnp/cph.3c39438.

262. Which of the following statements describes a provision of the 1867 Reconstruction Act?

(A) The law established a system to end Reconstruction.

(B) The law forced states to create new constitutions to allow African-American males to vote.

(C) The law created a system of sharecropping to boost the Southern economy.

(D) The law allowed for the legalization of Black Codes.

263. Which political viewpoint is most logically being depicted by this image?

   (A) the views of the Radical Republicans

   (B) the views of Andrew Johnson

   (C) the views of former members of the Confederacy

   (D) the views of the Democratic party

264. Beyond what is depicted in the image, President Johnson was impeached officially because he

   (A) voted for the Radical Republican plans for Reconstruction

   (B) illegally removed a cabinet member from office

   (C) illegally used Reconstruction funds for personal gain

   (D) refused to send the military to the South, as required by the 1867 Reconstruction Act

265. The 1869 Supreme Court decision in *Texas v. White* stated that to further Andrew Johnson's view of Reconstruction,

   (A) Texas, based on its annexation into the Union, still had the right to secede

   (B) the notion of "separate but equal" was legal

   (C) it was illegal for states to secede from the Union

   (D) citizens could not be denied rights based on race or color

Use the image and your knowledge of the time period to answer questions 266 to 272.

Source: Wales, James Albert (1880). The "Strong" government 1869–1877—The "weak" government 1877–1881. Retrieved from Library of Congress Prints and Photographs Division. http://hdl.loc.gov/loc.pnp/cph.3g02623.

266. What criticism is being made in the images above?

    (A) The policies of Rutherford B. Hayes forced the South to remain agricultural.

    (B) Rutherford B. Hayes' weak government policy could not effectively help the South.

    (C) The Reconstruction efforts of Grant were an undue burden on the South.

    (D) The end of military occupation of the South limited Southern Reconstruction efforts.

267. Which of the following actions was *not* taken by Ulysses S. Grant as president during Reconstruction?

    (A) overseeing the ratification of the Fifteenth Amendment

    (B) passing legislation to suppress the influence of the Ku Klux Klan

    (C) extending pardons to a broader number of Confederates

    (D) increasing the size of the Northern military in the South

268. As illustrated in the second image, during Reconstruction, most former slaves found employment mainly as

(A) factory workers

(B) sharecroppers

(C) skilled craftsmen

(D) members of the military

269. The Depression of 1873 most directly resulted in

(A) Ulysses S. Grant failing to be renominated for president

(B) Republicans losing control of the presidency in the following election

(C) Republicans losing control of the Senate in the following election

(D) Republicans losing control of the House of Representatives in the following election

270. Which corruption scandal is most associated with the administration of Ulysses S. Grant?

(A) Whiskey Ring Scandal

(B) Teapot Dome Scandal

(C) Whitewater Scandal

(D) Star Route Scandal

271. As illustrated in the images, in return for helping Rutherford B. Hayes win the presidency, the Republicans promised the Democrats that

(A) they would repeal the 1875 Civil Rights Act

(B) the occupation of the South by federal troops would be ended

(C) the U.S. Treasury would adopt a policy of bimetallism to help Southern farmers

(D) the practice of separate but equal would be upheld

272. Which of the following was *not* a result of the Compromise of 1877?

(A) Military occupation of the South ended.

(B) The Republicans maintained control of the White House.

(C) The Force Acts were overturned.

(D) Reconstruction was ended.

Use the image and your knowledge of the time period to answer questions 273 to 277.

Source: Nast, Thomas (1874). The Union as it was the lost cause, worse than slavery. Retrieved from Library of Congress Prints and Photographs Division. http://hdl.loc.gov/loc.pnp/cph.3c28619.

273. As illustrated in the cartoon, the Ku Klux Klan formed during Reconstruction with the purpose of

(A) fighting Union armies stationed in the South

(B) keeping African Americans from exercising rights

(C) restarting the Confederacy

(D) helping poor whites improve their economic status

274. In relation to the image, the purpose of the Force Acts was primarily to

(A) limit the actions of the Ku Klux Klan

(B) impose segregated accommodations in the South

(C) force Southerners to take loyalty oaths

(D) divide the South into military districts

275. Following the Civil War, the rights of freedmen were restricted by Southern governments through

   (A) the refusal to ratify the Thirteenth Amendment
   (B) the holding of constitutional conventions
   (C) the creation of Black Codes
   (D) the refusal to pay debts remaining from the war

276. In relation to the image, in the case of *United States v. Cruikshank*, the Supreme Court found that

   (A) the 1875 Civil Rights Act was unconstitutional
   (B) voter qualification requirements were illegal
   (C) "separate but equal" was legal
   (D) only states could enforce the Ku Klux Klan Act of 1871

277. In relation to the image, what are Jim Crow laws?

   (A) actions created by the federal government but not enforced by the states
   (B) laws creating segregated accommodations
   (C) laws limiting actions of groups such as the Ku Klux Klan
   (D) actions or laws enforced only through social conventions

CHAPTER 12

The Gilded Age and the American West

Use the image and your knowledge of the time period to answer questions 278 and 279.

OUR GOVERNMENT FARM.—PRESIDENT CLEVELAND FINDS AN EFFECTUAL PROTECTION AGAINST THE TWENTY-FIVE-YEAR LOCUSTS.

Source: Zimmerman, Eugene. Our government farm—President Cleveland finds an effectual protection against the twenty-five-year locusts. (1885) Accessed from the Library of Congress. http://hdl.loc.gov/loc.pnp/ppmsca.28123.

278. The Civil Service Commission ended the spoils system by

(A) allowing the president to offer supporters government jobs

(B) forbidding the government from hiring employees who belonged to the same party as the president

(C) requiring anyone applying for a government job to take a competitive exam

(D) not hiring people who were acquainted personally with the president

279. The Pendleton Act was created in response to the

    (A) Whiskey Ring Scandal

    (B) Colfax Massacre

    (C) Battle of Wounded Knee

    (D) assassination of President Garfield

Use the image and your knowledge of the time period to answer questions 280 to 283.

Source: Strobridge & Co. Lith. "Gift for the Grangers" (1873). Retrieved from the Library of Congress, http://hdl.loc.gov/loc.pnp/pga.04170.

280. As illustrated in the image, the primary function of the Grange movement was to

(A) allow western state governments to sell land quickly

(B) purchase large areas of land in the West to sell later for a profit

(C) help farmers create cooperatives

(D) allow Americans and immigrants to buy land directly from the federal government

281. The Grange movement began in part as a response to which of the following changes in the practice of post–Civil War agriculture?

(A) The government ended all Homestead Acts.

(B) The use of machinery on farms increased.

(C) The size of the average farm decreased.

(D) There was a lack of open land in the Great Plains.

282. Another factor leading to the formation of the Grange was that, during the late nineteenth century, the reduction in price of American agricultural products led to

(A) farmers facing less of a debt burden

(B) more workers shifting to agricultural work

(C) farmers being compelled to increase production

(D) less land being cultivated

283. Unlike the Grange, farmers of the late nineteenth century did *not* benefit from the

(A) Farmers' Alliances

(B) Homestead Acts

(C) McKinley Tariff

(D) Populist Party

Use the document and your knowledge of the time period to answer questions 284 to 286.

Homestead Act (1862)

An Act to secure Homesteads to actual Settlers on the Public Domain.

Be it enacted by the Senate and House of Representatives of the United States of America in Congress assembled, That any person who is the head of a family, or who has arrived at the age of twenty-one years, and is a citizen of the United States, or who shall have filed his declaration of intention to become such, as required by the naturalization laws of the United States, and who has never borne arms against the United States Government or given aid and comfort to its enemies, shall, from and after the first January, eighteen hundred and. sixty-three, be entitled to enter one quarter section or a less quantity of unappropriated public lands, upon which said person may have filed a preemption claim, or which may, at the time the application is made, be subject to preemption at one dollar and twenty-five cents, or less, per acre; or eighty acres or less of such unappropriated lands, at two dollars and fifty cents per acre, to be located in a body, in conformity to the legal subdivisions of the public lands, and after the same shall have been surveyed: Provided, That any person owning and residing on land may, under the provisions of this act, enter other land lying contiguous to his or her said land, which shall not, with the land so already owned and occupied, exceed in the aggregate one hundred and sixty acres.

---

284. Which of the following statements was *not* true of the 1862 Homestead Act?

(A) It provided a system for the federal government to provide land directly to settlers.

(B) It made land available to citizens and to immigrants who planned to become citizens.

(C) Farmers were given ownership of land after living on it for five years.

(D) Land speculators were effectively kept from abusing the act.

285. In addition to the Homestead Act, which of the following factors played the largest role in increasing the settlement of the Great Plains?

(A) construction of railroads

(B) removal of the Great Plains Indians

(C) increase in foreign demand for agricultural foods

(D) increase in price of agricultural goods

286. The Morrill Land-Grant Act of 1862 was also designed to help develop the West by

(A) assisting western states with establishing colleges

(B) helping farmers establish cooperatives

(C) promoting the construction of a transcontinental railroad

(D) providing land for landless former slaves

Use the image and your knowledge of the time period to answer question 287.

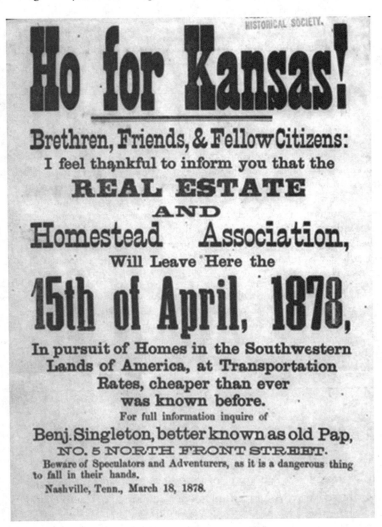

Source: Singleton, Benjamin, Ho for Kansas! Brethren, Friends, & Fellow Citizens: I feel thankful to inform you that the real estate and Homestead Association, will leave here the 15th of April, In pursuit of Homes in the Southwestern Lands of America. Kansas Tennessee, None. [Between 1980 and 1990?] [Photograph] Retrieved from the Library of Congress, https://www.loc.gov/item/98501335/.

287. What was a primary motivation for the Kansas Exodus of many African Americans to the West following the Civil War?

  (A) The increased military presence in the South threatened former slaves.

  (B) The decrease in agricultural jobs forced many to look for work elsewhere.

  (C) Institutionalized racism and discrimination forced many to look for a better place to live.

  (D) African Americans were not eligible for the Homestead Act, so Kansas was their only chance of owning land.

Use the document and your knowledge of the time period to answer questions 288 and 289.

Dawes Act (1887)

Be it enacted by the Senate and House of Representatives of the United States of America in Congress assembled, That in all cases where any tribe or band of Indians has been, or shall hereafter be, located upon any reservation created for their use, either by treaty stipulation or by virtue of an act of Congress or executive order setting apart the same for their use, the President of the United States be, and he hereby is, authorized, whenever in his opinion any reservation or any part thereof of such Indians is advantageous for agricultural and grazing purposes, to cause said reservation, or any part thereof, to be surveyed, or resurveyed if necessary, and to allot the lands in said reservation in severalty to any Indian located thereon in quantities as follows:

> To each head of a family, one-quarter of a section;
> To each single person over eighteen years of age, one-eighth of a section;
> To each orphan child under eighteen years of age, one-eighth of a section; and
> To each other single person under eighteen years now living, or who may be born prior to the date of the order of the President directing an allotment of the lands embraced in any reservation, one-sixteenth of a section . . .

---

288. As illustrated in the document, the 1887 Dawes Act was passed to

  (A) compensate Native Americans for prior illegal land contracts

  (B) move Native Americans onto western reservations

  (C) force Native Americans to adopt Western culture and farming practices

  (D) extend constitutional protections to Native American males

289. In addition to the Dawes Act, what did the events that took place between Chief Joseph of the Nez Percé and the federal government illustrate about U.S.–Native American relations in the late nineteenth century?

(A) The government became more active in protecting traditional Native American lands.

(B) Native Americans became more willing to accept the reservation system.

(C) Violent conflicts continued to be waged between the Native Americans and the government.

(D) Native Americans were willing to abandon traditional practices for sedentary agriculture.

Use the document and your knowledge of the time period to answer question 290.

Rm 24 Mc S 93 Paid Govt
Pine Ridge Agcy SF 422 Nov 24 [1890]
Chicago 24 Via Rushville

Major General Comdg the army is of opinion that the *ghost dances* should not be disturbed for the present nor anything be done to precipitate a conflict and that when the troops are all concentrated Ready for action it can be better judged of the measures that may be necessary and advisable. This opinion has been already anticipated by the Divn Commander In his instructions previously sent to you by command of Major Genl Miles.

R. Williams
Asst Adjt Genl

290. How was the focus of the Ghost Dance movement similar to that of Tenskwatawa, the Shawnee leader also known as the Prophet, in his movement prior to the War of 1812?

(A) They both called for assimilation into American culture.

(B) They both called for a rejection of white culture and technology.

(C) They both called for violent actions to stop encroachment onto their traditional lands.

(D) They both called for the peaceful acceptance of the reservation system.

Use the document and your knowledge of the time period to answer questions 291 and 292.

Frontier Thesis of American History Frederick Jackson Turner, 1893

In the settlement of America we have to observe how European life entered the continent, and how America modified and developed that life and reacted on Europe. . . . The frontier is the line of most rapid and effective Americanization. The wilderness masters the colonist. It finds him a European in dress . . . and thought. . . . It strips off the garments of civilization and arrays him in the hunting shirt and the moccasin. . . . He must accept the conditions which it furnishes or perish, and so he fits himself into the Indian clearings and follows the Indian trails.

   Little by little he transforms the wilderness, but the outcome is not the old Europe. . . . The fact is, that here is a new product that is American. At first, the frontier was the Atlantic coast. It was the frontier of Europe in a very real sense. Moving westward, the frontier became more and more American . . . a steady growth of independence on American lines. And to study this advance, the men who grew up under these conditions, and the political, economic, and social results of it, is to study the really American part of our history.

   American democracy is . . . the outcome of the experiences of the American people in dealing with the West. Western democracy . . . tended to the production of a society of which the most distinctive fact was the freedom of the individual to rise under conditions of social mobility. . . . This conception has vitalized all American democracy. . . . The problem of the United States is not to create democracy, but to conserve democratic institutions and ideals.

---

291. Based on the document, Frederick Jackson Turner's thesis argued that America's frontier

    (A) was a major obstacle that stood in the way of progress
    (B) was a fundamental factor in the American government and individualism
    (C) would continue despite the closing of the West
    (D) allowed immigrants to retain their culture

292. Frederick Jackson Turner's thesis focused on

    (A) European ideals in North America
    (B) the frontier and American democracy
    (C) cultural diversity among western settlers
    (D) the issue of slavery and westward expansion

Use the image and your knowledge of the time period to answer questions 293 to 296.

Source: Newell, Peter. From the Collections of the Pennsylvania Department, The Carnegie Library of Pittsburgh.

293. Based on the image, during the late nineteenth century, a "robber baron" would be best defined as

(A) a powerful industrialist

(B) the leader of a large criminal organization

(C) the head of a large political machine

(D) a leader of a large labor union

294. As illustrated in the image, a monopoly is best defined as

(A) a market situation where there is only a single provider of a good or service

(B) negotiation by workers as a group with business owners over compensation

(C) an arrangement of similar businesses created to regulate production and control pricing

(D) a business that provides a necessity to the general public

295. As depicted in the image, Andrew Carnegie engaged in the practice of vertical integration by

(A) monopolizing a single product by eliminating all competition

(B) controlling all aspects of the production process from beginning to end

(C) artificially inflating the value of his companies' stock to attract investors

(D) using private detective agencies to break strikes

296. Contrasting the business strategy illustrated in the image, *horizontal integration* is best illustrated by

(A) John D. Rockefeller eliminating all competing firms that produced the same products

(B) Cornelius Vanderbilt issuing noncompetitive railroad rebates

(C) John P. Morgan artificially inflating the price of his own stocks

(D) Henry Frick using private detective agencies to break strikes

Use the image and your knowledge of the time period to answer questions 297 to 299.

Source: Crawford, W. (1911) The fog/Will Crawford., 1911. N.Y.: Published by Keppler & Schwarzmann, Puck Building. [Photograph] Retrieved from the Library of Congress, https://www.loc.gov/item/2011649081/.
Ship labeled American Business
Buoy labeled US Justice Department
Fog labeled the Sherman Law

297. The goal of the Sherman Antitrust Act was to

(A) encourage the creation of labor unions

(B) encourage the growth of trusts

(C) create greater fairness in industry

(D) increase tax review on large businesses

298. The creator of the cartoon is most likely trying to convey which idea about the Sherman Act?

(A) The act creates clear guidelines for business practice.

(B) The act creates an uncertain business environment.

(C) The act negatively impacts labor.

(D) The act creates an undo tax burden on business.

299. Despite the initial intent of the Sherman Act, how did the government use the act in response to the 1894 Pullman strike?

(A) It nationalized the company.

(B) It tried the company owners under antitrust laws.

(C) It used federal troops to subdue the workers.

(D) It forced the striking workers to collectively bargain.

Use the document and your knowledge of the time period to answer questions 300 and 301.

Wabash, St. Louis, and Pacific Railroad Company v. Illinois (1886)

Although the precise point presented by this case may not have been heretofore decided by this court, the general subject of the power of the State legislature to regulate taxes, fares, and tolls for passengers and transportation of freight over railroads within their limits has been very much considered recently . . . and the question how far such regulations, made by the States and under State authority are valid or void, as they may affect the transportation of goods through more than one State, in one voyage, is not entirely new here . . . the State of Illinois and undertaking for itself to apportion the rates charged over the whole route, decides that the contract and the receipt of the money for so much of it as was performed within the State of Illinois violate the statute of the State on that subject . . .

Of the justice or propriety of the principle which lies at the foundation of the Illinois statute it is not the province of this court to speak. As restricted to a transportation which begins and ends within the limits of the State, it may be very just and equitable . . . But when it is attempted to apply to transportation through an entire series of States a principle of this kind, and each one of the States shall attempt to establish its own rates of transportation, its own methods to prevent discrimination in rates, or to permit it, the deleterious influence upon the freedom of commerce among the States, and upon the transit of goods through those States, cannot be overestimated.

---

300. Based on the document, the *Wabash* case allowed for the passage of which law?

(A) the Hepburn Act

(B) the Elkins Act

(C) the Interstate Commerce Act

(D) the Comstock Law

301. The main purpose of that act in relation to the court decision was to

   (A) control unfair railroad rate and rebate practices
   (B) better regulate free-range cattle grazing
   (C) increase taxes on businesses that profited from interstate commerce
   (D) limit union actions that could negatively affect interstate commerce

Use the documents and your knowledge of the time period to answer questions 302 to 304.

Preamble and Declaration of Principles of the Knights of Labor of America (1886)

The alarming development and aggressiveness of great capitalists and corporations, unless checked, will inevitably lead to the pauperization and hopeless degradation of the toiling masses.

It is imperative, if we desire to enjoy the full blessings of life, that a check be placed upon unjust accumulation, and the power for evil of aggregated wealth.

This much-desired object can be accomplished only by the united efforts of those who obey the divine injunction, "In the sweat of they face shalt thou eat bread."

Therefore we have formed the Order of Knights of Labor, for the purpose of organizing and directing the power of the industrial masses, not as a political party, for it is more—in it are crystallized sentiments and measures for the benefit of the whole people, but it should be borne in mind, when exercising the right of suffrage, that most of the objects herein set forth can only be obtained through legislation, and that it is the duty of all to assist in nominating and supporting with their votes only such candidates as will pledge their support to those measures, regardless of party. . . . We declare to the world that are our aims are:

1. To make individual and moral worth, not wealth, the true standard of individual and National greatness.
2. To secure to the workers the full enjoyment of the wealth they create, sufficient leisure in which to develop their intellectual, moral, and social faculties: all of the benefits, recreation and pleasures of association; in a word, to enable them to share in the gains and honors of advancing civilization.

Samuel Gompers President of American Federation of Labor (1913)

With the power of wealth and concentration of industry, the tremendous development in machinery, and power to drive machinery; with the improvement of the tools of labor, so that they are wonderfully tremendous machines, and with these all on the one hand; with labor, the workers, performing a given part of the whole product, probably an infinitesimal part, doing the thing a thousand or thousands of times over and over again in a day—labor divided and subdivided and specialized, so that a working man is but a mere cog in the great industrial modern plant; his individuality lost, alienated from the tools of labor; with concentration of wealth, concentration of industry, I wonder whether any of us can imagine what would be the actual condition of the working people of our country today without their organizations to protect them.

What would be the condition of the working men in our country in our day by acting as individuals with as great a concentrated wealth and industry on every hand? It is horrifying even to permit the imagination full swing to think what would be possible. Slavery! Slavery! Demoralized, degraded slavery. Nothing better.

302. Both The Knights of Labor and the American Federation of Labor raise which concern about the growth of American industry?

(A) Government regulations of businesses are hurting the wages of workers.

(B) The government must move away from capitalism and adopt socialism as an economic model.

(C) The growth of large corporations and trusts if unchecked will hurt the American worker.

(D) More laws like the Sherman Act were needed to protect the worker.

303. In what way did the Knights of Labor differ from the American Federation of Labor (AFL)?

(A) Unlike the AFL, the Knights of Labor limited membership to skilled labor only.

(B) Unlike the Knights of Labor, the AFL limited membership to skilled labor only.

(C) Unlike the Knights of Labor, the AFL allowed women to be members.

(D) Unlike the Knights of Labor, the AFL allowed farmers to be members.

304. How did the events of the Haymarket Square Riot of 1886 impact labor organizations such as the Knights of Labor?

(A) It led the public to become highly critical of unions.

(B) It led to increased public sympathy for organized labor.

(C) It led to increased support for labor reform.

(D) It led for stronger government actions to protect organized labor.

Use the document and your knowledge of the time period to answer questions 305 to 307.

Official Proceedings of the Democratic National Convention held in Chicago, Illinois 1896

I shall not slander the fair state of Massachusetts nor the state of New York by saying that when citizens are confronted with the proposition, "Is this nation able to attend to its own business?"—I will not slander either one by saying that the people of those states will declare our helpless impotency as a nation to attend to our own business. It is the issue of 1776 over again. Our ancestors, when but 3 million, had the courage to declare their political independence of every other nation upon earth. Shall we, their descendants, when we have grown to 70 million, declare that we are less independent than our forefathers? No, my friends, it will never be the judgment of this people. Therefore, we care not upon what lines the battle is fought. If they say bimetallism is good but we cannot have it till some nation helps us, we reply that, instead of having a gold standard because England has, we shall restore bimetallism, and then let England have bimetallism because the United States have.

If they dare to come out in the open field and defend the gold standard as a good thing, we shall fight them to the uttermost, having behind us the producing masses of the nation and the world. Having behind us the commercial interests and the laboring interests and all the toiling masses, we shall answer their demands for a gold standard by saying to them, you shall not press down upon the brow of labor this crown of thorns. You shall not crucify mankind upon a cross of gold.

---

305. This quotation is associated with which late-nineteenth-century leader?

(A) Eugene V. Debs

(B) William Jennings Bryan

(C) William McKinley

(D) W. E. B. Dubois

306. Based on the passage and your knowledge of history, the author of this passage lost his 1896 campaign for the presidency because he

(A) lacked ability as a persuasive speaker

(B) supported the silver standard

(C) was unable to win the support of western farmers

(D) could not win the support of eastern urban centers

307. In addition to the ideas noted in the speech, which of the following was *not* part of the Populist Party's platform?

(A) institution of a secret ballot

(B) private ownership of the railroads

(C) banking reform

(D) a graduated income tax

Use the document and your knowledge of the time period to answer question 308.

George Washington Plunkett in an interview with a newspaper reporter, 1905.

Everybody is talkin' these days about Tammany men growin' rich on graft, but nobody thinks of drawin' the distinction between honest graft and dishonest graft. There's all the difference in the world between the two. Yes, many of our men have grown rich in politics. I have myself. I've made a big fortune out of the game, and I'm getting' richer every day, but I've not gone in for dishonest graft—blackmailin' gamblers, saloon-keepers, disorderly people, etc.—and neither has any of the men who have made big fortunes in politics.

There's an honest graft, and I'm an example of how it works. I might sum up the whole thing by sayin': "I seen my opportunities and I took 'em."

Just let me explain by examples. My party's in power in the city, and it's goin' to undertake a lot of public improvements. Well, I'm tipped off, say, that they're goin' to lay out a new park at a certain place . . . I go to that place and I buy up all the land I can in the neighborhood. Then the board of this or that makes its plan public, and there's a rush to get my land, which nobody cared particular for before.

Ain't it perfectly honest to charge a good price and make a profit on my investment and foresight? Of course it is. Well, that's honest graft.

---

308. Based on the document, Tammany Hall of the late nineteenth century was

(A) the location that became the basis of the *Plessey v. Ferguson* decision

(B) a Democratic political machine that controlled New York City politics

(C) the headquarters for the newly formed NAACP

(D) the base of organization for the Populist Party joining with the Grange movement

U.S. Imperialism and the Progressive Movement

Use the graphic and your knowledge of the time period to answer questions 309 to 313.

United States Imperialism—1865 to 1904

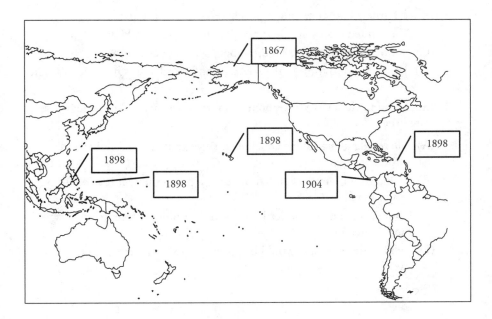

309. In relation to the map, Seward's Folly refers to the

(A) U.S. annexation of Hawaii

(B) U.S. purchase of Alaska

(C) events that led to the Spanish–American War

(D) Gadsden Purchase

310. Based on the map, which of the following territories were acquired by the United States as a result of the Spanish–American War?

(A) Guam, the Philippines, and Cuba

(B) Hawaii, Guam, and the Philippines

(C) Cuba, Puerto Rico, and the Philippines

(D) the Philippines, Guam, and Puerto Rico

311. In relation to the map, the Hay–Bunau Treaty allowed for the

(A) U.S. acquisition of Midway

(B) U.S. control over Hawaii

(C) construction of the Panama Canal

(D) Open Door Policy in China

312. Which of the following actions illustrated the usage of the Monroe Doctrine in the second half of the nineteenth century?

(A) Matthew Perry opening up trade relations with Japan

(B) the United States dominating sugar production in Hawaii

(C) John Hay's insistence on the Open Door Policy

(D) the U.S. arbitration in the Venezuelan boundary dispute with Britain

313. In relation to the map, the Supreme Court's decision in the "insular cases" stated that

(A) all people living under U.S. control are granted equal rights and protections

(B) Cuba could join the United States as a protectorate if it chose to by popular vote

(C) some people living under U.S. control would not receive equal rights and protections

(D) while Puerto Ricans would be given full rights as citizens, Filipinos would not

Use the document and your knowledge of the time period to answer questions 314 to 318.

The Influence of Sea Power upon History
Alfred Thayer Mahan, 1890

. . . The interesting and significant feature of this changing attitude is the turning of the eyes outward, instead of inward only, to seek the welfare of the country. To affirm the importance of distant markets, and the relation to them of our own immense powers of production, implies logically the recognition of the link that joins the products and the markets, that is, the carrying trade; the three together constituting that chain of maritime power to which Great Britain owes her wealth and greatness. Further, is it too much to say that, as two of these links, the shipping and the markets, are exterior to our own borders, the acknowledgment of them carries with it a view of the relations of the United States to the world radically distinct from the simple idea of self sufficientness? We shall not follow far this line of thought before there will dawn the realization of America's unique position, facing the older worlds of the East and West, her shores washed by the oceans which touch the one or the other, but which are common to her alone . . .

Despite a certain great original superiority conferred by our geographical nearness and immense resources,—due, in other words, to our natural advantages, and not to our intelligent preparations,—the United States is woefully unready, not only in fact but in purpose to assert in the Caribbean and Central America a weight of influence proportioned to the extent of her interests. We have not the navy, and, what is worse, we are not willing to have the navy that will weigh seriously in any disputes with those nations whose interests will conflict there with our own. We have not, and we are not anxious to provide, the defense of the seaboard which will leave the navy free for its work at sea. We have not, but many other powers have, positions, either within or on the borders of the Caribbean . . .

Yet, were our sea frontier as strong as it now is weak, passive self-defense, whether in trade or war, would be but a poor policy, so long as the world continues to be one of struggle and vicissitude . . .

---

314. Which of following policies would *not* have been supported by Alfred T. Mahan?

(A) creation of a modern navy

(B) creation of a large modern land army

(C) construction of a canal through Central America

(D) establishment of coaling stations throughout the Pacific

315. What factors did Mahan state the United States lacked in order to make its influence equal to its interests?

(A) It lacked a navy and motivation to build one.

(B) It lacked the financial resources for expansion.

(C) It lacked materials to participate in the global market.

(D) It lacked the geographic location to serve as a naval power.

316. In relation to the document, which of the following factors provided economic justification for U.S. expansion in the second part of the nineteenth century?

(A) Increased production led to the need for new markets abroad.

(B) U.S. industry was suffering from a severe shortage of labor.

(C) The U.S. domestic markets were flooded with less expensive imports.

(D) The United States would be considered an industrial power only if it had colonies.

317. In relation to the text, why was the Open Door Policy important to the United States?

(A) It gave the United States colonial territory in Asia.

(B) It ensured that the United States would have access to Chinese markets.

(C) It locked European nations out of Chinese markets.

(D) It further secured the legitimacy of the Monroe Doctrine.

318. In relation to the document, which of the following would *not* be an argument of the Anti-Imperialist League?

(A) Imperialism caused the need for an expanded military.

(B) Imperialism hurt manufacturers' ability to obtain raw materials.

(C) Imperialism would encourage people from different races to enter the United States.

(D) Imperial empires are too costly to maintain.

Use the image and your knowledge of the time period to answer questions 319 to 322.

Source: Goff, E. A. W., Goff, H. S. & Fort Dearborn Publishing Co. (1898) Goff's historical map of the Spanish-American War in the West Indies. [S.l] [Map] Retrieved from the Library of Congress, https://www.loc.gov/item/98687149/.

319. Which leader's atrocities helped lead the United States to war with Spain during the end of the nineteenth century?

(A) Valeriano Weyler

(B) Emilio Aguinaldo

(C) José Martí

(D) Victoriano Huerta

320. The destruction of which of the following American ships directly resulted in the Spanish–American War?

(A) the *Constitution*

(B) the *Maine*

(C) the *Maddox*

(D) the *Chesapeake*

321. Following the Spanish–American War, Cuban independence was protected with the

(A) signing of the 1898 Treaty of Paris

(B) passage of the Platt Amendment

(C) signing of the Hay–Bunau Treaty

(D) passage of the Teller Amendment

322. In relation to the conflict depicted in the map, the quote "You furnish the pictures, and I'll furnish the war" illustrates what type of late-nineteenth-century journalism?

(A) muckraking journalism

(B) yellow journalism

(C) citizen journalism

(D) red journalism

Use the documents and your knowledge of the time period to answer questions 323 to 328.

Theodore Roosevelt (Sept. 2, 1901)

A good many of you are probably acquainted with the old proverb: "Speak softly and carry a big stick—you will go far . . ."

. . . This is the attitude we should take as regards the Monroe Doctrine. There is not the least need of blustering about it. Still less should it be used as a pretext for our own aggrandizement at the expense of any other American state. But, most emphatically, we must make it evident that we intend on this point ever to maintain the old American position. Indeed, it is hard to understand how any man can take any other position, now that we are all looking forward to the building of the Isthmian Canal. The Monroe Doctrine is not international law; but there is no necessity that it should be. All that is needful is that it should continue to be a cardinal feature of American policy on this continent; and the Spanish–American states should, in their own interests, champion it as strongly as we do.

We do not by this doctrine intend to sanction any policy of aggression by one American commonwealth at the expense of any other, nor any policy of commercial discrimination against any foreign power whatsoever. Commercially, as far as this doctrine is concerned, all we wish is a fair field and no favor; but if we are wise we shall strenuously insist that under no pretext whatsoever shall there be any territorial aggrandizement on American soil by any European power, and this, no matter what form the territorial aggrandizement may take.

William Howard Taft (1912)

The foreign relations of the United States actually and potentially affect the state of the Union to a degree not widely realized and hardly surpassed by any other factor in the welfare of the whole nation. The position of the United States in the moral, intellectual, and material relations of the family of nations should be a matter of vital interest to every patriotic citizen . . .

Whether we have a farseeing and wise diplomacy and are not recklessly plunged into unnecessary wars, and whether our foreign policies are based upon an intelligent grasp of present-day world conditions and a clear view of the potentialities of the future, or are governed by a temporary and timid expediency or by narrow views befitting an infant nation, are questions in the alternative consideration of which must convince any thoughtful citizen that no department of national polity offers greater opportunity for promoting the interests of the whole people on the one hand, or greater chance on the other of permanent national injury, than that which deals with the foreign relations of the United States.

The fundamental foreign policies of the United States should be raised high above the conflict of partisanship and wholly dissociated from differences as to domestic policy. In its foreign affairs the United States should present to the world a united front. The intellectual, financial, and industrial interests of the country and the publicist, the wage earner, the farmer, and citizen of whatever occupation must cooperate in a spirit of high patriotism to promote that national solidarity which is indispensable to national efficiency and to the attainment of national ideals . . .

The diplomacy of the present administration has sought to respond to modern ideas of commercial intercourse. This policy has been characterized as substituting dollars for bullets. It is one that appeals alike to idealistic humanitarian sentiments, to the dictates of sound policy and strategy, and to legitimate commercial aims. It is an effort frankly directed to the increase of American trade upon the axiomatic principle that the government of the United States shall extend all proper support to every legitimate and beneficial American enterprise abroad . . .

Woodrow Wilson (October 27, 1913)

The future . . . is going to be very different for this hemisphere from the past. These States lying to the south of us, which have always been our neighbors, will now be drawn closer to us by innumerable ties, and, I hope, chief of all, by the tie of a common understanding of each other. Interest does not tie nations together; it sometimes separates them. But sympathy and understanding does [sic] unite them, and I believe that by the new route that is just about to be opened, while we physically cut two continents asunder, we spiritually unite them. It is a spiritual union which we seek. . . . What these States are going to see, therefore, is an emancipation from the subordination, which has been inevitable, to foreign enterprise and an assertion of the splendid character which, in spite of these difficulties, they have again and again been able to demonstrate. The dignity, the courage, the self-possession, the self-respect of the Latin American States, their achievements in the face of all these adverse circumstances, deserve nothing but the admiration and applause of the world. . . . We must prove ourselves their friends, and champions upon terms of equality and honor. You cannot be friends upon any other terms than upon the terms of equality. You cannot be friends at all except upon the terms of honor. We must show ourselves friends by comprehending their interest whether it squares with our own interest or not. . . . I want to take this occasion to say that the United States will never again seek one additional foot of territory by conquest. She will devote herself to showing that she knows how to make honorable and fruitful use of the territory she has, and she must regard it as one of the duties of friendship to see that from no quarter are material interests made superior to human liberty and national opportunity.

323. Which of the following ideas would *not* be part of the Roosevelt Corollary?

(A) The United States would continue limiting European influence in the Western Hemisphere.

(B) Latin America would be seen as an agent for U.S. commercial interests.

(C) The Monroe Doctrine would be expanded to include Asia as well as the Americas.

(D) The United States had the right to intervene in Latin American conflicts.

324. Which aspect of the Monroe Doctrine is supported by the three presidents?

(A) the continued notion of not allowing further colonization in the Western Hemisphere

(B) the role of the United States as an international police presence

(C) the ability to use military force to protect U.S. economic interests

(D) the maintenance of neutrality in international actions

325. Dollar diplomacy is most associated with the presidency of

(A) William McKinley
(B) Theodore Roosevelt
(C) William Taft
(D) Woodrow Wilson

326. Moral diplomacy, as described in the third passage, was best illustrated by

(A) Woodrow Wilson's use of the military in Nicaragua and Haiti
(B) William Taft's urging of U.S. banks to refinance Haiti's national debt
(C) Woodrow Wilson's response to the Tampico Incident
(D) the U.S. refusal to recognize the government of Victoriano Huerta

327. Based on the passages, Wilson strongly supported which of Roosevelt's policies?

(A) the Gentleman's Agreement
(B) the Panama Canal
(C) Big Stick diplomacy
(D) military intervention in the Western Hemisphere

328. Which action would not illustrate Roosevelt's notion of "Speak softly and carry a big stick, and you will go far?"

(A) the tour of the Great White Fleet
(B) Roosevelt's involvement in the Venezuelan dispute with Great Britain
(C) Roosevelt's Square Deal
(D) U.S. military intervention in Latin American countries

Use the document and your knowledge of the time period to answer questions 329 to 333.

Of Mr. Booker T. Washington and Others
W. E. B. DuBois, 1903

Mr. Washington distinctly asks that black people give up, at least for the present, three things, —

First, political power, Second, insistence on civil rights, Third, higher education of Negro youth, and concentrate all their energies on industrial education, the accumulation of wealth, and the conciliation of the South. . . . As a result of this tender of the palm-branch, what has been the return? In these years there have occurred:

1. The disfranchisement of the Negro.
2. The legal creation of a distinct status of civil inferiority for the Negro.
3. The steady withdrawal of aid from institutions for the higher training of the Negro.

These movements are not, to be sure, direct results of Mr. Washington's teachings; but his propaganda has, without a shadow of doubt, helped their speedier accomplishment. The question then comes: Is it possible, and probable, that nine millions of men can make effective progress in economic lines if they are deprived of political rights, made a servile caste, and allowed only the most meagre chance for developing their exceptional men? If history and reason give any distinct answer to these questions, it is an emphatic No.

. . . Mr. Washington's position is the object of criticism by two classes of colored Americans. One class is spiritually descended from Toussaint the Savior, through Gabriel, Vesey, and Turner, and they represent the attitude of revolt and revenge; they hate the white South blindly and distrust the white race generally, and so far as they agree on definite action, think that the Negro's only hope lies in emigration beyond the borders of the United States.

---

329. Though Booker T. Washington and W. E. B. DuBois both believed in improving conditions for African Americans, in what way did their views differ?

   (A) They both fought for social equality, but only DuBois fought for economic equality as well.

   (B) They both fought for social equality, but only Washington fought for economic equality as well.

   (C) DuBois fought only for social equality, while Washington fought only for economic equality.

   (D) DuBois felt African Americans should focus only on vocational training, while Washington called for liberal arts education.

330. When W. E. B. DuBois refers to "Toussaint the Savior," he is referring to Toussaint L'Ouverture who:

(A) led the Haitian Independence movement

(B) led a slave uprising in the United States in the early nineteenth century

(C) was the first African American in the House of Representatives

(D) was the African-American inventor who surveyed the land for Washington, D.C.

331. To further the aims described, Dubois helped begin the Niagara movement, which sought to

(A) further the views of the Anti-Imperialism League

(B) promote nativism and stem immigration

(C) achieve civil liberties for all African Americans

(D) grant suffrage to African-American women

332. The National Association for the Advancement of Colored People (NAACP) was created primarily to

(A) fight discrimination in American legal courts

(B) create a political party to represent African Americans

(C) promote the "Back to Africa" movement

(D) further the cultural advancements of the Harlem Renaissance

333. The Supreme Court's decision in *Plessy v. Ferguson* created a challenge to movements like those described in the passage by

(A) ending segregation in the United States

(B) upholding the doctrine of "separate but equal"

(C) overturning the earlier Dred Scott decision

(D) stating that "separate but equal" applied only to private businesses

Use the image and your knowledge of the time period to answer questions 334 to 336.

Source: Rogers, W. A. (1924) Whither, Old Woman, Whither So High – To Rake the Cobwebs from the Sky?., 1924. [?] [Photograph] Retrieved from the Library of Congress, https://www.loc.gov/item/2010717825/.
Caption: *Whither, old woman, whither so high–to rake the cobwebs from the sky?*
Plume text: *Scandal Monger*

334. The image above provides a commentary of what journalistic movement associated with the Progressive Era?

(A) yellow journalism

(B) muckraking journalism

(C) political satire

(D) alternative facts

335. Based on the image, the creator of the comic is most likely conveying which notion?

(A) strong support for the integrity of the journalistic movement

(B) a push to begin political witch hunts to stop socialist movements

(C) a negative criticism of the type of stories being produced by the journalistic movement

(D) a criticism of the role women played within the journalistic movement

336. Which of the following Progressive Period journalists is *not* correctly matched with the focus of his or her reporting?

(A) Ida Tarbell—the unscrupulous practices of the road industry

(B) Lincoln Steffens—political corruption

(C) Upton Sinclair—abuses in the meatpacking industry

(D) Jacob Riis—the harsh conditions in New York's slums

Use the document and your knowledge of the time period to answer questions 337 to 341.

Progressive Party Platform of 1912
November 5, 1912

The conscience of the people, in a time of grave national problems, has called into being a new party, born of the nation's sense of justice. We of the Progressive party here dedicate ourselves to the fulfillment of the duty laid upon us by our fathers to maintain the government of the people, by the people and for the people whose foundations they laid.

. . . In accordance with the needs of each generation the people must use their sovereign powers to establish and maintain equal opportunity and industrial justice, to secure which this Government was founded and without which no republic can endure.

This country belongs to the people who inhabit it. Its resources, its business, its institutions and its laws should be utilized, maintained or altered in whatever manner will best promote the general interest.

It is time to set the public welfare in the first place.

The Rule of the People

The National Progressive party, committed to the principles of government by a self-controlled democracy . . ., pledges itself to secure such alterations in the fundamental law . . . as shall insure the representative character of the government.

In particular, the party declares for direct primaries for the nomination of . . . officers, for nation-wide preferential primaries for … the presidency; for the direct election of United States Senators by the people; and we urge on the States the policy of the short ballot, with responsibility to the people secured by the initiative, referendum and recall.

Equal Suffrage

The Progressive party . . . pledges itself to the task of securing equal suffrage to men and women alike.

Social and Industrial Justice

. . . We pledge ourselves to work unceasingly in State and Nation for:

- Effective legislation looking to the prevention of industrial accidents, occupational diseases, overwork, involuntary unemployment, and other injurous effects incident to modern industry;
- The fixing of minimum safety and health standards for the various occupations, and the exercise of the public authority of State and Nation, including the Federal Control over interstate commerce, and the taxing power, to maintain such standards;
- The prohibition of child labor;
- Minimum wage standards for working women, to provide a "living wage" in all industrial occupations;
- The general prohibition of night work for women and the establishment of an eight hour day for women and young persons;
- The eight hour day in continuous twenty-four hour industries;

337. Based on the document, which of the following is *not* an example of a political reform made during the Progressive Era?

   (A) the initiative

   (B) party nominating conventions

   (C) the referendum

   (D) the direct election of senators

338. How did socialists and progressives differ in their views on how to bring about social change?

   (A) The socialists supported child safety laws, while the progressives did not.

   (B) The socialists supported immigration, while the progressives did not.

   (C) Socialists sought to end or reduce private ownership of the means of production, while the progressives did not.

   (D) The progressives supported women's suffrage, while the socialists did not.

339. Florence Kelley's efforts helped address which issue stated in the Progressive platform noted above?

(A) child labor

(B) segregation of public facilities

(C) machine politics

(D) yellow dog contracts

340. The 1911 fire in the Triangle Shirtwaist factory reflected the Progressive platform by directly leading to the

(A) outlawing of sweatshops in New York

(B) push for comprehensive safety laws

(C) decline in political machines in New York

(D) decline of the International Ladies' Garment Workers' Union

341. The Supreme Court's decisions in *Muller v. Oregon* and *Bunting v. Oregon* addressed the Progressive Party platform by stating that

(A) child labor is illegal

(B) employers need to provide pensions to employees

(C) states can limit working hours

(D) only the federal government can regulate interstate commerce

Use the passage and your knowledge of the time period to answer questions 342 to 345.

New Nationalism Speech
Theodore Roosevelt (August 31, 1910)

I stand for the square deal. But when I say that I am for the square deal, I mean not merely that I stand for fair play under the present rules of the game, but that I stand for having those rules changed so as to work for a more substantial equality of opportunity and of reward for equally good service. One word of warning, which, I think, is hardly necessary in Kansas. When I say I want a square deal for the poor man, I do not mean that I want a square deal for the man who remains poor because he has not got the energy to work for himself. If a man who has had a chance will not make good, then he has got to quit. And you men of the Grand Army, you want justice for the brave man who fought, and punishment for the coward who shirked his work. Is that not so?

Now, this means that our government, national and state, must be freed from the sinister influence or control of special interests. Exactly as the special interests of cotton and slavery threatened our political integrity before the Civil War, so now the great special business interests too often control and corrupt the men and methods of government for their own profit. We must drive the special interests out of politics. That is one of our tasks to-day. Every special interest is entitled to justice—full, fair, and complete—and, now, mind you, if there were any attempt by mob-violence to plunder and work harm to the special interest, whatever it may be, that I most dislike, and the wealthy man, whomsoever he may be, for whom I have the greatest contempt, I would fight for him, and you would if you were worth your salt. He should have justice. For every special interest is entitled to justice, but not one is entitled to a vote in Congress, to a voice on the bench, or to representation in any public office. The Constitution guarantees protection to property, and we must make that promise good. But it does not give the right of suffrage to any corporation.

342. Which of the following objectives was *not* considered part of Theodore Roosevelt's Square Deal?

(A) controlling the corporations
(B) providing consumer protection
(C) protecting business from extreme union demands
(D) expanding America's international influence

343. Both the Elkins Act and the Hepburn Act illustrated the notion of the Square Deal by allowing the government to

(A) use federal troops to break strikes
(B) regulate unfair business practices by railroads
(C) limit the power of corrupt political machines
(D) limit child labor in mines and factories

344. Which of the following policies of Theodore Roosevelt was continued by William Taft?

(A) Roosevelt's strong advocacy for women's suffrage
(B) the continued attempts to break up monopolies and trusts
(C) furthering the policy of New Nationalism
(D) continuation of Big Stick diplomacy

345. How did Woodrow Wilson's reform platform during the 1912 campaign differ from Theodore Roosevelt's platform?

(A) Wilson and Roosevelt differed on how trusts should be dealt with.

(B) Wilson supported lowering tariffs, while Roosevelt did not.

(C) Roosevelt supported a strong executive office, while Wilson did not.

(D) Wilson supported women's suffrage, while Wilson did not.

Use the document and your knowledge of the time period to answer questions 346 and 347.

New Freedom
Woodrow Wilson, 1913

. . . If the government is to tell big business men how to run their business, then don't you see that big business men have to get closer to the government even than they are now? Don't you see that they must capture the government, in order not to be restrained too much by it? . . .

. . . I don't care how benevolent the master is going to be, I will not live under a master. That is not what America was created for. America was created in order that every man should have the same chance as every other man to exercise mastery over his own fortunes . . . If you will but hold off the adversaries, if you will but see to it that the weak are protected, I will venture a wager with you that there are some men in the United States, now weak, economically weak, who have brains enough to compete with these gentlemen and who will presently come into the market and put these gentlemen on their mettle.

---

346. Concerns noted by Wilson were addressed by the Clayton Antitrust Act in all of the following ways *except*

(A) labor unions were subject to antitrust laws

(B) people could not sit on multiple boards of companies within the same business

(C) companies were required to notify federal regulators prior to merging

(D) holding companies were clearly defined

347. Woodrow Wilson's main objective in calling for the establishment of the Federal Reserve was to

(A) better enforce the Federal Trade Act

(B) better organize the federal banking system

(C) nationalize the American banking system

(D) rescue farmers suffering from the recession

CHAPTER 14

The First World War and the Roaring Twenties

Use the document and your knowledge of the time period to answer questions 348 to 353.

Second Inaugural Address, Woodrow Wilson, 1917

. . . We are a composite and cosmopolitan people. We are of the blood of all the nations that are at war. The currents of our thoughts as well as the currents of our trade run quick at all seasons back and forth between us and them. The war inevitably set its mark from the first alike upon our minds, our industries, our commerce, our politics and our social action. To be indifferent to it, or independent of it, was out of the question . . .

It is in this spirit and with this thought that we have grown more and more aware, more and more certain that the part we wished to play was the part of those who mean to vindicate and fortify peace. We have been obliged to arm ourselves to make good our claim to a certain minimum of right and of freedom of action. We stand firm in armed neutrality since it seems that in no other way we can demonstrate what it is we insist upon and cannot forget. We may even be drawn on, by circumstances, not by our own purpose or desire, to a more active assertion of our rights as we see them and a more immediate association with the great struggle itself. But nothing will alter our thought or our purpose. They are too clear to be obscured. . . . We desire neither conquest nor advantage. We wish nothing that can be had only at the cost of another people. We always professed unselfish purpose and we covet the opportunity to prove our professions are sincere . . .

. . . but we realize that the greatest things that remain to be done must be done with the whole world for stage and in cooperation with the wide and universal forces of mankind, and we are making our spirits ready for those things.

---

348. Wilson's statement, "We desire neither conquest nor advantage. We wish nothing that can be had only at the cost of another people," illustrates the policy of

(A) Big Stick diplomacy

(B) Dollar diplomacy

(C) Moral diplomacy

(D) Good Neighbor policy

349. Wilson's speech illustrates what aspect of American society during the first part of the First World War?

(A) The U.S. population initially being divided over the two sides of the conflict.

(B) The United States' strong desire for overseas expansion.

(C) The U.S. desire to reduce overseas investment.

(D) The U.S. eagerness to enter the European conflict.

350. Which of the following was *not* a direct factor leading to World War I?

(A) rise of militarism

(B) creation of secret alliances

(C) increased jingoism within states

(D) rise of fascism within European states

351. Which of the following was *not* a reason for the initial American neutrality during the First World War?

(A) Wilson hoped neutrality would allow him to lead the peace at the end of the war.

(B) American military treaties prevented direct involvement.

(C) Neutrality allowed American businesses to trade with both sides of the conflict.

(D) Americans generally supported a policy of isolation.

352. Despite the intentions of Wilson's speech, which of the following events most directly brought the United States into the First World War?

(A) Britain's use of a naval blockade

(B) Germany's resumption of unrestricted submarine warfare

(C) success of the communist revolution in Russia

(D) collapse of the French Army

353. In relation to the document, a major goal of Woodrow Wilson's League of Nations was to

(A) provide agricultural aid internationally to countries in need

(B) provide all nations with open access to trade

(C) create military equality among the world's major powers

(D) promote international security and peace among nations

Use the image and your knowledge of the time period to answer questions 354 to 356.

Source: Smith, D. (ca. 1919) World War—in the service of the nation / Dan Smith., ca. 1919. [Photograph] Retrieved from the Library of Congress, https://www.loc.gov/item/2002719506/. Text: Let there be no misunderstanding. Our present and immediate task is to win the war, and nothing shall turn us aside from it until it is accomplished. Every power and resource we possess, whether of men, of money, or of materials, is being devoted and will continue to be devoted to that purpose until it is achieved. —Woodrow Wilson

354. Despite what is being depicted in the image, which statement is most accurate concerning African Americans serving in the First World War?

    (A) As many African Americans served in the war as white Americans.

    (B) African Americans predominantly served in combat roles.

    (C) African Americans were barred from military service.

    (D) The military segregated African-American soldiers and they were rarely given combat assignments.

355. In relation to the African American in the military, what was the Great Migration during the First World War?

(A) the increased number of European migrants coming to America, hoping to escape the war

(B) the mass exodus of Midwestern farmers looking for factory jobs in war industries

(C) the increased numbers of African Americans moving into Northern cities

(D) the massive transition of women to do work once solely carried out by men

356. In relation to the text accompanying the poster, which of the following was a major power of the War Industry Board during World War I?

(A) hosting massive rallies to sell war bonds

(B) censoring seditious materials

(C) setting government prices on agricultural goods

(D) setting production quotas and allocating raw materials

Use the image and your knowledge of the time period to answer questions 357 and 358.

Source: Carleton, C. He is keeping the world safe for democracy Enlist and help him / / C. Carleton. United States, None. [Erie, PA: Erie Lithograph Co., between 1916 and 1918] [Photograph] Retrieved from the Library of Congress, https://www.loc.gov/item/00652148/.

357. In relation to the image, the purpose of the Selective Service during the First World War was to

   (A)   raise money for the war effort through the sales of war bonds

   (B)   call on females to work in industries that were once open only to males

   (C)   create more-selective requirements for young men wishing to serve in the military

   (D)   institute a draft to bolster the number of men in the military

358. In relation to the image, Eugene V. Debs was arrested during World War I for

   (A)   selling fraudulent war bonds

   (B)   discouraging enlistment and registration for selective service

   (C)   declaring his candidacy against Woodrow Wilson

   (D)   organizing a strike during the war

Use the passage and your knowledge of the time period to answer questions 359 to 362.

Return to Normalcy
by Warren G. Harding, 1920

There isn't anything the matter with world civilization, except that humanity is viewing it through a vision impaired in a cataclysmal war . . . and men have wandered far from safe paths, but the human procession still marches in the right direction. . . .

It is one thing to battle successfully against world domination by military autocracy, because the infinite God never intended such a program, but it is quite another thing to revise human nature and suspend the fundamental laws of life and all of life's acquirements . . . .

This republic has its ample tasks. If we put an end to false economics, which lure humanity to utter chaos, ours will be the commanding example of world leadership today. If we can prove a representative popular government under which a citizenship seeks what it may do for the government rather than what the government may do for individuals, we shall do more to make democracy safe for the world than all armed conflict ever recorded. . . .

The world needs to be reminded that all human ills are not curable by legislation, and that quantity of statutory enactment and excess of government offer no substitute for quality of citizenship.

359. Based on the passage, the Republican administrations of the 1920s would best be described as

(A) possessing a foreign policy based on expansion and heavy domestic business regulation

(B) supporting isolationism and laissez-faire business policies domestically

(C) strongly focused on building up the armed forces

(D) open to increased immigration and less stringent quotas

360. Harding's statement, "that all human ills are not curable by legislation, and that quantity of statutory enactment and excess of government offer no substitute for quality of citizenship," serves as a rejection of

(A) the military strategy of naval dominance outlined by Alfred T. Mahan

(B) the temperance movement and prohibition

(C) the reforms under the progressive movement

(D) the increased consolidation of business

361. Harding's statement, "government under which a citizenship seeks what it may do for the government rather than what the government may do for individuals," most closely illustrates the sentiment stated by which president?

(A) Franklin D. Roosevelt

(B) Gerald Ford

(C) John F. Kennedy

(D) William McKinley

362. Which of the following statements best illustrates a challenge faced by the United States following the First World War?

(A) The United States found itself the world's largest debtor nation.

(B) The United States found itself with a severe labor shortage.

(C) The United States lacked a plan to reintegrate soldiers into society.

(D) The U.S. government continued to tightly control the economy.

Use the image and your knowledge of the time period to answer questions 363 to 366.

Source: Put them out and keep them out (1919). Retrieved from https://www.baruch.cuny.edu/library/alumni/online _exhibits/digital/redscare/HTMLCODE/CHRON/RS073.HTM.

Dagger: Bolshevism
Hat: Reds
Torch: Anarchy

363. In relation to the image, the Palmer Raids of the 1920s were a response to

(A) organized crime developing after Prohibition

(B) fears of communism following the Russian Revolution

(C) the reemergence of the Ku Klux Klan during the 1920s

(D) government corruption as illustrated in the Teapot Dome Scandal

364. Which of the following events best illustrates the nativist sentiments depicted in the image?

(A) the feats of Charles Lindbergh and Amelia Earhart

(B) the Washington Naval Conference and the Kellogg–Briand Pact

(C) the reemergence of the Ku Klux Klan and the passage of the National Origins Act

(D) the works produced by the Lost Generation and the Harlem Renaissance

365. The Supreme Court decision of *Schenk v. United States* furthered the ideas noted in the image by establishing the precedent for the idea that

(A) speech that presents a "clear and present danger" is not protected

(B) labor unions are exempt from antitrust laws

(C) groups such as the Ku Klux Klan are protected under the First Amendment

(D) "separate but equal" is constitutional

366. Like the image, the trial of Sacco and Vanzetti illustrated America's fear of

(A) African Americans' migration to Northern cities

(B) the reemergence of hate groups such as the Ku Klux Klan

(C) immigrants who possessed radical or leftist beliefs

(D) treaties that might bring the United States into more European conflicts

Use the document and your knowledge of the time period to answer questions 367 and 368.

Kellogg–Briand Pact 1928

. . . Deeply sensible of their solemn duty to promote the welfare of mankind;

Persuaded that the time has, come when a frank renunciation of war as an instrument of national policy should be made to the end that the peaceful and friendly relations now existing between their peoples may be perpetuated;

Convinced that all changes in their relations with one another should be sought only by pacific means and be the result of a peaceful and orderly process, and that any signatory Power which shall hereafter seek to promote its national interests by resort to war a should be denied the benefits furnished by this Treaty;

Hopeful that, encouraged by their example, all the other nations of the world will join in this humane endeavor and by adhering to the present Treaty as soon as it comes into force bring their peoples within the scope of its beneficent provisions, thus uniting the civilized nations of the world in a common renunciation of war as an instrument of their national policy;

Have decided to conclude a Treaty and for that purpose. . . .

Article I
The High Contracting Parties solemnly declare in the names of their respective peoples that they condemn recourse to war for the solution of international controversies, and renounce it, as an instrument of national policy in their relations with one another.

Article II
The High Contracting Parties agree that the settlement or solution of all disputes or conflicts of whatever nature or of whatever origin they may be, which may arise among them, shall never be sought except by pacific means.

---

367. Why was the Kellogg–Briand Pact significant?

(A) The nations involved agreed not to use the threat of war against each other.

(B) It limited the sizes of the participating nations' navies.

(C) It called for the voluntary disarmament of nations.

(D) It led to the passage of the Nineteenth Amendment.

368. The Kellogg–Briand Pact of 1928 was similar to the earlier League of Nations in that

(A) both promised that if a member of the agreement was attacked, all signing parties would come to that state's defense

(B) both were agreements designed to prevent further global wars

(C) both created a multinational army to secure peace

(D) both were designed to maintain the balance of power amongst global states

Use the passage and your knowledge of the time period to answer questions 369 and 370.

Philip Randolph recounting a 1916 encounter with Marcus Garvey

I was on a soapbox speaking on socialism, when someone pulled my coat and said, "There's a young man here from Jamaica." I said, "What does he want to talk about?" He said, "He wants to talk about a movement to develop a back-to-Africa sentiment in America."

Garvey got up on the platform, and you could hear him from 135th to 125th Street. He had a tremendous voice. When he finished speaking he sat near the platform with a sheaf of paper on which he was constantly writing, and he had stamps and envelopes, ready to send out his propaganda. I could tell from watching him even then that he was one of the greatest propagandists of his time . . .

---

369. In relation to the passage, how was Marcus Garvey's plan for African Americans similar to the plans of the eighteenth-century colonization societies?

(A) They both called for a mass migration of African Americans back to Africa.

(B) They both sought to promote assimilation into white culture.

(C) They both promoted the creation of greater political activism within African-American community.

(D) They both called for an end of segregation policies.

370. In contrast with the observations made in the passage, what was the 1920s Harlem Renaissance?

(A) the refusal of African Americans to submit quietly to the practices of Jim Crow laws

(B) the emergence of civic-minded African-American business leaders

(C) the migration of African Americans from the South to Northern cities

(D) a period of artistic achievement in multiple fields by African Americans

Use the passage and your knowledge of the time period to answer question 371.

William Jennings Bryan being cross-examined by Clarence Darrow, at the end of day seven, of the Scopes Trial, July 20, 1925

Mr. Bryan: I am simply trying to protect the word of God against the greatest atheist or agnostic in the United States. (Prolonged applause.) I want the papers to know I am not afraid to get on the stand in front of him and let him do his worst. I want the world to know. (Prolonged applause.) . . .

Mr. Bryan: Your honor, I think I can shorten this testimony. The only purpose Mr. Darrow has is to slur at the Bible, but I will answer his question. I will answer it all at once, and I have no objection in the world, I want the world to know that this man, who does not believe in God, is trying to use a court in Tennessee

Mr. Darrow: I object to that.

Mr. Bryan: to slur at it, and while it will require time, I am willing to take it.

Mr. Darrow: I object to your statement. I am exempting you on your fool ideas that no intelligent Christian on earth believes.

---

371. As illustrated in the transcript, the Scopes Trial illustrated the nation's debate over

(A) immigration and fears of leftist radicals

(B) religious conservatism versus modern scientific theories

(C) the rural versus urban split within the nation

(D) women's suffrage versus the cult of domesticity

Use the image and your knowledge of the time period to answer question 372.

Source: Hoover vs. Smith coattals flyer.jpg. (2017, October 1). Wikimedia Commons, the free media repository.

372. The election of Herbert Hoover over Al Smith illustrated

(A) America's general rejection of Prohibition

(B) discontentment with Republican policies

(C) nativist opinions concerning religion

(D) fears of impending economic uncertainty

CHAPTER 15

The Great Depression and the Second World War

Use the chart and your knowledge of the time period to answer questions 373 and 374.

U.S. Tariff Rates 1913 to 1935

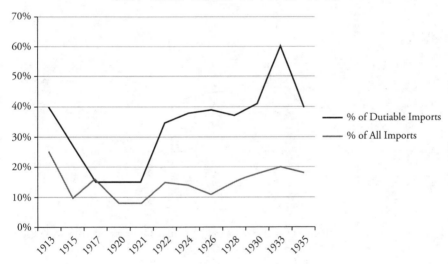

373. Based on the chart, what inferences can be made between political parties in control of the presidency and tariff rates between 1913 and 1932?

   (A) Republican and Democratic presidents tended to both support high tariffs.
   (B) Republican presidencies coincided with higher tariff rates.
   (C) Democratic presidencies coincided with higher tariff rates.
   (D) Republican and Democratic presidents tended to both support lower tariffs.

374. The impact of the Fordney–McCumber of 1924 and Hawley–Smoot tariffs of 1930 could be best described as

(A) upsetting the balance of trade among European nations

(B) crippling Europe's ability to pay off its war debts and damaging American industry

(C) illustrating America's willingness to disarm following the First World War

(D) greatly benefiting Midwestern farmers during the 1920s

Use the chart and your knowledge of the time period to answer questions 375 to 378.

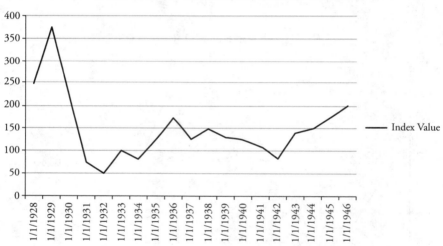

Dow Jones Industrial Index Value

375. In relation to the chart, at the start of the Great Depression, Black Tuesday (October 29, 1929) occurred when

(A) investors began to buy large numbers of stocks on margin

(B) bankers responded to Black Tuesday by offering loan and mortgage forgiveness

(C) President Hoover declared a national bank holiday to stabilize the market

(D) investors raced to sell their stock holdings

376. What is the practice of buying on margin?

(A) purchasing stocks without any prior knowledge of the company

(B) using bank loans to purchase stocks

(C) pooling money with a group of investors to buy stock

(D) buying stocks when they are low and selling them when they are high

377. How might the practice of buying on margin impact the market value illustrated in the chart?

(A) It allowed stock values to recover more quickly.

(B) It led to a deflation in stock values prior to the market's decline.

(C) It led to inflated stock values prior to the market's dramatic decline.

(D) It allowed for quicker bank recovery following the crash.

378. In relation to the chart, how would the economy of 1937 be best described?

(A) The economy faced another recession.

(B) Stock prices regained their pre-depression values.

(C) There was continued strong economic growth.

(D) Stock prices fell to their lowest point of the Depression.

Use the document and your knowledge of the time period to answer questions 379 to 382.

Radio Address to the Nation on Unemployment Relief
Herbert Hoover (October 18, 1931)

My fellow citizens:

This broadcast tonight marks the beginning of the mobilization of the whole Nation for a great undertaking to provide security for those of our citizens and their families who, through no fault of their own, face unemployment and privation during the coming winter. Its success depends upon the sympathetic and generous action of every man and woman in our country. No one with a spark of human sympathy can contemplate unmoved the possibilities of suffering that can crush many of our unfortunate fellow Americans if we shall fail them.

The depression has been deepened by events from abroad which are beyond the control either of our citizens or our Government. Although it is but a passing incident in our national life, we must meet the consequences in unemployment . . . with that completeness of effort and that courage and . . .

As an important part of our plans for national unity of action in this emergency I have created a great national organization . . . to cooperate with the Governors, the State and the local agencies, and with the many national . . . so that the countless streams of human helpfulness which have been the mainstay of our country in all emergencies may be directed wisely and effectively . . .

No governmental action, no economic doctrine, no economic plan or project can replace that God-imposed responsibility of the individual man and woman to their neighbors. That is a vital part of the very soul of a people. If we shall gain in this spirit from this painful time, we shall have created a greater and more glorious America. The trial of it is here now. It is a trial of the heart and the conscience, of individual men and women . . .

379. When faced with the start of the Depression, Hoover supported

    (A) government deficit spending to help bring relief

    (B) lowering tariffs to revive international trade

    (C) creating federal relief programs for the average worker

    (D) encouraging voluntary reforms within private businesses

380. In relation to the passage, the main purpose of the Reconstruction Finance Corporation under Hoover was to

    (A) provide low-cost mortgages to homeowners facing foreclosure

    (B) provide government credit to secure failing banks

    (C) raise farm prices by encouraging farmers to reduce output

    (D) provide work relief for the unemployed through public projects

381. In contrast to Hoover's idea noted in the document, what did economist John Maynard Keynes say was necessary to restart the economy during the Depression?

    (A) using government spending to increase consumer demand for goods

    (B) cutting taxes on businesses and investors so they could grow

    (C) adopting bimetallism to provide relief to farmers

    (D) maintaining a strict policy of laissez-faire and letting the economy recover naturally

382. The Bonus Army at the start of the Depression could be seen as a rejection to Hoover's statement because they wanted to

    (A) allow veterans to receive their promised army pensions early

    (B) distribute food aid to the multitude of people suffering from malnutrition

    (C) provide federal aid to farmers who had lost their farms

    (D) support the Norris–La Guardia Anti-Injunction Act to protect unions

Use the passage and your knowledge of the time period to answer questions 383 to 389.

First Inaugural Speech
Franklin D. Roosevelt, 1933

So, first of all, let me assert my firm belief that the only thing we have to fear is fear itself—nameless, unreasoning, unjustified terror which paralyzes needed efforts to convert retreat into advance. . . .

Happiness lies not in the mere possession of money; it lies in the joy of achievement, in the thrill of creative effort. The joy and the moral stimulation of work no longer must be forgotten in the mad chase of evanescent profits. . . .

Recognition of the falsity of material wealth as the standard of success goes hand in hand with the abandonment of the false belief that public office and high political position are to be valued only by the standards of pride of place and personal profit; and there must be an end to a conduct in banking and in business which too often has given to a sacred trust the likeness of callous and selfish wrongdoing. . . .

Restoration calls, however, not for changes in ethics alone. This Nation is asking for action and action now. . . .

Our greatest primary task is to put people to work. This is no unsolvable problem if we face it wisely and courageously. It can be accomplished in part by direct recruiting by the Government itself, treating the task as we would treat the emergency of a war, but at the same time, through this employment, accomplishing greatly needed projects to stimulate and reorganize the use of our great natural resources.

---

383. Based on the passage, how did Roosevelt's response to the Great Depression differ from that of Hoover?

(A) While Hoover felt that aid should be supplied directly to the people, Roosevelt felt that government should only try to stabilize the corporations and banks.

(B) Roosevelt believed that the Depression should be corrected by voluntary self-regulation in business, while Hoover advocated heavy government regulation.

(C) Hoover's reforms focused on providing aid to farmers, while Roosevelt focused on industrial workers.

(D) While Roosevelt felt that aid should be supplied directly to the people, Hoover felt that government should only try to stabilize the corporations and banks.

384. Which of the following people would be most critical of Roosevelt's assertions of the "falsity of material wealth" and an end to the "conduct in banking and business," because they would be viewed as an attack on the financial industry and the wealthy?

(A) Alfred Smith

(B) Henry A. Wallace

(C) Huey Long

(D) Upton Sinclair

385. Which New Deal program most directly illustrated "direct recruiting by the Government itself"?

(A) Emergency Banking Relief Act

(B) National Recovery Administration

(C) Agricultural Adjustment Agency

(D) Civilian Conservation Corps

386. Which New Deal action would be most intended to curtail what Roosevelt noted as, "The conduct in banking . . . which too often has given to a sacred trust the likeness of callous and selfish wrongdoing"?

(A) Federal Emergency Relief Act

(B) National Labor Relations Board

(C) Securities and Exchange Commission

(D) Federal Deposit Insurance Corporation

387. Which of the following New Deal agencies was created to assist businesses most directly?

(A) Home Owners' Loan Corporation

(B) Works Progress Administration

(C) National Recovery Administration

(D) Tennessee Valley Authority

388. In President Roosevelt implementing the platform noted in the passage, what was Franklin Roosevelt's "Brain Trust"?

(A) the heads of Roosevelt's executive agencies

(B) a collection of intellectuals who served as unofficial advisors

(C) the appointed heads of the agencies created under the New Deal

(D) students who attended colleges with New Deal grants

389. How did the Second New Deal differ from the First New Deal during the Depression?

(A) The Second New Deal was less focused on the welfare of citizens.

(B) The Second New Deal did not focus on job relief.

(C) The Second New Deal gave more support to unions.

(D) The Second New Deal loosened business regulations by the federal government.

Use the passage and your knowledge of the time period to answer questions 390 to 392.

Share Our Wealth Radio Speech
Senator Huey P. Long, February 23, 1934

So, we have in America today, my friends, a condition by which about 10 men dominate the means of activity in at least 85 percent of the activities that you own. They either own directly everything or they have got some kind of mortgage on it . . . They own the banks, they own the steel mills, they own the railroads, they own the bonds, they own the mortgages, they own the stores, and they have chained the country from one end to the other until there is not any kind of business that a small, independent man could go into today and make a living . . . and still they have got little enough sense to think they ought to be able to get more business out of it anyway. . . .

Both of these men, Mr. Hoover and Mr. Roosevelt, came out and said there had to be a decentralization of wealth, but neither one of them did anything about it . . . The fact that neither one of them ever did anything about it is their own problem that I am not undertaking to criticize; but had Mr. Hoover carried out what he says ought to be done, he would be retiring from the President's office, very probably, 8 years from now, instead of 1 year ago; and had Mr. Roosevelt proceeded along the lines that he stated were necessary for the decentralization of wealth . . . within a few months he would have probably reached a solution of all of the problems that afflict this country today.

But I wish to warn you now that nothing that has been done up to this date has taken one dime away from these big fortune-holders; they own just as much as they did, and probably a little bit more; they hold just as many of the debts of the common people as they ever held, and probably a little bit more; and unless we, my friends, are going to give the people of this country a fair shake of the dice, by which they will all get something out of the funds of this land, there is not a chance on the topside of this God's eternal earth by which we can rescue this country and rescue the people of this country.

Every man a king, so there would be no such thing as a man or woman who did not have the necessities of life . . . What do we propose by this society? We propose to limit the wealth of big men in the country. There is an average of $15,000 in wealth to every family in America. That is right here today.

We do not propose to divide it up equally. We do not propose a division of wealth, but we propose to limit poverty that we will allow to be inflicted upon any man's family . . . enough for a home, an automobile, a radio, and the ordinary conveniences, and the opportunity to educate their children; a fair share of the income of this land thereafter to that family so there will be no such thing as merely the select to have those things, and so there will be no such thing as a family living in poverty and distress.

390. Based on the passage, individuals like Huey Long and Upton Sinclair criticized the New Deal on the grounds that

(A) it was moving the country too far in the direction of socialism

(B) shifting the tax burden onto the wealthy was unfair

(C) they disagreed with tighter government regulations on private banks

(D) they believed the reforms did not go far enough to redistribute wealth

391. Father Charles Coughlin parallels the criticisms made by Huey Long by supporting

(A) a move toward a fascist state

(B) greater nationalization of industry and resources

(C) a flat income tax

(D) nationalized healthcare

392. Individuals such as William Randolph Hearst would reject the notions put forth by Long because

(A) they saw them as socialist

(B) they went against his lifelong republican values

(C) they felt they were not radical enough to address the challenges of the Depression

(D) they strongly supported the moderate nature of the New Deal

Use the excerpt and your knowledge of the time period to answer questions 393 and 394.

WHY WE COME TO CALIFORNY
Flora Robertson Shafter, 1940

Here comes the dust-storm Watch the sky turn blue. You better git out quick Or it will smother you.

Here comes the grasshopper, He comes a-jumpin' high. He jumps away across the state An' never bats an eye.

Here comes the river it sure knows its stuff. It takes our home and cattle, An' leaves us feelin' tough.

Californy, Californy, Here I come too. With a coffee pot and skillet, I'm a-comin' to you!

Source: Robertson, F. (1940). Why We Come to California. Shafter FSA Camp, CA. [Manuscript/Mixed Material] Retrieved from the Library of Congress, https://www.loc.gov/item/toddbib000522/.

---

393. "Here comes the dust-storm" refers to the Dust Bowl of the Great Depression, which occurred because

(A) the region was hit with heavy rains and tornadoes

(B) farmers lacked modern irrigation capabilities

(C) intense agriculture had depleted the topsoil

(D) increased crop prices led to severe overproduction

394. Which New Deal Program was designed specifically to aid struggling farmers?

(A) Civil Works Administration

(B) Home Owners' Loan Corporation

(C) Agricultural Adjustment Act

(D) Wagner Act

Use the image and your knowledge of the time period to answer questions 395 and 396.

Source: (ca. 1938) Twenty Afro-American members of Franklin Roosevelt's "Black Cabinet," posed, standing outside of building. United States, Washington D.C., ca. 1938. New York: Crown Publishers, Inc. [Photograph] Retrieved from the Library of Congress, https://www.loc.gov/item/93503008/.

395. During the Great Depression, the "Black Cabinet" referred to

    (A) African-American public policy advisors

    (B) African Americans who served in Roosevelt's executive cabinet

    (C) supporters of the civil rights leader A. Philip Randolph

    (D) African Americans who openly opposed the New Deal

396. African Americans during the Depression often experienced

    (A) access to low-paying industrial jobs once available only to whites

    (B) increased discrimination in employment and in relief programs

    (C) greatly improved civil rights and opportunities

    (D) the end of many of the Jim Crow laws in the South

Use the document and your knowledge of the time period to answer questions 397 to 399.

America First Committee Speech
Senator Burton K. Wheeler (1940)

During the past eight years, we have gone far down the road toward one-man government. We have granted to President Roosevelt more power than was ever given to any peacetime president in the history of this nation. . . . But now the American people are asked, by H.R. 1776, to give in effect to the president of the United States the power to wage an undeclared war. Not in the defense of our shores, our freedom, or our independence, but in the defense of foreign powers.

. . . This bill specifically provides that, notwithstanding any other provisions of law, the president may sell, transfer, exchange, lease or otherwise dispose of any defense article. And this includes any material necessary for the manufacture of guns, munitions, warships, or any other defense article. And the president is given authority to repair any implement of war for one belligerent and deny the same privilege to the other. Military or naval secrets, however vital to American defense, may be given to a foreign power by the president.

In plain language, this bill means that the president can give to any foreign nation our entire navy, our entire air force, all our guns, all our tanks, all our munitions, and all our military secrets can be disclosed to Russia to China to Greece to England or to any other country, though they are cautiously withheld from you, the American people, and your Senators, and your Congressmen. The Russians can be trusted—if the president says so—but you, and I, cannot be.

---

397. The main goal of the America First Committee was to

(A) preemptively enter the Second World War to avoid a surprise attack

(B) continue American isolationism by ending the Lend–Lease program

(C) trade with both Axis and Allied nations to bolster the American economy

(D) stop the influx of Latin American immigrants from entering the United States

398. The main purpose of the Lend–Lease program described in the passage was to

(A) provide aid against communist insurgencies in Spain

(B) attempt to convince Italy to maintain neutrality

(C) end the Depression through wartime production

(D) aid nations deemed vital to American security

399. The argument made by Senator Burton K. Wheeler reflects which earlier criticism of Roosevelt and the New Deal?

(A) President Roosevelt's policies under the New Deal seemed passive and limited in scope.

(B) President Roosevelt's New Deal was too isolationist in scope.

(C) President Roosevelt's New Deal relied too heavily on self-correction in the free market.

(D) President Roosevelt's New Deal illustrated an overreach in executive authority.

Use the document and your knowledge of the time period to answer questions 400 to 402.

To Senator William E. Borah
Washington, February 23, 1932

You have asked my opinion whether . . . present conditions in China have in any way indicated that the so-called Nine Power Treaty has become inapplicable or ineffective or rightly in need of modifications, and if so, what I considered should be the policy of this Government . . .

This Treaty thus represents a carefully developed and matured international policy intended . . . to assure to all of the contracting parties their rights and interests in and with regard to China . . . to assure to the people of China the fullest opportunity to develop without molestation their sovereignty and independence . . . At the time this Treaty was signed, it was known that China was engaged in an attempt to develop the free institutions of a self-governing republic after her recent revolution from an autocratic form of government. . . . It was believed—and the whole history of the development of the "Open Door" policy reveals that faith— that only by such a process, under the protection of such an agreement, could the fullest interests not only of China but of all nations which have intercourse with her best be served . . .

The recent events which have taken place in China, especially the hostilities which having been begun in Manchuria have latterly been extended to Shanghai . . . have tended to bring home the vital importance of the faithful observance of the covenants therein to all of the nations interested in the Far East . . . It is clear beyond peradventure that a situation has developed which cannot . . . be reconciled with the obligations of the covenants of these two treaties . . . The signatories of the Nine Power Treaty and of the Kellogg–Briand Pact who are not parties to that conflict are not likely to see any reason for modifying the terms of those treaties. To them the real value of the faithful performance of the treaties has been brought sharply home by the perils and losses to which their nationals have been subjected in Shanghai . . .

On January 7th last . . . this Government formally notified Japan and China that it would not recognize any situation, treaty or agreement entered into by those governments in violation of the covenants of these treaties, which affected the rights of our Government or its citizens in China. If a similar decision should be reached and a similar position taken by the other governments of the world . . . will effectively bar the legality hereafter of any title or right sought to be obtained by pressure or treaty violation . . . will eventually lead to the restoration to China of rights and titles of which she may have been deprived.

In the past our Government, as one of the leading powers on the Pacific Ocean, has rested its policy upon an abiding faith in the future of the people of China and upon the ultimate success in dealing with them of the principles of fair play, patience, and mutual goodwill . . .

Very sincerely yours,
Henry L. Stimson

400. In response to the Japanese invasion of Manchuria in 1931, the United States

(A) declared war on Japan

(B) adopted its Good Neighbor policy

(C) adopted the first Neutrality Act

(D) adopted the Stimson Doctrine

401. The main focus of the Nine Power Treaty was to

(A) maintain the Open Door Policy by protecting Chinese sovereignty

(B) divide China into nine separate spheres to promote trade and development

(C) stop Japanese economic and military development in the Pacific

(D) establish limitations on the expansion of naval forces by the nine signatories of the agreement

402. The continuation of Japanese expansion is illustrated by General Douglas MacArthur forced withdraw from

(A) the Philippines

(B) Korea

(C) Pearl Harbor

(D) French-held Indochina

Use the document and your knowledge of the time period to answer questions 403 to 408.

Atlantic Charter
President Franklin D. Roosevelt (August 21, 1941)

TO THE CONGRESS OF THE UNITED STATES:

The Congress and the President having heretofore determined through the Lend Lease Act on the national policy of American aid to the democracies which East and West are waging war against dictatorships, the military and naval conversations at these meetings made clear gains in furthering the effectiveness of this aid.

Furthermore, the Prime Minister and I are arranging for conferences with the Soviet Union to aid it in its defense against the attack made by the principal aggressor of the modern world—Germany.

Finally, the declaration of principles at this time presents a goal which is worthwhile for our type of civilization to seek. It is so clear cut that it is difficult to oppose in any major particular without automatically admitting a willingness to accept compromise with Nazism; or to agree to a world peace which would give to Nazism domination over large numbers of conquered nations. Inevitably such a peace would be a gift to Nazism to take breath—armed breath—for a second war to extend the control over Europe and Asia to the American Hemisphere itself.

It is perhaps unnecessary for me to call attention once more to the utter lack of validity of the spoken or written word of the Nazi government.

It is also unnecessary for me to point out that the declaration of principles includes of necessity the world need for freedom of religion and freedom of information. No society of the world organized under the announced principles could survive without these freedoms which are a part of the whole freedom for which we strive.

---

403. Based on the passage, the Atlantic Charter was an agreement between

   (A) the United States and France
   (B) the United States and Britain
   (C) the United States and Russia
   (D) the United States and Germany

404. The Nazi Party was an extreme example of what political ideology?

   (A) communism
   (B) socialism
   (C) fascism
   (D) democratic socialism

405. Which of the following was *not* a term of the Atlantic Charter?

    (A) The nations involved formally rejected the communist government of the Soviet Union.

    (B) The nations agreed that territorial expansion would be pursued during the conflict.

    (C) The nations involved pronounced continued support for free trade.

    (D) The United States would continue its Lend–Lease Program.

406. The focus of the Atlantic Charter was most similar to which previous pronouncement?

    (A) The Fourteen Points

    (B) The Platt Amendment

    (C) The Gentleman's Agreement

    (D) The Roosevelt Corollary

407. In relation to the document, the main function of the Office of War Mobilization during the Second World War was to

    (A) create a system of selective service

    (B) coordinate government agencies involved in the war effort

    (C) ration industrial materials that would be needed for the war effort

    (D) use the media to stir popular support for the war

408. In addition to the Atlantic Charter, during the Second World War, Tehran, Yalta, and Potsdam were

    (A) pivotal military victories for the Allied nations

    (B) sites of conferences held by the Big Three

    (C) key beaches during the invasion of Normandy

    (D) decisive victories for the Axis powers

Use the document and your knowledge of the time period to answer questions 409 and 410.

Executive Order No. 9066: Authorizing the Secretary of War to Prescribe Military Areas
Franklin D. Roosevelt (February 19, 1942)

Whereas the successful prosecution of the war requires every possible protection against espionage and against sabotage to national-defense material, national-defense premises, and national-defense utilities . . .

Now, therefore, by virtue of the authority vested in me as President of the United States, and Commander in Chief of the Army and Navy, I hereby authorize and direct the Secretary of War . . . to prescribe military areas in such places and of such extent as he or the appropriate Military Commander may determine, from which any or all persons may be excluded, and with respect to which, the right of any person to enter, remain in, or leave shall be subject to whatever restrictions the Secretary of War . . . The Secretary of War is hereby authorized to provide for residents of any such area who are excluded therefrom . . . accommodations as may be necessary . . . to accomplish the purpose of this order. The designation of military areas in any region or locality shall supersede designations of prohibited and restricted areas by the Attorney General . . .

I hereby further authorize and direct the Secretary of War . . . to take such other steps as he . . . may deem advisable to enforce compliance with the restrictions applicable to each Military area hereinabove authorized to be designated, including the use of Federal troops and other Federal Agencies, with authority to accept assistance of state and local agencies.

I hereby further authorize and direct all Executive Departments . . . to assist the Secretary of War or the said Military Commanders in carrying out this Executive Order, including the furnishing of medical aid, hospitalization, food, clothing, transportation, use of land, shelter, and other supplies, equipment, utilities, facilities, and services . . .

---

409. What was the main function of President Roosevelt's Executive Order 9066?

(A) to force Americans deemed as a threat into internment camps

(B) to make striking in a wartime industry a crime

(C) to ban discriminatory hiring within the federal government

(D) to ban the sale or shipment of arms to belligerent nations

410. Which group was the most targeted in relation to the executive order?

(A) Japanese Americans

(B) German Americans

(C) Italian Americans

(D) Irish Americans

411. The United States formally apologized for the Executive Order and began to give redress payments to surviving victims during which presidency?

(A) Gerald Ford

(B) Jimmy Carter

(C) Ronald Reagan

(D) George H. W. Bush

Use the map and and your knowledge of the time period to answer questions 412 and 413.

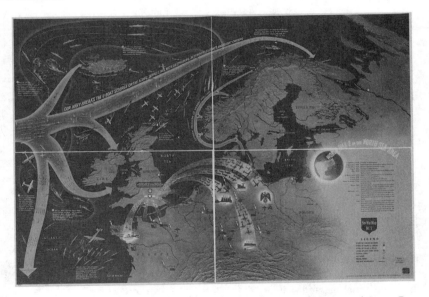

Source: United States Bureau Of Naval Personnel. Training Aids & United States Bureau Of Naval Personnel. Educational Services Section. (1939) World War 2 in the North Sea area / Training Aids. [Washington, D.C.: Distributed by the Educational Services Section, Bureau of Naval Personnel, Navy Dept] [Map] Retrieved from the Library of Congress, https://www.loc.gov/item/2013593061/.

412. The Allied invasion of Normandy, France, was code-named

(A) Operation Barbarossa
(B) Operation Torch
(C) Operation Overlord
(D) Operation Cartwheel

413. How does the map illustrate the main war strategy agreed upon by Franklin Roosevelt and Winston Churchill?

(A) It concentrates on defeating the Axis Powers in Africa.
(B) It focuses on defeating the Axis Powers in Europe.
(C) It concentrates on fighting the Japanese in the Pacific.
(D) It concentrates on reopening sea lanes in the northern Atlantic.

Use the passage and your knowledge of the time period to answer questions 414 to 419.

Hirohito Speech
Emperor Hirohito (August 14, 1945)

To our good and loyal subjects:

After pondering deeply the general trends of the world and the actual conditions obtaining in our empire today, we have decided to effect a settlement of the present situation by resorting to an extraordinary measure.

We have ordered our Government to communicate to the Governments of the United States, Great Britain, China and the Soviet Union that our empire accepts the provisions of their joint declaration.

To strive for the common prosperity and happiness of all nations as well as the security and well-being of our subjects is the solemn obligation which has been handed down by our imperial ancestors and which we lay close to the heart.

Indeed, we declared war on America and Britain out of our sincere desire to insure Japan's self-preservation and the stabilization of East Asia, it being far from our thought either to infringe upon the sovereignty of other nations or to embark upon territorial aggrandizement.

But now the war has lasted for nearly four years. Despite the best that has been done by everyone—the gallant fighting of our military and naval forces, the diligence and assiduity of out servants of the State and the devoted service of our 100,000,000 people—the war situation has developed not necessarily to Japan's advantage, while the general trends of the world have all turned against her interest.

Moreover, the enemy has begun to employ a new and most cruel bomb, the power of which to do damage is, indeed, incalculable, taking the toll of many innocent lives.

Should we continue to fight, it would not only result in an ultimate collapse and obliteration of the Japanese nation, but also it would lead to the total extinction of human civilization.

Let the entire nation continue as one family from generation to generation, ever firm in its faith of the imperishableness of its divine land, and mindful of its heavy burden of responsibilities, and the long road before it. Unite your total strength to be devoted to the construction for the future. Cultivate the ways of rectitude, nobility of spirit, and work with resolution so that you may enhance the innate glory of the Imperial State and keep pace with the progress of the world.

414. Based on the passage, why did Japan enter the war?

    (A) to defend itself from European colonization

    (B) to protect itself from the expansion of communism

    (C) to protect Japanese interests and bring stability to the region

    (D) to protect itself from the advancement of Nazi Germany

415. Which was *not* a reason for surrender noted by the Emperor?

    (A) the bombings of Hiroshima and Nagasaki

    (B) the united efforts of the Allied Powers

    (C) the lack of ability of the Japanese forces

    (D) the potential for future loss of Japanese lives

416. Which of the following battles is considered to be a turning point in the Pacific Campaign against Japan during World War II?

    (A) Battle of Guadalcanal

    (B) Battle of Iwo Jima

    (C) Battle of the Coral Sea

    (D) Battle of Midway

417. In relation to the passage, the purpose of the Manhattan Project was to

    (A) assassinate the emperor to hasten the end of the war

    (B) develop improved jet technology to gain superiority

    (C) develop an atomic bomb

    (D) coordinate an Allied invasion of the Japanese mainland

418. The Japanese officially surrendered by signing a treaty

    (A) on the battleship Missouri

    (B) on the island of Okinawa

    (C) in the city of Tokyo

    (D) in the Japanese emperor's palace

419. A major limitation of this document for a historian researching the Second World War would be

    (A) it only offers the Japanese viewpoint of the conflict

    (B) it fails to address why the Japanese entered the conflict

    (C) it is biased by the U.S. viewpoint

    (D) it fails to account for the impact of the conflict upon the Japanese people

CHAPTER 16

The Cold War and Postwar America

Use the passage and your knowledge of the time period to answer questions 420 to 423.

Truman Doctrine (1947)

To ensure the peaceful development of nations, free from coercion, the United States has taken a leading part in establishing the United Nations . . . We shall not realize our objectives, however, unless we are willing to help free peoples to maintain their free institutions and their national integrity against aggressive movements that seek to impose upon them totalitarian regimes. This is no more than a frank recognition that totalitarian regimes imposed on free peoples . . . undermine the foundations of international peace and hence the security of the United States.

The peoples of a number of countries of the world have recently had totalitarian regimes forced upon them against their will. The Government of the United States has made frequent protests against coercion and intimidation, in violation of the Yalta agreement, in Poland, Rumania, and Bulgaria. I must also state that in a number of other countries there have been similar developments.

At the present moment in world history nearly every nation must choose between alternative ways of life. The choice is too often not a free one.

One way of life is based upon the will of the majority, and is distinguished by free institutions, representative government, free elections, guarantees of individual liberty, freedom of speech and religion, and freedom from political oppression.

The second way of life is based upon the will of a minority forcibly imposed upon the majority. It relies upon terror and oppression, a controlled press and radio; fixed elections, and the suppression of personal freedoms.

I believe that it must be the policy of the United States to support free peoples who are resisting attempted subjugation by armed minorities or by outside pressures. I believe that we must assist free peoples to work out their own destinies in their own way. I believe that our help should be primarily through economic and financial aid which is essential to economic stability and orderly political processes.

420. Which of the following events most directly led to the creation of this document?

(A) the end of the Second World War

(B) the creation of the United Nations

(C) the withdrawal of British economic aid to Greece and Turkey

(D) the construction of the Berlin Wall

421. The Truman Doctrine and the Marshall Plan were similar in that they

(A) provided justification for military actions against authoritarian governments

(B) provided economic aid while containing Soviet influence

(C) focused on expanding American business interests in Latin America

(D) were used as the basis for creating the United Nations

422. The Truman Doctrine was similar to George F. Kennan's policy in they both called for which policy?

(A) containment

(B) massive retaliation

(C) mutually assured destruction

(D) creation of NATO

423. How could the Berlin Airlift be seen as a continuation of the Truman Doctrine?

(A) The United States coordinated the massive evacuations of diplomats following the Soviet takeover of West Berlin.

(B) The United States engineered the evacuation of West German citizens following the construction of the Berlin Wall.

(C) The United States coordinated the delivery of goods and necessities after a Soviet blockade of West Berlin.

(D) The United States stopped the delivery of Soviet propaganda to West Berlin in an attempt to fuel a revolution.

Use the document and your knowledge of the time period to answer questions 424 and 425.

2nd Annual Message to the Congress on the State of the Union, Harry S. Truman (January 5, 1949)

In this society, we are conservative about the values and principles which we cherish; but we are forward-looking in protecting those values and principles and in extending their benefits. We have rejected the discredited theory that the fortunes of the Nation should be in the hands of a privileged few. We have abandoned the "trickledown" concept of national prosperity. Instead, we believe that our economic system should rest on a democratic foundation and that wealth should be created for the benefit of all . . .

The American people have decided that poverty is just as wasteful and just as unnecessary as preventable disease. We have pledged our common resources to help one another in the hazards and struggles of individual life. We believe that no unfair prejudice or artificial distinction should bar any citizen of the United States of America from an education, or from good health, or from a job that he is capable of performing . . .

. . . Since the boom year of 1929, while our population has increased by only 20 percent, our agricultural production has increased by 45 percent, and our industrial production has increased by 75 percent. We are turning out far more goods and more wealth per worker than we have ever done before.

This progress has confounded the gloomy prophets—at home and abroad who predicted the downfall of American capitalism. The people of the United States, going their own way, confident in their own powers, have achieved the greatest prosperity the world has even seen.

But, great as our progress has been, we still have a long way to go. As we look around the country, many of our shortcomings stand out in bold relief.

- We are suffering from excessively high prices.
- Our production is still not large enough to satisfy our demands.
- Our minimum wages are far too low.
- Small business is losing ground to growing monopoly.
- Our farmers still face an uncertain future. And too many of them lack the benefits of our modern civilization.
- Our schools, in many localities, are utterly inadequate.
- Our democratic ideals are often thwarted by prejudice and intolerance.
- Each of these shortcomings is also an opportunity—an opportunity for the Congress and the President to work for the good of the people.
- Our first great opportunity is to protect our economy against the evils of "boom and bust."

424. President Harry Truman's domestic program, outlined in the passage above, was called the

(A) Fair Deal

(B) Great Society

(C) New Frontier

(D) New Deal

425. As noted in the passage, during the decade following the Second World War, the U.S. national economy

(A) more than doubled

(B) fell back into depression

(C) suffered from a decade-long recession

(D) remained mostly unchanged

Use the document and your knowledge of the time period to answer questions 426 to 431.

I Shall Go to Korea
Dwight D. Eisenhower (October 25, 1952)

In this anxious autumn for America, one fact looms above all others in our people's mind. One tragedy challenges all men dedicated to the work of peace. One word shouts denial to those who foolishly pretend that ours is not a nation at war. This fact, this tragedy, this word is: Korea.

A small country, Korea has been, for more than two years, the battleground for the costliest foreign war our nation has fought, excepting the two world wars. It has been the burial ground for 20,000 America dead. It has been another historic field of honor for the valor and skill and tenacity of American soldiers.

The biggest fact about the Korean War is this: It was never inevitable, it was never inescapable, no fantastic fiat of history decreed that little South Korea—in the summer of 1950—would fatally tempt Communist aggressors as their easiest victim. No demonic destiny decreed that America had to be bled this way in order to keep South Korea free and to keep freedom itself self-respecting. We are not mute prisoners of history. That is a doctrine for totalitarians; it is no creed for free men. There is a Korean war and we are fighting it—for the simplest of reasons: Because free leadership failed to check and to turn back Communist ambition before it savagely attacked us. The Korean war—more perhaps than any other war in history—simply and swiftly followed the collapse of our political defenses. There is no other reason than this: We failed to read and to outwit the totalitarian mind.

---

426. Based on the passage, what conclusion can be made about the U.S. involvement in the Korean War?

    (A) The United States shifted to economic sanctions rather than military action.

    (B) The United States applied the policy of containment in Asia as well as in Europe.

    (C) The United States did not suffer from war weariness following the Second World War.

    (D) The United States felt a unilateral policy was necessary in Korea.

427. As a result of the Korean War, the Korean Peninsula was divided at what latitude?

    (A) 48° North

    (B) 17° North

    (C) 54°40' North

    (D) 38° North

428. Why was Douglas MacArthur removed from command during the Korean War?

    (A) He relied too heavily on negotiations with the Chinese.

    (B) He had lost the support of the South Koreans.

    (C) MacArthur showed insubordination to President Truman.

    (D) He was seen as too inexperienced.

429. Which of the following was *not* a result of the Korean War?

    (A) peace treaty between the United States and Japan

    (B) passage of the Montgomery GI Bill

    (C) establishment of a military-industrial complex

    (D) racial integration of the armed forces

430. The Eisenhower Doctrine deviated from the passage as well as the Truman Plan by focusing on

    (A) a more relaxed approach to the spread of communism

    (B) a rejection of the Truman Doctrine and the Marshall Plan

    (C) the increased role of petroleum in American foreign policy

    (D) the return of American isolationism

431. In relation to his foreign policy, which of the following was an accomplishment of President Eisenhower's domestic policy?

(A) expansion of the Tennessee Valley Authority

(B) launch of the first satellite into space

(C) creation of a national interstate highway system

(D) creation of the Department of Housing and Urban Affairs

Use the excerpt and your knowledge of the time period to answer questions 432 to 435.

Testimony before the House Committee on Un-American Activities
Paul Robeson, June 12, 1956

Mr. ARENS: Now, during the course of the process in which you were applying for this passport, in July of 1954, were you requested to submit a non-Communist affidavit?

Mr. ROBESON: We had a long discussion—with my counsel . . . with the State Department, about just such an affidavit and I was very precise . . . that under no conditions would I think of signing any such affidavit, that it is a complete contradiction of the rights of American citizens.

. . .

Mr. ARENS: Are you now a member of the Communist Party?

. . .

Mr. ROBESON: What do you mean by the Communist Party? As far as I know it is a legal party like the Republican Party and the Democratic Party. Do you mean a party of people who have sacrificed for my people, and for all Americans and workers, that they can live in dignity? Do you mean that party?

Mr. ARENS: Are you now a member of the Communist Party?

. . .

Mr. ROBESON: I stand upon the Fifth Amendment of the American Constitution.

. . .

THE CHAIRMAN: You are directed to answer that question.

. . .

Mr. ROBESON: Gentlemen, in the first place, wherever I have been in the world, Scandinavia, England, and many places, the first to die in the struggle against Fascism were the Communists and I laid many wreaths upon graves of Communists. It is not criminal, and the Fifth Amendment has nothing to do with criminality. The Chief Justice of the Supreme Court, Warren, has been very clear on that in many speeches, that the Fifth Amendment does not have anything to do with the inference of criminality. I invoke the Fifth Amendment.

432. The major function of the House Un-American Activities Committee (HUAC) was to

(A) stop domestic infiltration of communism

(B) contain the spread of communism in Europe

(C) demobilize the American economy from wartime production

(D) investigate the actions taken by Joseph McCarthy

433. The House Un-American Activities Committee is most similar to the Senate Subcommittee headed by

(A) Joseph McCarthy

(B) Alan K. Simpson

(C) John Stewart Service

(D) Edward R. Murrow

434. When Paul Robeson invoked his Fifth Amendment right, he was referring to which constitutional protection?

(A) right to a fair trial

(B) protection from self-incrimination

(C) right to due process

(D) protection from warrantless searches

435. In relation to the passage, *The Crucible* by Arthur Miller was an analogy of the acts of House Committee on Un-American Activities and

(A) the events of the Holocaust

(B) the Salem Witch Trials

(C) racism in the Southern states

(D) the plight of slavers during the Antebellum period

Use the document and your knowledge of the time period to answer questions 436 to 438.

Special Message to the Congress on Urgent National Needs, John F. Kennedy (May 25, 1961)

The great battleground for the defense and expansion of freedom today is the whole southern half of the globe—Asia, Latin America, Africa and the Middle East—the lands of the rising peoples. Their revolution is the greatest in human history. They seek an end to injustice, tyranny, and exploitation. More than an end, they seek a beginning.

And theirs is a revolution which we would support regardless of the Cold War, and regardless of which political or economic route they should choose to freedom.

For the adversaries of freedom did not create the revolution; nor did they create the conditions which compel it. But they are seeking to ride the crest of its wave—to capture it for themselves . . .

The first and basic task confronting this nation this year was to turn recession into recovery. An affirmative anti-recession program, initiated with your cooperation, supported the natural forces in the private sector; and our economy is now enjoying renewed confidence and energy. The recession has been halted. Recovery is under way.

But the task of abating unemployment and achieving a full use of our resources does remain a serious challenge for us all. Large-scale unemployment during a recession is bad enough, but large-scale unemployment during a period of prosperity would be intolerable.

I am therefore transmitting to the Congress a new Manpower Development and Training program, to train or retrain several hundred thousand workers, particularly in those areas where we have seen chronic unemployment as a result of technological factors in new occupational skills over a four-year period, in order to replace those skills made obsolete by automation and industrial change with the new skills which the new processes demand . . .

In line with these developments, I have directed a further reinforcement of our own capacity to deter or resist non-nuclear aggression. In the conventional field, with one exception, I find no present need for large new levies of men. What is needed is rather a change of position to give us still further increases in flexibility.

Therefore, I am directing the Secretary of Defense to undertake a reorganization and modernization of the Army's divisional structure, to increase its non-nuclear firepower, to improve its tactical mobility in any environment, to insure its flexibility to meet any direct or indirect threat, to facilitate its coordination with our major allies, and to provide more modern mechanized divisions in Europe and bring their equipment up to date, and new airborne brigades in both the Pacific and Europe . . .

Third, I am directing the Secretary of Defense to expand rapidly and substantially, in cooperation with our Allies, the orientation of existing forces for the conduct of non-nuclear war, para-military operations and sub-limited or unconventional wars.

In addition, our Special Forces and unconventional warfare units will be increased and reoriented. Throughout the services new emphasis must be placed on the special skills and languages which are required to work with local populations.

Fourth, the Army is developing plans to make possible a much more rapid deployment of a major portion of its highly trained reserve forces . . . In short, these new plans will allow us to almost double the combat power of the Army in less than two months, compared to the nearly nine months heretofore required.

436. How did President Kennedy's policy of "flexible response" differ from Eisenhower's New Look Policy?

(A) Kennedy focused his policy more on deterrence than Eisenhower.

(B) Kennedy focused on reducing the number of missiles held by both the United States and the Soviet Union.

(C) Kennedy focused on preparing multiple options in response to Soviet actions.

(D) Kennedy focused more on conventional warfare than Eisenhower's policy.

437. The use of paramilitary forces noted by Kennedy is best illustrated in which of the following events?

(A) the Vienna Summit

(B) the Bay of Pigs

(C) the Cuban Missile Crisis

(D) the establishment of the Peace Corps

438. In relation to the passage, which of the following was *not* a consequence of the 1962 Cuban Missile Crisis?

(A) The Soviet Union agreed to remove its nuclear missiles from Cuba.

(B) The United States agreed to remove its nuclear missiles from Turkey.

(C) The Moscow–Washington hotline was created.

(D) President Kennedy launched the Bay of Pigs invasion of Cuba.

Use the image and your knowledge of the time period to answer questions 439 to 441.

Source: File: Family watching television 1958.jpg. (2018, January 5).
Wikimedia Commons, the free media repository.

439. The 1950s literary and cultural movement that would reject the decade of the 1950s social conformity depicted was called the

(A) Lost Generation

(B) Beat Generation

(C) Yippies

(D) Hippies

440. Which pair of events best illustrates the incongruence of the domestic trends of the 1950s?

(A) the emergence of rock and roll and of televangelists

(B) the popularity of rock and roll and the decline in movie attendance

(C) the work of Dr. Spock and the reemergence of the cult of domesticity

(D) suburban sprawl and the growth of the automotive industry

441. In relation to the image, William J. Levitt helped the expansion of the American suburbs by

(A) designing an interstate highway system

(B) establishing the installment plan

(C) introducing mass-produced housing developments

(D) creating the Federal Housing Administration

CHAPTER 17

Civil Rights, the 1960s, and Vietnam

Use the document and your knowledge of the time period to answer questions 442 to 445.

Transcript of *Brown v. Board of Education* (1954)

We conclude that, in the field of public education, the doctrine of "separate but equal" has no place. Separate educational facilities are inherently unequal. Therefore, we hold that the plaintiffs and others similarly situated for whom the actions have been brought are, by reason of the segregation complained of, deprived of the equal protection of the laws guaranteed by the Fourteenth Amendment. This disposition makes unnecessary any discussion whether such segregation also violates the Due Process Clause of the Fourteenth Amendment.

Because these are class actions, because of the wide applicability of this decision, and because of the great variety of local conditions, the formulation of decrees in these cases presents problems of considerable complexity. On re-argument, the consideration of appropriate relief was necessarily subordinated to the primary question—the constitutionality of segregation in public education. We have now announced that such segregation is a denial of the equal protection of the laws. In order that we may have the full assistance of the parties in formulating decrees, the cases will be restored to the docket, and the parties are requested to present further argument on Questions 4 and 5 previously propounded by the Court for the re-argument this Term The Attorney General of the United States is again invited to participate. The Attorneys General of the states requiring or permitting segregation in public education will also be permitted to appear as amici curiae upon request to do so by September 15, 1954, and submission of briefs by October 1, 1954.

---

442. Based on the document, which constitutional amendment served as the basis of the court's decision?

(A) the Thirteenth Amendment

(B) the Fourteenth Amendment

(C) the Fifteenth Amendment

(D) the Sixteenth Amendment

443. The Supreme Court decision in *Brown v. Board of Education* overturned

(A) *Plessy v. Ferguson*

(B) the Taft–Hartley Act

(C) *Youngstown Sheet & Tube Co. v. Sawyer*

(D) the Civil Rights Act

444. Which action actively protested this court decision?

(A) the issuing of the Southern Manifesto

(B) the federalizing Arkansas's National Guard

(C) the deployment of the 101st Airborne Division to Arkansas

(D) the issuing of the Civil Rights Act in 1964

Use the passage and your knowledge of the time period to answer questions 445 to 449.

"We Must Free Ourselves"

John Lewis, Chairman of the Student Non-Violent Coordinating Committee (SNCC) (1963)

In good conscience, we cannot support the administration's civil rights bill, for it is too little, and too late. There's not one thing in the bill that will protect our people from police brutality.

I want to know, which side is the Federal Government on? The revolution is at hand, and we must free ourselves of the chains of political and economic slavery. The nonviolent revolution is saying, "We will not wait for the courts to act, for we have been waiting for hundreds of years. We will not wait for the President, the Justice Department, nor Congress, but we will take matters into our own hands and create a source of power, outside of any national structure, that could and would assure us a victory."

To those who have said, "Be patient and wait," we must say that "patience" is a dirty and nasty word. We cannot be patient, we do not want to be free gradually. We want our freedom, and we want it now. We cannot depend on any political party, for both the Democrats and the Republicans have betrayed the basic principles of the Declaration of Independence. . . .

The revolution is a serious one. Mr. Kennedy is trying to take the revolution out of the streets and put it into the courts. Listen, Mr. Kennedy. Listen, Mr. Congressman. Listen, fellow citizens. The black masses are on the march for jobs and freedom, and we must say to the politicians that there won't be a "cooling-off" period.

---

445. Based on the passage, why would fellow members of the rally, such as civil rights leader A. Philip Randolph, object to this speech?

(A) They fully endorsed the Democratic Party in the South.

(B) They did not want the rally to be political in nature.

(C) They were concerned that the language would ultimately hurt the movement.

(D) They felt the speech went against the socialist principles of the movement.

446. Which statement best describes the shift within the Student Nonviolent Coordinating Committee (SNCC) over the course of the 1960s?

(A) It became more militant over time.

(B) It was slowly absorbed by the hippie movement.

(C) It moved away from militancy and focused on changes through the legislative process.

(D) It became more interracial over time and focused more on women's rights.

447. Unlike Student Nonviolent Coordinating Committee (SNCC), CORE and the SCLC were similar in that both organizations continued to

(A) use militant protest

(B) be church-based organizations

(C) advocate change through nonviolence

(D) not allow white membership

448. In the speech, Lewis is critical of the Civil Rights Act. Which of the following was *not* part of the 1964 Civil Rights Act that may have led to this criticism?

(A) banning of different voter registration practices based on race

(B) banning of discrimination in public accommodations

(C) creation of the Equal Employment Opportunity Commission

(D) outlawing of poll taxes

449. The civil rights movement spread to other aspects of society. Which leader is *not* paired with the cause he or she is associated with?

(A) Betty Friedan—women's rights

(B) César Chávez—migrant workers' rights

(C) Dennis Banks—Native American rights

(D) Rachel Carson—Japanese-American rights

Use the passage and your knowledge of the time period to answer questions 450 to 452.

The Ballot or the Bullet
Malcolm X (April 3, 1964)

The question tonight, as I understand it, is "The Negro Revolt, and Where Do We Go From Here?" or What Next?" In my little humble way of understanding it, it points toward either the ballot or the bullet.

Before we try and explain what is meant by the ballot or the bullet, I would like to clarify something concerning myself. I'm still a Muslim; my religion is still Islam. That's my personal belief. Just as . . . Dr. Martin Luther King is a Christian minister down in Atlanta, Georgia, who heads another organization fighting for the civil rights of black people in this country; . . . well, I myself am a minister, not a Christian minister, but a Muslim minister; and I believe in action on all fronts by whatever means necessary.

Although I'm still a Muslim, I'm not here tonight to discuss my religion. I'm not here to try and change your religion . . . we have the same problem, a common problem . . . we all are going to catch the same hell from the same man. He just happens to be a white man. All of us have suffered here, in this country, political oppression at the hands of the white man, economic exploitation at the hands of the white man, and social degradation at the hands of the white man.

Now in speaking like this, it doesn't mean that we're anti-white, but it does mean we're anti-exploitation, we're anti-degradation, we're anti-oppression. And if the white man doesn't want us to be anti-him, let him stop oppressing and exploiting and degrading us.

If we don't do something real soon, I think you'll have to agree that we're going to be forced either to use the ballot or the bullet. It's one or the other in 1964. It isn't that time is running out—time has run out!

. . . If the black man in these Southern states had his full voting rights, the key Dixiecrats in Washington, D.C., which means the key Democrats in Washington, D.C., would lose their seats. The Democratic Party itself would lose its power. It would cease to be powerful as a party.

---

450. Based on the passage, Malcolm X's argument most closely resembles W. E. B. DuBois notion that

(A) the African-American community should isolate itself from "white politics"

(B) the African American community must politically empower itself

(C) the African-American community should be patient in political empowerment

(D) African Americans should reject Christianity because it was a means of white political control

451. The approaches of Dr. Martin Luther King Jr. and Malcolm X to the civil rights movement differed in that

(A) King was part of the SCLC, and Malcolm X created SNCC

(B) Malcolm X adopted a view of the "alleged inferiority of the Negro," while King did not

(C) Malcolm X, unlike King, was a follower of Stokely Carmichael

(D) King fought for desegregation, while Malcolm X supported a separate identity for African Americans

452. The civil rights movement's Freedom Summer and the Selma March further highlighted what issue that was also illustrated in Malcolm X's speech?

(A) They illustrated the lack of African-American voting rights.

(B) They brought attention to the black power movement.

(C) They led to the creation of the Southern Manifesto.

(D) They led to the Civil Rights Act of 1964.

Use the document and your knowledge of the time period to answer questions 453 to 455.

Acceptance of the Democratic Party Nomination for the Presidency
John F. Kennedy (July 15, 1960)

For I stand tonight facing west on what was once the last frontier. From the lands that stretch three thousand miles behind me, the pioneers of old gave up their safety, their comfort and sometimes their lives to build a new world here in the West. They were not the captives of their own doubts, the prisoners of their own price tags. Their motto was not "every man for himself"—but "all for the common cause." They were determined to make that new world strong and free, to overcome its hazards and its hardships, to conquer the enemies that threatened from without and within.

Today some would say that those struggles are all over—that all the horizons have been explored—that all the battles have been won—that there is no longer an American frontier.

But I trust that no one in this vast assemblage will agree with those sentiments. For the problems are not all solved and the battles are not all won—and we stand today on the edge of a New Frontier—the frontier of the 1960's—a frontier of unknown opportunities and perils—a frontier of unfulfilled hopes and threats.

Woodrow Wilson's New Freedom promised our nation a new political and economic framework. Franklin Roosevelt's New Deal promised security and succor to those in need. But the New Frontier of which I speak is not a set of promises—it is a set of challenges. It sums up not what I intend to offer the American people, but what I intend to ask of them. It appeals to their pride, not to their pocketbook—it holds out the promise of more sacrifice instead of more security.

But I tell you the New Frontier is here, whether we seek it or not. Beyond that frontier are the uncharted areas of science and space, unsolved problems of peace and war, unconquered pockets of ignorance and prejudice, unanswered questions of poverty and surplus. It would be easier to shrink back from that frontier, to look to the safe mediocrity of the past, to be lulled by good intentions and high rhetoric—and those who prefer that course should not cast their votes for me, regardless of party.

But I believe the times demand new invention, innovation, imagination, decision. I am asking each of you to be pioneers on that New Frontier. My call is to the young in heart, regardless of age—to all who respond to the Scriptural call: "Be strong and of a good courage; be not afraid, neither be thou dismayed."

453. Which action would *not* be considered part of President Kennedy's New Frontier?

   (A) the Trade Expansion Act
   (B) the Fair Labor Standards Act
   (C) the Equal Pay Act
   (D) the signing of the Nuclear Test Ban Treaty

454. Which statement best describes the election of Kennedy to the presidency?

   (A) It illustrated an end of anti-Catholic sentiments in the United States.
   (B) Kennedy's wide margin of victory gave him a strong mandate.
   (C) The narrow margin of victory denied Kennedy an initial mandate as president.
   (D) Kennedy was able to secure a victory on the fast economic growth of the previous administration.

455. Which event ultimately led to the end of Kennedy's New Frontier initiative?

   (A) the failed Bay of Pigs Invasion
   (B) the military escalation of Vietnam
   (C) the Cuban Missile Crisis
   (D) Kennedy's assassination in 1963

Use the document and your knowledge of the time period to answer questions 456 and 457.

Transcript of Tonkin Gulf Resolution (1964)

Whereas naval units of the Communist regime in Vietnam, in violation of the principles of the Charter of the United Nations and of international law, have deliberately and repeatedly attacked United States naval vessels lawfully present in international waters, and have thereby created a serious threat to international peace; and

Whereas these attackers are part of deliberate and systematic campaign of aggression that the Communist regime in North Vietnam has been waging against its neighbors and the nations joined with them in the collective defense of their freedom; and

Whereas the United States is assisting the peoples of southeast Asia to protest their freedom and has no territorial, military or political ambitions in that area, but desires only that these people should be left in peace to work out their destinies in their own way: Now, therefore be it

Resolved by the Senate and House of Representatives of the United States of America in Congress assembled, That the Congress approves and supports the determination of the President, as Commander in Chief, to take all necessary measures to repel any armed attack against the forces of the United States and to prevent further aggression . . .

---

456. President Johnson escalated the Vietnam War in response to the

(A) My Lai Massacre

(B) Second Gulf of Tonkin incident

(C) establishment of the Viet Cong

(D) release of the Pentagon Papers

457. Prior to the resolution, President Kennedy tried to keep communism out of Vietnam by

(A) providing military assistance to Ho Chi Minh

(B) launching a bombing campaign against Cambodia

(C) providing the Southern Vietnamese government with American military advisors

(D) allying with the Viet Cong against the Ngo Dinh Diem

Use the document and your knowledge of the time period to answer questions 458 to 460.

Address to the Nation Announcing Steps to Limit the War in Vietnam and Reporting His Decision Not to Seek Reelection
President Lyndon B. Johnson (March 31, 1968)

For years, representatives of our Government and others have traveled the world—seeking to find a basis for peace talks.

Since last September, they have carried the offer that I made public at San Antonio. That offer was this:

That the United States would stop its bombardment of North Vietnam when that would lead promptly to productive discussions—and that we would assume that North Vietnam would not take military advantage of our restraint. Hanoi denounced this offer, both privately and publicly. Even while the search for peace was going on, North Vietnam rushed their preparations for a savage assault on the people, the government, and the allies of South Vietnam.

. . . Their attack—during the Tet holidays—failed to achieve its principal objectives. It did not collapse the elected government of South Vietnam or shatter its army—as the Communists had hoped.

Our goal of peace and self-determination in Vietnam is directly related to the future of all of Southeast Asia—where much has happened to inspire confidence during the past 10 years. We have done all that we knew how to do to contribute and to help build that confidence. . . .

I think every American can take a great deal of pride in the role that we have played in bringing this about in Southeast Asia. We can rightly judge—as responsible Southeast Asians themselves do—that the progress of the past 3 years would have been far less likely—if not completely impossible—if America's sons and others had not made their stand in Vietnam.

---

458. The major North Vietnamese and Viet Cong offensive launched on the Vietnamese New Year in 1968 is referred to as

(A) the My Lai Massacre

(B) Operation Rolling Thunder

(C) the Tet Offensive

(D) the Ho Chi Minh Trail

459. The Vietnam War finally ended when

(A) the United Nations divided the nation at the 17th Parallel

(B) the United States led a successful invasion of Cambodia

(C) the United States withdrew its armed forces

(D) the North Vietnamese army successfully captured South Vietnam

460. Which of the following terms was *not* part of the 1973 Paris Peace Agreement signed between the United States and Vietnam?

(A) agreement by North and South Vietnam to hold free elections

(B) removal of all American military forces from the region

(C) release of all war prisoners

(D) end of military actions in Cambodia and Laos

Use the document and your knowledge of the time period to answer questions 461 and 462.

War Powers Resolution
Joint Resolution

PURPOSE AND POLICY

SEC. 2. (a) It is the purpose of this joint resolution to fulfill the intent of the framers of the Constitution of the United States and insure that the collective judgement of both the Congress and the President will apply to the introduction of United States Armed Forces into hostilities, or into situations where imminent involvement in hostilities is clearly indicated by the circumstances, and to the continued use of such forces in hostilities or in such situations.

(b) Under article I, section 8, of the Constitution, it is specifically provided that the Congress shall have the power to make all laws necessary and proper for carrying into execution, not only its own powers but also all other powers vested by the Constitution in the Government of the United States, or in any department or officer thereof.

(c) The constitutional powers of the President as Commander-in-Chief to introduce United States Armed Forces into hostilities, or into situations where imminent involvement in hostilities is clearly indicated by the circumstances, are exercised only pursuant to (1) a declaration of war, (2) specific statutory authorization, or (3) a national emergency created by attack upon the United States, its territories or possessions, or its armed forces.

CONSULTATION

SEC. 3. The President in every possible instance shall consult with Congress before introducing United States Armed Forces into hostilities or into a situation where imminent involvement in hostilities is clearly indicated by the circumstances, and after every such introduction shall consult regularly with the Congress until United States Armed Forces are no longer engaged in hostilities or have been removed from such situations.

REPORTING
SEC. 4. (a) In the absence of a declaration of war, in any case in which United States Armed Forces are introduced–
(1) into hostilities or into situations where imminent involvement in hostilities is clearly indicated by the circumstances;
(2) into the territory, airspace or waters of a foreign nation, while equipped for combat, except for deployments which relate solely to supply, replacement, repair, or training of such forces; or
(3) in numbers which substantially enlarge United States Armed Forces equipped for combat already located in a foreign nation; the president shall submit within 48 hours to the Speaker of the House of Representatives and to the President pro tempore of the Senate a report, in writing, setting forth–
(A) the circumstances necessitating the introduction of United States Armed Forces;
(B) the constitutional and legislative authority under which such introduction took place; and
(C) the estimated scope and duration of the hostilities or involvement.
(D) The President shall provide such other information as the Congress may request in the fulfillment of its constitutional responsibilities with respect to committing the Nation to war and to the use of United States Armed Forces abroad
(E) Whenever United States Armed Forces are introduced into hostilities or into any situation described in subsection (a) of this section, the President shall, so long as such armed forces continue to be engaged in such hostilities or situation, report to the Congress periodically on the status of such hostilities or situation as well as on the scope and duration of such hostilities or situation, but in no event shall he report to the Congress less often than once every six months.

461. Which of the following provisions was *not* part of the 1973 War Powers Act?

(A) The president must notify Congress within 48 hours after deploying the military abroad.

(B) Only Congress has the power to declare war.

(C) The president must provide Congress with justification for his actions after deploying the military abroad.

(D) Troops cannot be deployed for more than 60 days without congressional approval.

462. The War Powers Act was first used in response the actions of which presidency?

(A) Richard Nixon

(B) Gerald Ford

(C) Jimmy Carter

(D) Ronald Reagan

Use the passage and your knowledge of the time period to answer questions 463 to 465.

Remarks at the University of Michigan
Lyndon B. Johnson (May 22, 1964)

The challenge of the next half century is whether we have the wisdom to use that wealth to enrich and elevate our national life, and to advance the quality of our American civilization.

Your imagination, your initiative, and your indignation will determine whether we build a society where progress is the servant of our needs, or a society where old values and new visions are buried under unbridled growth. For in your time we have the opportunity to move not only toward the rich society and the powerful society, but upward to the Great Society.

The Great Society rests on abundance and liberty for all. It demands an end to poverty and racial injustice, to which we are totally committed in our time. But that is just the beginning.

The Great Society is a place where every child can find knowledge to enrich his mind and to enlarge his talents. It is a place where leisure is a welcome chance to build and reflect, not a feared cause of boredom and restlessness. It is a place where the city of man serves not only the needs of the body and the demands of commerce but the desire for beauty and the hunger for community.

It is a place where man can renew contact with nature. It is a place which honors creation for its own sake and for what it adds to the understanding of the race. It is a place where men are more concerned with the quality of their goals than the quantity of their goods.

But most of all, the Great Society is not a safe harbor, a resting place, a final objective, a finished work. It is a challenge constantly renewed, beckoning us toward a destiny where the meaning of our lives matches the marvelous products of our labor.

So I want to talk to you today about three places where we begin to build the Great Society—in our cities, in our countryside, and in our classrooms.

463. Which of the following actions would *not* be considered part of Johnson's Great Society?

(A) the 1968 Civil Rights Act
(B) the creation of the Department of Housing and Urban Development
(C) the Elementary and Secondary Education Act
(D) the creation of NASA

464. Which program of the Great Society was designed to address healthcare costs for low-income families?

(A) Head Start
(B) Medicare
(C) Medicaid
(D) the VISTA program

465. Which of the following was *not* a factor leading to the end of the Great Society?

(A) The cost of the Vietnam War put a strain on funding Great Society programs.
(B) It failed to have any impact on poverty rates in the United States.
(C) Concern grew that the federal government was overstepping its role.
(D) Concerns grew that the program was socialist and spent too much on the poor.

CHAPTER 18

End of the Cold War, the 1970s to the Present

Use the passage and your knowledge of the time period to answer questions 466 to 469.

Address Accepting the Presidential Nomination
Richard M. Nixon (August 8, 1968)

We are going to win because at a time that America cries out for the unity that this Administration has destroyed, the Republican Party—after a spirited contest for its nomination for President and for Vice President—stands united before the nation tonight . . .

The choice we make in 1968 will determine not only the future of America but the future of peace and freedom in the world for the last third of the Twentieth Century.

And the question that we answer tonight: can America meet this great challenge? . . .

Listen to the answer to those questions. It is another voice. It is the quiet voice in the tumult and the shouting. It is the voice of the great majority of Americans, the forgotten Americans—the non-shouters; the non-demonstrators. They are not racists or sick; they are not guilty of the crime that plagues the land. They are black and they are white—they're native born and foreign born—they're young and they're old. They work in America's factories.

They run America's businesses. They serve in government. They provide most of the soldiers who died to keep us free. They give drive to the spirit of America. They give lift to the American Dream. They give steel to the backbone of America. They are good people, they are decent people; they work, and they save, and they pay their taxes, and they care.

Like Theodore Roosevelt, they know that this country will not be a good place for any of us to live in unless it is a good place for all of us to live in. This I say to you tonight is the real voice of America. In this year 1968, this is the message it will broadcast to America and to the world . . .

And this great group of Americans, the forgotten Americans, and others know that the great; question Americans must answer by their votes in November is this: Whether we shall continue for four more years the policies of the last five years . . .

466. Which group would most likely reject Nixon's message as stated above?

(A) American conservatives

(B) White Southern voters

(C) Eisenhower Republicans

(D) the antiwar movement

467. Following his election to the presidency, Richard Nixon's "Southern strategy" policy focused on

(A) cutting funding to Southern schools that were still segregated

(B) gaining popular African-American support in the South

(C) making it easier to meet desegregation requirements

(D) furthering the implementation of the 1965 Voting Rights Act

468. Nixon's domestic policy became known as New Federalism, which

(A) continued the Great Society's expansion of programs at a federal level

(B) shifted federal programs to the state level through block grants

(C) successfully ended social services such as welfare and Medicaid

(D) successfully implemented the family assistance plan to help low-income families

469. The combination of inflation and economic recession faced in the United States in 1973 was caused in part by

(A) the opening of diplomatic relations with China and the Soviet Union

(B) OPEC's increasing the price of oil

(C) the signing of the Camp David Accords

(D) the signing of the SALT I agreement

Use the document and your knowledge of the time period to answer questions 470 and 471.

Opening Remarks
Dr. Henry Kissinger, October 22, 2007

. . .We felt we owed it to the American public to demonstrate a permanent commitment to a period of what President Nixon called negotiation, a commitment to the desirability of peaceful resolutions of disputes, and to make permanent efforts to bridge the gaps that existed between us and the Soviet Union, between us and China, and to solve the Vietnam War on a basis which we considered honorable, which meant that we were not prepared to turn over the people who, in reliance on American promises by our predecessors, had staked their fate on America . . .

Once it became clear that the channel existed, in late '72, then each of the elements in this process would put forward their maximum position . . . by the time I became Secretary of State . . . the bureaucratic backup for it was breaking down, Détente got on a violent controversy . . . the channel in its old sense didn't exist anymore because it moved into the State Department. I could use State Department backup, and all it was then was a very intense conversation between the Secretary of State and the Soviets, and the Soviet Ambassador, who was outstanding.

One of the attributes of this channel was that we could spend time on philosophical issues. We did not come to each meeting with a formal position and begin negotiating. We would have sessions . . . which we described to each other, as thinking out loud . . . And I think that . . . helped negotiations...

And it is based on these assumptions that a number of agreements were made. And for example, the Strategic Arms Limitation Agreement, which was really an attempt by us to cap the growth of the Soviet missile force, and whose numbers, even though it became very controversial, whose numbers were never altered in the 25 years that followed it or in the 20 years that followed it . . .

---

470. In foreign affairs, President Nixon's policy of détente was illustrated by

  (A) relaxing Cold War tensions by engaging in talks with China and the Soviet Union

  (B) rejecting the ideals of realpolitik

  (C) his bombing campaign of Cambodia

  (D) rejecting the SALT I agreement

471. The SALT I and SALT II Agreements were created primarily to

  (A) create diplomatic ties between the United States and China

  (B) further the U.S. policy of containment of communism

  (C) negotiate arms control between the major superpowers

  (D) reduce tensions within the Middle East

Use the document and your knowledge of the time period to answer questions 472 to 474.

Pardon Proclamation
President Gerald Ford (September 8, 1974)

Pursuant to resolutions of the House of Representatives, its Committee on the Judiciary conducted an inquiry and investigation on the impeachment of the President . . . The hearings of the Committee and its deliberations . . . resulted in votes adverse to Richard Nixon on recommended Articles of Impeachment.

As a result of certain acts or omissions occurring before his resignation . . . Richard Nixon has become liable to possible indictment and trial for offenses against the United States. Whether or not he shall be so prosecuted depends on findings of the appropriate grand jury and on the discretion of the authorized prosecutor. Should an indictment ensue, the accused shall then be entitled to a fair trial by an impartial jury, as guaranteed to every individual by the Constitution.

It is believed that a trial of Richard Nixon . . . could not fairly begin until a year or more has elapsed. In the meantime, the tranquility to which this nation has been restored by the events of recent weeks could be irreparably lost by the prospects of bringing to trial a former President of the United States. The prospects of such trial will cause prolonged and divisive debate over the propriety of exposing to further punishment and degradation a man who has already paid the unprecedented penalty of relinquishing the highest elective office of the United States . . .

472. What action did Gerald Ford take to attempt to heal the nation following the Watergate Scandal?

   (A) He asked citizens to wear WIN buttons.

   (B) He pardoned Richard Nixon.

   (C) He provided military support to the South Vietnamese government.

   (D) He ordered a full investigation of the Nixon administration.

473. What was the primary reason behind the Watergate break-in in 1972?

   (A) Nixon wanted to purge his administration of possible communist infiltration.

   (B) CREEP wanted to spy on the Democratic Party.

   (C) The FBI was monitoring the Democratic Party's election campaign.

   (D) President Nixon wanted to recapture the leaked Pentagon Papers.

474. In relation to the passage, Jimmy Carter won the 1976 presidential election by

(A) flaunting his knowledge of nuclear technology

(B) capturing the support of the Moral Majority

(C) promoting himself as a Washington outsider

(D) increasing government regulations on industries

Use the passage and your knowledge of the time period to answer questions 475 and 476.

Text of Letter from President Carter to Prime Minister Begin August 3, 1978

To Prime Minister Begin

This is a private and personal letter, and I would appreciate your honoring its confidentiality. I want to express myself frankly and directly to you personally.

During the past year under your leadership of Israel we have made remarkable progress toward peace. The boldness and leadership qualities exhibited by you and President Sadat have contributed to a new and better relationship between Israel and Egypt which was not anticipated by the rest of the world. In my opinion, you are the leader who, in the foreseeable future, can and must continue this progress. You have a strong hold on the government, loyalty among your associates, and the well-deserved confidence of the people of your country.

It is imperative that every effort be made to capitalize on this unprecedented opportunity to consummate a definitive peace treaty between Israel and Egypt and then to match this achievement with other agreements between your nation and your other neighbors.

Although the recent discussions have produced minimal progress, broad areas of agreement do exist, providing a basis for sustained hope. Unless we take advantage of this opportunity now, however, those of us who presently serve as leaders of our respective nations may not again have such a chance to advance the cause of peace in the Middle East.

After hours of detailed discussions on several occasions with both you and President Sadat, in private and in group sessions, I am convinced of your mutual desire for peace. That desire is obviously shared by the people of both nations. Nevertheless, the high hopes of last winter have now been dissipated, with potentially serious consequences.

It is time, therefore, for a renewed effort at the highest level. My hope is that during this visit by Secretary Vance to the Middle East progress and harmony will be indicated by positive statements and the avoidance of public disputes.

Then, as soon as is convenient, I would like to meet personally with you and President Sadat to search for additional avenues toward peace . . .

475. The 1978 peace agreement between Israel and Egypt was called the

(A) Helsinki Accords

(B) Geneva Accords

(C) Peace of Paris

(D) Camp David Accords

476. What international incident helped Ronald Reagan defeat Jimmy Carter in 1980?

(A) First Persian Gulf War

(B) Iran hostage crisis

(C) Iran–Contra Affair

(D) signing of SALT I

Use the document and your knowledge of the time period to answer questions 477 to 482.

Inaugural Address
Ronald Reagan (January 20, 1981)

The business of our nation goes forward. These United States are confronted with an economic affliction of great proportions. We suffer from the longest and one of the worst sustained inflations in our national history. It distorts our economic decisions, penalizes thrift, and crushes the struggling young and the fixed-income elderly alike. It threatens to shatter the lives of millions of our people.

Idle industries have cast workers into unemployment, human misery, and personal indignity. Those who do work are denied a fair return for their labor by a tax system which penalizes successful achievement and keeps us from maintaining full productivity.

But great as our tax burden is, it has not kept pace with public spending. For decades we have piled deficit upon deficit, mortgaging our future and our children's future for the temporary convenience of the present. To continue this long trend is to guarantee tremendous social, cultural, political, and economic upheavals.

You and I, as individuals, can, by borrowing, live beyond our means, but for only a limited period of time. Why, then, should we think that collectively, as a nation, we're not bound by that same limitation? We must act today in order to preserve tomorrow. And let there be no misunderstanding: We are going to begin to act, beginning today.

The economic ills we suffer have come upon us over several decades. They will not go away in days, weeks, or months, but they will go away. They will go away because we as Americans have the capacity now, as we've had in the past, to do whatever needs to be done to preserve this last and greatest bastion of freedom.

In this present crisis, government is not the solution to our problem; government is the problem. From time to time we've been tempted to believe that society has become too complex to be managed by self-rule, that government by an elite group is superior to government for, by, and of the people. Well, if no one among us is capable of governing himself, then who among us has the capacity to govern someone else? All of us together, in and out of government, must bear the burden. The solutions we seek must be equitable, with no one group singled out to pay a higher price.

477. What were the two major areas of focus of Ronald Reagan's economic plan?

(A) expanding federal assistance programs and increasing government

(B) adopting Keynesian economics and cutting military spending

(C) funding urban development and lowering taxes on the wealthy

(D) lowering taxes and reducing government regulations

478. Which statement best describes the impact of President Reagan's domestic policy?

(A) While economic growth did occur, the gap between the rich and poor increased.

(B) Both economic growth and income economy were achieved.

(C) Federal spending increased for federal programs, reducing urban poverty.

(D) While the gap between the rich and poor decreased, economic growth was limited.

479. Reagan's view of government regulation is most similar to

(A) the Progressives of the first decade of the twentieth century

(B) the Republicans of the 1920s

(C) the Johnson administration of the 1960s

(D) the New Deal under Franklin Roosevelt

480. In relation to the passage, which statement best describes the national debt under President Reagan?

(A) Despite cutting in federal domestic programs, the national debt greatly increased.

(B) Through tax cuts and reduction in federal spending, the national debt was decreased.

(C) Through economic regulation and balanced spending measures, the national debt became revenue neutral.

(D) Though spending and tax cuts were implemented, the national debt was only reduced slightly.

481. Ronald Reagan made history by appointing which individual as the first female to sit on the Supreme Court?

(A) Ruth Joan Bader Ginsburg

(B) Sandra Day O'Connor

(C) Frances Perkins

(D) Sonia Sotomayor

482. During his presidency, the controversy in which members of President Reagan's administration illegally sold arms in violation of a congressional embargo has become known as

(A) the S&L crisis

(B) the HUD scandal

(C) Whitewater

(D) the Iran–Contra Affair

Use the document and your knowledge of the time period to answer questions 483 and 484.

Speech Given to Party Conference
Soviet Premier Mikhail Gorbachev (June 28, 1988)

We are facing many intricate questions. But which one of them is the crucial one? As the C.C. C.P.S.U. sees it, the crucial one is that of reforming our political system . . .

It follows that the political objective of our conference is to examine the period after the April 1985 . . . to enrich the strategy and specify the tactics of our changes, and define the ways, means and methods that would assure the steady advancement and irreversibility of our perestroika, and to do so in the spirit of Lenin's traditions and with reference to available experience . . .

Just now it is often being said and written by people in various localities that perestroika has not reached them; they ask when this will happen. But perestroika is not manna from the skies, instead of waiting for it to be brought in from somewhere, it has to be brought about by the people themselves in their town or village, in their work collective. What are needed today more than ever are deeds, actions, not talk about perestroika. Much here depends on our personnel, on leaders at the district, town, region, republic and all-union level.

But it is not leaders alone who are to blame for the fact that we still have plenty of places where perestroika is riding at anchor. Pointing an accusing finger at the people in charge is known to be the easiest thing to do and it is a very widespread thing with us. This habit could be somehow understood when the social atmosphere in the country, and the activities of party and state bodies, were not creating the proper groundwork for people to take an active civic stand. But now, comrades, everything is changing radically, and many people have joined energetically in all the processes of perestroika. Therefore, we must put a blunt question to people who persist in complaining and pointing a finger at those in charge, at the "higher-ups": what have you yourself done for perestroika?

483. What was the overall impact of perestroika and glasnost on the Cold War?

(A) They strengthened the communist system in Eastern Europe.

(B) They brought an end to the strategic arms race between the United States and Soviet Union.

(C) They helped lead to the collapse of communist regimes in Eastern Europe.

(D) They led to the SALT I and II agreements.

484. Which of the following statements does *not* describe American foreign policy concerning Russia after the Soviet Union collapsed?

(A) The United States attempted to assist the nation's transition to democracy.

(B) The United States provided assistance in the establishment of a free market economy.

(C) The United States assisted in the Soviet Union's collapse by backing a coup against Boris Yeltsin.

(D) The United States supplied direct financial aid to the former Soviet Union.

Use the passage and your knowledge of the time period to answer questions 485 and 486.

Iraqi Aggression in the Persian Gulf
George H. W. Bush (1991)

We gather tonight, witness to events in the Persian Gulf as significant as they are tragic. In the early morning hours of August 2nd, following negotiations and promises by Iraq's dictator, Saddam Hussein, not to use force, a powerful Iraqi army invaded its trusting and much weaker neighbor, Kuwait. Within three days, 120,000 Iraqi troops with 850 tanks had poured into Kuwait, and moved south to threaten Saudi Arabia. It was then I decided to check that aggression.

At this moment, our brave servicemen and women stand watch in that distant desert and on distant seas, side by side with the forces of more than 20 other nations.

They are some of the finest men and women of the United States of America. And they're doing one terrific job.

These valiant Americans were ready at a moment's notice to leave their spouses, their children to serve on the front line halfway around the world. They remind us who keeps America strong. They do.

In the trying circumstances of the gulf, the morale of our servicemen and women is excellent. In the face of danger, they are brave, well trained and dedicated . . .

Our objectives in the Persian Gulf are clear, our goals defined and familiar: Iraq must withdraw from Kuwait completely, immediately and without condition. Kuwait's legitimate government must be restored. The security and stability of the Persian Gulf must be assured. American citizens abroad must be protected.

These goals are not ours alone. They have been endorsed by the U.N. Security Council five times in as many weeks. Most countries share our concern for principle. And many have a stake in the stability of the Persian Gulf. This is not, as Saddam Hussein would have it, the United States against Iraq. It is Iraq against the world . . .

---

485. The First Persian Gulf War began when Saddam Hussein

(A) launched an attack on Israel

(B) overthrew the democratic Iraqi government

(C) launched an invasion of Kuwait

(D) attempted to assassinate George H. W. Bush

486. Prior to the U.S. actions in Iraq under President George H. W. Bush, Operation Just Cause was a U.S. action in response to

(A) the Chinese government's actions in the Tiananmen Square protests

(B) the admittance of the unified Germany into NATO

(C) the military over through of Manuel Noriega in Panama

(D) the creation of the START Treaty

Use the document and your knowledge of the time period to answer questions 487 to 489.

President's Address to Congress on Health Care William J. Clinton (September 23, 1993)

From the settling of the frontier to the landing on the moon, ours has been a continuous story of challenges defined, obstacles overcome, new horizons secured. That is what makes America what it is and Americans what we are.

Now we are in a time of profound change and opportunity. The end of the cold war, the information age, the global economy have brought us both opportunity and hope and strife and uncertainty.

Our purpose in this dynamic age must be to change, to make change our friend and not our enemy.

To achieve that goal, we must face all our challenges with confidence, with faith and with discipline, whether we're reducing the deficit, creating tomorrow's jobs and training our people to fill them, converting from a high-tech defense to a high-tech domestic economy, expanding trade, reinventing government, making our streets safer or rewarding work over idleness. All these challenges require us to change.

If Americans are to have the courage to change in a difficult time, we must first be secure in our most basic needs. Fixing a Broken System. Tonight I want to talk to you about the most critical thing we can do to build that security. This health care system of ours is badly broken and it is time to fix it. Despite the dedication of literally millions of talented health care professionals, our health care is too uncertain and too expensive, too bureaucratic and too wasteful. It has too much fraud and too much greed.

At long last, after decades of false starts, we must make this our most urgent priority: giving every American health security, health care that can never be taken away, health care that is always there. That is what we must do tonight.

On this journey, as on all others of true consequence, there will be rough spots in the road and honest disagreements about how we should proceed. After all, this is a complicated issue. But every successful journey is guided by fixed stars, and if we can agree on some basic values and principles, we will reach this destination and we will reach it together.

---

487. In attempting to reform the nation's healthcare system, President Clinton wanted to

(A) provide health insurance to all Americans

(B) provide healthcare coverage for the poor

(C) offer loans to students pursuing a career in medicine

(D) provide health insurance to the elderly

488. In response to President Clinton's domestic agenda, the Republican Party's 1994 Contract with America pledged to

(A) fully fund the "Star Wars" program

(B) end the federal welfare system

(C) tighten immigration laws

(D) balance the federal budget

489. Which of the following statements is true of the impeachments of both President Clinton and President Johnson?

(A) Both presidents were accused of committing perjury while under oath.

(B) Both presidents were found not guilty by the Senate.

(C) Because of the impeachments, neither president sought reelection.

(D) Both presidents were accused of illegally firing advisors.

Use the document and your knowledge of the time period to answer questions 490 to 492.

GEORGE W. BUSH, et al., *PETITIONERS v. ALBERT GORE*, Jr., et al.
December 12, 2000

The Supreme Court of Florida has said that the legislature intended the State's electors to "participate fully in the federal electoral process" . . . That statute, in turn, requires that any controversy or contest that is designed to lead to a conclusive selection of electors be completed by December 12. That date is upon us, and there is no recount procedure in place under the State Supreme Court's order that comports with minimal constitutional standards. Because it is evident that any recount seeking to meet the December 12 date will be unconstitutional for the reasons we have discussed, we reverse the judgment of the Supreme Court of Florida ordering a recount to proceed.

Seven Justices of the Court agree that there are constitutional problems with the recount ordered by the Florida Supreme Court that demand a remedy . . . The only disagreement is as to the remedy. Because the Florida Supreme Court has said that the Florida Legislature intended to obtain the safe-harbor benefits of 3 U.S.C. § 5 Justice Breyer's proposed remedy—remanding to the Florida Supreme Court for its ordering of a constitutionally proper contest until December 18—contemplates action in violation of the Florida election code . . .

None are more conscious of the vital limits on judicial authority than are the members of this Court, and none stand more in admiration of the Constitution's design to leave the selection of the President to the people, through their legislatures, and to the political sphere. When contending parties invoke the process of the courts, however, it becomes our unsought responsibility to resolve the federal and constitutional issues the judicial system has been forced to confront.

490. The verdict of the *Bush v. Gore* court case resulted in

(A) the state of Florida being forced to perform a recount of ballots

(B) the state legislature of Florida deciding which candidate would receive the electoral votes

(C) the termination of the recounting of ballots in the state of Florida

(D) Florida's electoral votes not being counted in the election

491. In the 2000 election, "hanging chads" referred to

(A) Somali militiamen loyal to Mohamed Farrah Aidid

(B) improperly punched election ballots

(C) the bombing of Serbia supply lines in the war in Bosnia and Herzegovina

(D) a 21-day government shutdown

492. The 2000 presidential election was similar to the 1824 election in that

(A) the House of Representatives decided the election

(B) neither candidate won enough electoral votes to win the presidency

(C) the candidate who received a majority of the popular vote lost the election

(D) the Supreme Court had to decide the final outcome

Use the passage and your knowledge of the time period to answer questions 493 to 495.

Address to the Nation on the Terrorist Attacks
George W. Bush (September 11, 2001)

Today our fellow citizens, our way of life, our very freedom came under attack in a series of deliberate and deadly terrorist acts. The victims were in airplanes or in their offices: secretaries, business men and women, military and Federal workers, moms and dads, friends and neighbors. Thousands of lives were suddenly ended by evil, despicable acts of terror.

The pictures of airplanes flying into buildings, fires burning, huge structures collapsing have filled us with disbelief, terrible sadness, and a quiet, unyielding anger. These acts of mass murder were intended to frighten our Nation into chaos and retreat, but they have failed. Our country is strong.

A great people has been moved to defend a great nation. Terrorist attacks can shake the foundations of our biggest buildings, but they cannot touch the foundation of America. These acts shattered steel, but they cannot dent the steel of American resolve. America was targeted for attack because we're the brightest beacon for freedom and opportunity in the world. And no one will keep that light from shining.

493. The events of September 11th can be compared to the burning of Washington during the War of 1812 and the Pearl Harbor attack in that

(A) they resulted in mass panic among the citizenship

(B) they led to popular calls for increased isolationism

(C) the events became a rallying cry for national unity

(D) they were used to justify the curtailment of civil liberties

494. Which of the following events is *not* associated with Al Qaeda?

(A) the bombing of the USS *Cole*

(B) the 1998 bombing of the U.S. Embassy

(C) the bombing of the Oklahoma City Federal Building

(D) the Madrid train bombings

495. Which of the following legislation was passed in direct response to the events of September 11, 2001?

(A) USA PATRIOT Act

(B) FISA Act

(C) McCain–Feingold Act

(D) Brady Bill

Use the document and your knowledge of the time period to answer questions 496 to 498.

The President's Address to a Joint Session of Congress
Barack Obama (February 24, 2009)

We have lived through an era where too often, short-term gains were prized over long-term prosperity; where we failed to look beyond the next payment, the next quarter, or the next election. A surplus became an excuse to transfer wealth to the wealthy instead of an opportunity to invest in our future. Regulations were gutted for the sake of a quick profit at the expense of a healthy market. People bought homes they knew they couldn't afford from banks and lenders who pushed those bad loans anyway. And all the while, critical debates and difficult decisions were put off for some other time on some other day. Well that day of reckoning has arrived, and the time to take charge of our future is here.

Now is the time to act boldly and wisely—to not only revive this economy, but to build a new foundation for lasting prosperity. Now is the time to jumpstart job creation, re-start lending, and invest in areas like energy, health care, and education that will grow our economy, even as we make hard choices to bring our deficit down. That is what my economic agenda is designed to do, and that's what I'd like to talk to you about tonight . . .

My budget does not attempt to solve every problem or address every issue. It reflects the stark reality of what we've inherited—a trillion dollar deficit, a financial crisis, and a costly recession. Given these realities, everyone in this chamber—Democrats and Republicans—will have to sacrifice some worthy priorities for which there are no dollars. And that includes me.

But that does not mean we can afford to ignore our long-term challenges. I reject the view that says our problems will simply take care of themselves; that says government has no role in laying the foundation for our common prosperity.

496. President Obama gave this address most directly to respond to what event?

(A) a government shutdown

(B) an economic recession

(C) the deficit caused by the wars in Iraq and Afghanistan

(D) the attempt to pass healthcare reform

497. In relation to the statement "A surplus became an excuse to transfer wealth to the wealthy," Obama is most likely crediting which administration with the creation of a surplus?

(A) the Reagan administration

(B) the administration of George H. W. Bush

(C) the Clinton administration

(D) the administration of George W. Bush

498. In stating the "surplus became an excuse to transfer wealth to the wealthy," Obama is criticizing which action?

(A) the tax cuts during the George W. Bush administration

(B) the budget compromise during the Clinton administration

(C) the passage of T.A.R.P.

(D) the implementation of the Affordable Care Act

Use the passage and your knowledge of the time period to answer questions 499 and 500.

Foreign Policy Speech
Barack Obama (July 16, 2008)

The challenge facing the greatest generation of Americans—the generation that had vanquished fascism on the battlefield—was how to contain this threat while extending freedom's frontiers. Leaders like Truman and Acheson, Kennan and Marshall, knew that there was no single decisive blow that could be struck for freedom. We needed a new overarching strategy to meet the challenges of a new and dangerous world . . .

Today's dangers are different, though no less grave. The power to destroy life on a catastrophic scale now risks falling into the hands of terrorists. The future of our security—and our planet—is held hostage to our dependence on foreign oil and gas. From the cave-spotted mountains of northwest Pakistan, to the centrifuges spinning beneath Iranian soil, we know that the American people cannot be protected by oceans or the sheer might of our military alone . . .

Imagine, for a moment, what we could have done in those days, and months, and years after 9/11. We could have deployed the full force of American power to hunt down and destroy Osama bin Laden, al-Qaida, the Taliban, and all of the terrorists responsible for 9/11, while supporting real security in Afghanistan . . .

We could have invested hundreds of billions of dollars in alternative sources of energy to grow our economy, save our planet, and end the tyranny of oil. We could have strengthened old alliances, formed new partnerships, and renewed international institutions to advance peace and prosperity . . . We could have rebuilt our roads and bridges, laid down new rail and broadband and electricity systems, and made college affordable for every American to strengthen our ability to compete. We could have done that.

Instead, we have lost thousands of American lives, spent nearly a trillion dollars, alienated allies and neglected emerging threats—all in the cause of fighting a war for well over five years in a country that had absolutely nothing to do with the 9/11 attacks.

---

499. In stating "all in the cause of fighting a war for well over five years in a country that had absolutely nothing to do with the 9/11 attacks," President Obama was most likely criticizing which action?

   (A) the War in Afghanistan
   (B) the War in Iraq
   (C) the Arab Spring
   (D) the Civil War in Syria

500. With regard to the passage, which of the following was a successful accomplishment of the Obama administration?

(A) capturing and killing Saddam Hussein

(B) closing the prisoner camps at Guantanamo Bay

(C) capturing and killing Osama bin Laden

(D) ending U.S. involvement in Iraq and Afghanistan

ANSWERS

Chapter 1

1. (A) The most commonly accepted theory about the populating of the Americas by humans is that a migration took place roughly 35,000 years ago when a land bridge was exposed. The bridge lasted for roughly 25,000 years, allowing people to pass from Siberia to the Americas.

2. (C) Throughout the last Ice Age, over the period of roughly 22,000 to 7,000 years ago, the climactic shift caused increased glaciations in both the Arctic and Antarctic, causing a global lowering of ocean levels. During this same period, other land bridges such as those connecting Australia to surrounding lands also appeared. Interestingly, D is incorrect because climatologists theorize that during this time period, there was a lack of precipitation caused by ocean currents and the location of regional mountain ranges.

3. (B) Maize first appeared circa 5000 BCE in the highland regions of Mexico. It reached North America in about 1200 BCE, though the spread of its cultivation in North America is believed to have been slower than in other parts of the Americas.

4. (A) The technique of growing beans, squash, and maize first appeared around CE 1000. The maize provided a structure for the beans, and the squash aided in maintaining moisture in the soil. This allowed populations' densities to increase within the Eastern Seaboard region of North America.

5. (B) Maize, commonly referred to as corn, is a New World crop originating from the area that is now modern-day Mexico. Wheat, cattle, horses, and coffee are Old World crops. The introduction of American agricultural products to Europe, and vice versa is part of what is called the Columbian Exchange.

6. (D) The Native American Mississippian Valley culture is often associated with vast complexes of mound structures constructed around CE 1200. Archaeological evidence shows that this group illustrated a much higher level of political organization than was common among most indigenous populations in North America, though the civilization began to decline and vanish nearly a century prior to European arrival in North America.

7. (C) Though the Native Americans had developed high-yielding agriculture illustrated by the Three Sisters (maize, beans, and squash) cultivated by groups such as the Creek and Cherokee, they did not develop the intensive farming techniques commonplace in Europe. This could be partly due to the commonly held reverence for the natural world. However, many groups did use slash-and-burn clearing techniques to open forest and clear areas for agriculture on a limited basis.

8. (D) The Iroquois League founded around the fifteenth century initially consisted of the Mohawk, Oneida, Onondaga, Cayuga, and Seneca and spanned what is now southeastern Canada into New York. While initially consisting of five nations, the league expanded to six when the Tuscarora joined in the 1700s. The league began to decline after its allies, the British, were defeated in the American Revolution. The Powhatan were a tribe from eastern Virginia that controlled a confederacy of roughly thirty tributary tribes. They are associated with the early history of the Jamestown settlement. Pocahontas, the daughter of a Powhatan chief, is stated to have rescued John Smith. The confederation declined after the two Powhatan Wars in the 1700s.

9. (B) While the males of the Iroquois League held the actual lordship or chief title, unlike most European nations, the lineage was passed through the female or maternal lineage, rather than the paternal or male lineage. While the time period did mark a period often referred to as the Age of Absolutism in Europe, codified laws were being established placing certain limitations and checking certain powers of European monarchs as illustrated by the Magna Carta, English Bill of Rights, and French Estates General.

10. (B) With the exception of groups such as the Cahokia settlement in the present-day Mississippi Basin and the Ancestral Puebloan (Anasazi) culture in the Four Corners region of the Southwest, most Native American groups in North America lived in small, impermanent, matrilineal groups right up to the arrival of European explorers. However, as evidenced by the passage, the Iroquois did establish codified laws in terms of lineage and intertribal relations.

11. (A) Native American groups across the North American continent shared the trait of using kinship networks to define their clans. They consisted of a group of related families (aunts, uncles, cousins, etc.) connected through common ancestry.

12. (D) While initially believed to be legend, archaeological evidence has confirmed Norse sagas that describe contact between Europeans and North American Native Americans. Most evidence illustrates that this contact may date back to CE 1000, predating Columbus's voyage by over four centuries. While settlements such as L'Anse aux Meadows were temporary, they do illustrate the earliest documented contact and trade between Europe and the indigenous populations of North America.

13. (A) L'Anse aux Meadows, located in present-day Newfoundland, marks the location where Norse seafarers arrived around CE 1000. The settlement was short-lived and soon forgotten except in Norse legend. Later archaeological finds rediscovered the settlement in the 1960s.

Chapter 2

14. (C) Pope Alexander VI established the Treaty of Tordesillas after Columbus returned from his expedition. Because of a 1481 papal declaration, Portugal declared all discovered lands its rightful property. Pope Alexander established the treaty, which was signed by Ferdinand II, Isabella I, and John II, to settle the dispute and allow both Spain and Portugal to continuing colonizing efforts. However, the king of Portugal was disappointed with the treaty because he felt it gave Portugal too little land and interfered with his attempts to establish a route to India. Later the treaty was renegotiated with Spain, moving the line farther west and allowing Portugal to claim newly discovered lands east of the line.

15. (D) The 1494 agreement created a line that would divide the unclaimed land left in the Americas between the Spanish and the Portuguese. The line of demarcation established in the treaty was roughly halfway between the Portuguese-held Cape Verde Islands and Spanish-held Hispaniola. Spain gained lands west of the line, while Portugal gained lands to the east.

16. (A) Because of the Treaty of Tordesillas and its establishment of the Line of Demarcation, the land that is now Brazil was controlled by Portugal. To this day, Portuguese remains the predominant language within that country, while Spanish is the primary language of the remainder of Latin America with the exception of small regions that were later dominated by other European nations such as Britain. Because both Portugal and Spain were Catholic powers, high levels of Catholicism can be seen in most South American nations into contemporary times.

17. (B) Starting with Christopher Columbus's first expedition to the Americas through the acts of conquistadors such as Cortés, the spread of Christianity served as a major function of exploration. While the papacy did play a role within the New World, such as the establishment of the line of demarcation under the Treaty of Tordesillas, the Spanish monarchy retained sovereignty over its possessions in the Americas.

18. (D) While the Spanish and French made religious conversion a major goal of New World settlement, the Spanish were able to export vast amounts of wealth from the Americas in the form of precious metals. The early French explorers in North America pursued an intensive fur trade.

19. (B) Even though the Dutch Reformed Church was maintained as the official church of Dutch settlements in North America, such as that of New Amsterdam (present-day New York), the Dutch attempted to attract many of the populations displaced by conflicts following the Reformation. By the 1700s, nearly half of the population in Dutch possessions was not Dutch and did not follow the Dutch Reformed Church. Furthermore, religious conversion do not hold the same level of priority as it did for the either the Spanish or the French, though it did occur.

20. (C) Under the encomienda system, Spanish colonists were granted not only land but also the labor of the indigenous people to guarantee a profit. This was initially offered with the understanding that the Spanish would ensure protection and fair treatment, but most indigenous workers were exploited under this arrangement. This system would become a foundation of the economy for Spanish colonies in the Americas and was also used later in the Philippines.

21. (D) The Reconquista was a roughly 781-year period when the Christian powers of the Iberian Peninsula removed Islamic forces from the region. Within the Reconquista the encomienda was created to exact tribute from Muslims and Jews who remained on the peninsula. The practice was formalized in 1503, and later abolished in 1720. The Hundred Years' War (1337–1453) was a conflict between France and England rooted in conflicts over succession of the French monarchy. The Anglo-Spanish War (1585–1604) was part of the broader Eighty Years' War (1568–1648), which saw the destruction of the Spanish Armada. The War of the Spanish Succession (1701–1713) was fought between European powers over the succession of the Spanish monarchy after the death of Charles II. This led to the colonial conflict known as Queen Anne's War in North America, part of the series of conflicts known as the French and Indian War.

22. (B) While the early English colonies such as that of the Virginia Bay Colony, including the area around Jamestown, attempted subjugation of the nearby Native American people, the low population density, which was further decimated by disease, made these attempts nearly futile. Instead the British were forced to find labor internally using systems such as indentured servitude, and then later African slave labor.

23. (A) In 1608, Quebec, France's first permanent settlement was established by Samuel de Champlain. Sieur Robert Cavelier de La Salle explored the lower Mississippi River in 1682 and claimed the surrounding territory for France, naming it Louisiana in honor of his sovereign, Louis XIV. In 1535, Cartier explored the Saint Lawrence River. Louis Joliet, a priest, explored the Great Lakes and upper Mississippi River with Jacques Marquette, a French trader, setting up missions and trading posts in 1637.

24. (A) Similar to the English experience in North America, the French colony of New France (Canada) would not yield the wealth of precious metals found by the Spanish in Mesoamerica. The French, however, will find value in the land for raw resources, especially through the fur trade. As the colony progressed, agriculture and lumber will take root; however, the population density will remain sparse in comparison to the English colonies established in North America.

Chapter 3

25. (B) Hakluyt argues that proprietary colonies would be more loyal to the government and be less likely to fall victim to corruption and mismanagement. This is illustrated in his statement where he notes privately funded joint stock company colonies would be "subject to rivalry, fraud, and envy."

26. (C) In a proprietary colony, the individuals who receive the charter to found the colony retain the rights to create laws for the colony and appoint the governor. Many colonies were founded in this manner, but the practice began to decline in the 1700s as the monarchy began to concentrate its control. By the outbreak of the American Revolution, only Delaware, Maryland, and Pennsylvania still held proprietary charters.

27. (C) The Puritans of the Arabella who left England in 1630, was one of eleven ships, making it one of the largest single venture to the New World by England. The Puritans were part of the Great Migration of Puritans where nearly 14,000 left England for New England. John Winthrop envisioned the development of an ideal Christian state that was based on the Puritan values rooted in Calvinism.

28. (D) In 1634, Lord Baltimore, who was a member of a prominent Catholic family in England, received a charter to establish Maryland. While profit was a main goal, the charter also was intended to provide a safe haven for his fellow Catholics who faced persecution in England under the Church of England—for example, not being allowed to marry in the Catholic Church.

29. (C) Roger Williams, though having separatist ideals, alienated himself from and was eventually exiled because of his rejection of Puritan practices in Boston. His belief in liberty of conscience called for individual freedom of religion and a separation of church and state. In 1636, he founded Providence, which stood apart from other North American colonies in that it practiced religious tolerance.

30. (C) Like, Massachusetts, an initial reason Maryland was established was to provide refuge for religious dissenters, but this time it was for Catholics who were persecuted in England. Lord Baltimore allowed freedom of worship from its founding, however, and many Protestants began to migrate into the region, threatening Catholic domination in the colony. The Toleration Act, while extending toleration to all Christians, was mainly to protect the rights of the Catholics settled there. It protected Christians, but non-Christians such as Jewish colonists did not receive any protections.

31. (C) As noted in the passage, the North American colonies provided the mother country, England, with large quantities of raw materials that aided in British manufacturing. As noted, this was important because it lessened dependency on trade with other nations and provided markets for British manufacturing and created other jobs in shipping.

32. (B) Mercantilism was a dominant economic philosophy during the sixteenth to eighteenth centuries. Under this system, international commerce existed to increase a country's wealth, especially in acquiring gold and foreign currency. Under mercantilism, exports were viewed as desirable, and imports as undesirable unless they led to even greater exports. Colonies were useful in this system because countries could use them to acquire raw materials and had access to markets without having to trade with foreign nations.

33. (C) The southern colonies' economy was dominated by the export of staple crops such as tobacco, rice, and indigo. Upland cotton initially was not a major cash crop but later dominated the Southern economy after the cotton gin was invented by Eli Whitney in 1793, making the removal of seeds and processing of the fiber economically viable. Slaves and indentured servants initially worked side by side. This illustrated a potential danger, however, after Bacon's Rebellion, in which they banded together against the plantation owners in 1676.

34. (D) The Navigation Acts were a series of English laws that restricted colonial trade to England. The first of the acts was enacted in 1651 and were revised through 1663. Ultimately they were repealed in 1849. The acts enforced mercantilist trade between England and its colonies, keeping trade within the Empire. The Act of Supremacy of 1534 English recognized Henry VIII as leader of the Church of England. The Dominion of New England was created in 1686 and lasted to 1689, when William of Orange took the throne following the Glorious Revolution. Under this action New England and the Mid-Atlantic Colonies were combined under a single colonial administration, with the exception of Pennsylvania. The dominion angered many colonists because the colonists lost many of their previously held rights along with their colonial charters. The Declaratory Act of 1766 stated that the British Parliament had the right to tax the colonies of North America.

35. (A) The Middle Passage was part of the triangle of trade routes that defined Atlantic colonial trade and brought Africans to the Americas, where they were sold into slavery. The first African slaves arrived in the English North American colonies in 1619, brought by Dutch traders. The movement of African Americans out of the southern United States during the early twentieth century is referred to as the Great Migration. The removal of Cherokee Indians to Oklahoma in 1838, often referred to as the Trail of Tears, resulted from President Andrew Jackson's Indian Removal Act of 1830.

36. (D) The scattering of African people and their culture during the three centuries that followed Columbus's arrival in the Western Hemisphere has been referred to as the African Diaspora. During this period, millions of Africans were forcibly relocated to the Americas. In some areas, such as the British West Indies and Haiti, they outnumbered European colonists. Slave codes were harsh laws put in place to maintain order within areas with slave populations. The African slaves were, however, able to hold onto many of their traditions and their culture through creolized language and religious practice.

37. (D) Even though laws concerning African slaves made it difficult for them to travel or communicate freely, several slave uprisings occurred, including the Stono Rebellion in 1739. New York City had slave uprisings as early as 1712.

38. (C) While the Spanish initially used the indigenous population as forced labor through policies such as the encomienda system, as did the Portuguese, these populations began to dwindle as a result of European disease and harsh labor conditions. In 1502, the Portuguese began trading slaves from West Africa to New World colonies. Nearly 11 million Africans became victims of this system of forced labor.

39. (A) The Piedmont is a plateau of forests and hills in the western part of Virginia leading to the Appalachian Mountains. When the fertile land of the Tidewater was taken, many poorer farmers and former indentured servants moved into this region. The farms in the Piedmont tended to be smaller, and many farmers in this region faced economic hardships. The disparity between the Piedmont and Tidewater eventually led to uprisings such as Bacon's Rebellion.

40. (A) In 1676, Nathaniel Bacon led an uprising in Virginia, marking the first rebellion in the colonies. The event became known as Bacon's Rebellion. It was sparked by Native American raids on the outskirts of the colony but illustrated a rejection of Governor William Berkley's policies, which favored the wealthy planters over the poor. The uprising inspired a similar revolt in Maryland later that year.

41. (D) During Bacon's Rebellion, poor whites (many former indentured servants) and blacks banded together against what was viewed as a ruling class. In response, the Virginia government moved to further institutionalize African slavery as a way to control one segment of the poor population.

42. (D) The headright system established in 1619 was introduced by the Virginia Company and offered 50 acres of land to any man who paid his own way to the Virginia Colony. It furthermore offered an additional 50 acres for each additional person he brought with him.

43. (D) The Massachusetts Bay Company established Massachusetts as a chartered corporate colony in 1630. It became a royal colony in 1691, but its citizens retained the ability to elect representation in the colonial government. Learning from earlier attempts to establish colonies such as Jamestown, which suffered from a period of starvation that nearly destroyed the colony over the winter of 1609–1610, Massachusetts was well provisioned. While slavery was legal in the Massachusetts Bay Colony, there were fewer slaves than in the southern colonies, and the practice was ended in the 1780s.

44. (C) The House of Burgesses was created in 1619 and was the first representative body of its kind in the Americas. While it did have the power to make laws concerning the colony, those laws could be vetoed by the governor, who was initially selected by the officials within the joint stock company and by the king after 1624, when Virginia became a royal colony. The House of Burgesses was allowed to remain even after Virginia became a royal colony.

45. (B) During the seventeenth century, roughly half of the European settlers who arrived in North America were indentured servants. Indentured servants were laborers who contracted to work for a set period of time in exchange for passage to the Americas. Unlike a slave, an indentured servant was required to work only for a limited term specified in a signed contract. This practice slowed, however, after Bacon's Rebellion, when poor farmers, including many former indentured servants, rose up against the wealthy landed planters. Afterward, the use of African slaves became more common.

46. (B) At the time William Penn received his charter from the Charles II on February 28th, 1681, he began advertising what he saw as the advantages of moving to Pennsylvania. Charles gave Penn the charter to Pennsylvania to repay a debt the king owed to Penn's father, making it one of the largest land grants given in history. Though he was a Quaker, he tried to attract both Quakers and non-Quakers. At the time of this document's publication, Penn had himself never been to the colony, though he strongly pronounced the advantages of moving there.

47. (A) During much of English history, the eldest male child inherited a majority of the land from the father, leaving the younger with little to no land. Furthermore, often their wealth was based on sums given to them by the elder son. Penn notes that these younger siblings would be able to buy their own land in Pennsylvania.

48. (D) Pennsylvania, which was established in 1681 by the Quaker William Penn and has been called one of the better-advertised colonies, as noted in the passage, attracted a diverse mix of artisans and craftsmen. Because of the Quaker faith, the Pennsylvania colony stressed fairer treatment of the Native Americans, though this effort was often undermined by others who joined the colony. While Pennsylvania did allow religious freedom and did not have a state-tax-sponsored church, because of pressures from England the colony did deny political rights to certain groups such as Catholics and Jews. Also, while the Pennsylvania colony did practice capital punishment, it was at a much lower rate than practiced in England.

49. (B) Both the proposed Albany Congress and the House of Representatives, established under the 1787 Constitution, were based on proportional representation. The Senate established under the 1787 Constitution was based off of equal representatives (two from each state). Similarly, under the Articles of Confederation, while each state could choose the number of representatives to attend, each state only had one vote, ensuring equal representation. The House of Burgesses, established in 1619, Virginia also had a set number of representatives, 2 representatives from each of the 11 plantations or settlements.

50. (C) Virginia, established in 1607, and Massachusetts, established in 1620, both had the largest number of apportioned seats. However, the newest colony of the ones noted, Pennsylvania, which was established in 1682, had the third-largest population.

51. (A) New England and other northern colonies such as New York often found themselves victims of raids from French-held Canada during times of conflict, such as King George's War (or the War of Austrian Succession), which ended in 1748. During this conflict, much of the fighting took place in the British colonies of New York, Massachusetts Bay, and New Hampshire. While indigenous tribes did present concerns and lead to conflicts along the western frontier of the colony, the main purpose of the Albany Plan was to formalize a treaty with the Iroquois Confederacy. The Spanish did also represent a threat in the South, but Georgia served as a buffer zone, though during the War of Jenkins' Ear, fighting did erupt briefly on the border. The Albany Plan, as noted in the first clause, was to serve under the crown, and its President-General was to be appointed by the crown. However, the Albany Plan would serve as a blueprint for the Second Continental Congress, which would raise an army against the crown on June 14th, 1775.

52. (D) The French and Indian War began in 1754 with George Washington's failed venture, under the orders of Governor Robert Dinwiddie, into the Ohio River Valley where he unsuccessfully faced French forces. King William's War, also referred to the War of the League of Augsburg (1689–1697), Queen Anne's War (1702–1713), also referred to as the War of Spanish Succession, and King George's War, also known as the War of Austrian Succession, were earlier conflicts between the French and English colonies of North America that laid the foundation for the French and Indian War. However, the French and Indian War, or Seven Years' War, was unique, as the fighting began in North America, spread back to Europe, then spread over the entire globe, making it, as Winston Churchill later noted, the first true world war.

53. (B) As noted in the passage, initially the major focus of Great Britain was to protect its holding in the western frontier of its North American colonies. However as time progressed, Great Britain established that its colonies would only be secure if France was removed entirely from North America. This would become a major focus of British foreign policy, later influencing Minister George Canning in a joint proposal following the Congress of Vienna, which would ultimately result in the creation of the U.S. Monroe Doctrine.

54. (B) When William Pitt took charge of the war effort in 1758, he changed the British strategy to focus on defeating the French in North America. In the process, Britain adopted the policy of the removal of the French from North America to protect their colonial interests.

Chapter 4

55. (C) After the conclusion of the French and Indian War with the Treaty of Paris in 1763, the British government sought out ways to efficiently manage the newly acquired lands that it received from France. Furthermore, it hoped to limit further military costs stirred by conflicts between the colonists and the indigenous Native Americans, such as that of Pontiac's Rebellion.

56. (B) In 1774, Britain issued the Quebec Act, also known as the Land Act, which like the Proclamation of 1763, limited the British colonies' ability to expand into the highly prized lands of the Ohio River Valley, leading to increased tensions amongst the colonists because their westward expansion was greatly hindered. However, unlike the Proclamation of 1763, which reserved the lands as tribal hunting grounds, the Quebec Act gave the lands of the region to the colony of Quebec.

57. (B) Both the Proclamation of 1763 and the Northwest Ordinance contained provisions designed to protect indigenous Native American land claims within the Ohio River Valley. The Ordinance notes in Article 3 that "lands and property shall never be taken from them without their consent." While the Northwest Ordinance does outlaw the expansion of slavery into the region as noted in Article 6, the Proclamation of 1763 does not reference this practice. Also, the Ordinance was designed to promote expansion of both settlement and industry into the region, while the Proclamation was specifically written to limit these practices.

58. (A) As early as the 1750s, colonists began to reject British taxes based on the notion "No taxation without representation." Boston lawyer James Otis argued that this taxation was "tyranny." Prime Minister George Grenville's rebuttal argument was that colonists were represented through virtual representation, meaning the government looked out for interests of all English subjects. This notion was further enforced with the 1766 Declaratory Act.

59. (C) Based on the fact that the document's origin is from 1765, the Stamp Act would be the most logical answer. Further, the Stamp Act was issued in part to pay off the debts raised by providing protection for the colonies during the French and Indian War. While the Townshend Acts were also issued to raise revenues, they were not instituted until 1767. The Declaratory Act dealt with the notion that the British Government could pass laws and taxes without the consent of the colonists, which is reflected in the passage, but it was issued with the repeal of the Stamp Act in 1766, after this document was created. The Coercive Acts passed in 1774 also were predated by this work, as was the Olive Branch Petition.

60. (B) While the Sugar Act, the Stamp Act, and the Townshend Acts were attempts to raise revenues from the colonies, it was the Declaratory Act that clearly made the argument that the British government had the right to levy taxes upon the colonists.

61. (C) In protest of such acts as the 1765 Stamp Act and the 1767 Townshend Acts, groups such as the Sons of Liberty organized colonial boycotts of British goods. These nonimportation societies attempted to use economic pressure to force Britain to acknowledge what colonists saw as their political rights. Before the French and Indian War (ending in 1763), the English government had limited direct interference with the American colonists, treating them with a policy referred to as salutary neglect. As long as the colonies exported raw materials to Britain and imported finished goods from Britain, Britain left them alone. This policy came to an end after 1763 as Prime Minister George Greenville ordered the British Navy to begin enforcing the Navigation Acts initially passed in 1651 to recoup funds and pay off debts accumulated during the French and Indian War. *Impressment* referred to the practice of capturing sailors and forcing them to serve on naval vessels, the action by the British would be a factor leading to the War of 1812.

62. (C) In the passage, Franklin states, "I never heard any objection to the right of laying duties to regulate commerce; but a right to lay internal taxes was never supposed to be in parliament, as we are not represented there." By saying this, he expressed that external taxes were acceptable because it was a tax on products produced outside of the colonies and later shipped in, such as the Sugar Act of 1764. The Stamp Act, however, placed a tax on goods within the colonies themselves. This type of taxation was traditionally performed by colonial assemblies and violated the notion of self-rule that had become a tradition in the colonies.

63. (C) Believing in all citizens' right to trial and the necessity of the rule of law, John Adams defended Captain Preston and other soldiers involved in the incident known as the Boston Massacre. During the event, five colonists were killed after an angry mob attacked the soldiers. It took place on March 5, 1770. In the end, Captain Preston and six other soldiers were acquitted. Two other soldiers were found guilty after evidence showed they had fired directly into the crowd.

64. (B) In the trial, Adams stated, "he saw a man come up to Montgomery with a club, and knock him down before he fired, and that he not only fell himself, but his gun flew out of his hand" and "had he not reason to think his life in danger, or did it not raise his passions and put him off his guard; so that it cannot be more than manslaughter." In other words, Adams argues that the man was being physically beaten to the point that it should be concluded that his life was being directly threatened.

65. (B) While the Declaration of Independence states, "All men are created equal," Jefferson implied that all free citizens are politically equal. Most scholars feel that this notion of equality did not apply to wealth. Furthermore, the statement did not apply to those not considered to be full citizens, such as women and slaves. The notion of equality has evolved over time, however, and it inspired abolitionists, suffragists, and other civil rights groups in later generations.

66. (D) The Enlightenment was an eighteenth-century intellectual movement with a strong focus on the individual, rationalism, and natural rights. Philosophers of this movement, such as John Locke and Jean-Jacques Rousseau, inspired Thomas Jefferson in his writing of the Declaration of Independence. The declaration's reference to "Life, Liberty, and the pursuit of Happiness" echoes the ideas from Locke's "Two Treatises of Government," though Locke originally referred to life, liberty, and property.

67. (D) Both *Common Sense* by Thomas Paine and the Declaration of Independence, whose preamble was written notably by Thomas Jefferson, show a marked contrast with earlier documents such as the Olive Branch Petition by specifically blaming colonial grievances directly on the actions taken by the king instead of just parliament. Paine's *Common Sense* was a notable "bestseller" in the colonies in part because it was written in common terms that the average citizen could understand. Furthermore, while Jefferson noted slavery in earlier drafts, they were removed to better ensure passage by the Second Continental Congress.

68. (D) By 1778, the patriots gained control of the Ohio River Valley and halted the British attempt to isolate New England from the rest of the colonies. Starting in 1778, the British began to focus their strategy in the South, hoping to incite Southern loyalist sympathizers and capture key ports such as Savannah and Charleston. General Cornwallis established a camp at Yorktown in Virginia. He found himself surrounded, however, and was forced to surrender after the patriots held siege on his position with the assistance of the French. The British government and Benedict Arnold did devise a plan to turn over West Point to the British in 1780, but the plan was foiled.

69. (C) After 1778, the British Army began to focus on the South, successfully capturing key Southern ports. General Cornwallis attempted to secure Yorktown, but the French Navy took control of the Chesapeake Bay at the Battle of Hampton Roads, cutting off British supply lines and allowing American and French forces to besiege the British position. Cornwallis surrendered on October 19, 1781, marking the last major battle of the American Revolution.

70. (B) The Battle of Saratoga has been considered by many historians to be the turning point of the war for the colonists. This battle ended the British plan to sever New England from the rest of the American colonies. It also convinced the French to extend their support to the patriots more openly, and it convinced the Spanish to enter the conflict as an ally of the French.

71. (A) The Battle of Saratoga, often considered the turning point of the American Revolution for the colonists, was led by Horatio Gates. At that time, General Washington was leading his troops at Brandywine. Here Washington was defeated, and Philadelphia fell to the British, forcing the Continental Congress to abandon the city.

72. (C) Going into the war, the British possessed many advantages. They held the greatest navy in the world, as well as the strongest army. The colonists had only a small, untrained group of volunteers, and their navy consisted of a few vessels. The British also had the manufacturing capability to make arms, as well as a treasury that could support the war effort. They were unable, however, to fully use their loyalist support.

73. (B) During the war, the British actively recruited slaves, especially those whose owners were patriots. During the war, a majority of African Americans fought for Britain under the promise that they would gain freedom. Though some African Americans fought for the patriot cause, the colonists were reluctant to enlist black soldiers. At the end of the war, the British took thousands of slaves with them as they withdrew from the South. Some were given freedom in Canada, while others remained enslaved and were forced into labor in the West Indies.

74. (B) Though certain slaves gained their freedom during the American Revolution, at the war's conclusion, the institution remained unchanged, and the freedoms granted by the revolution did not extend to most Africans living in the country. The Treaty of Paris indirectly referenced slavery in Article 7, stating that the British should leave American property, including slaves, unmolested as they withdrew.

75. (C) Overall, the conflict had a negative impact on the Native Americans. The Iroquois initially attempted to stay out of the conflict. However, the war served as a justification for many settlers to attempt to capture traditional lands, causing the Iroquois to side with the British government. This led to harsh treatment by the United States following the Treaty of Paris and a further loss of land within their region. The Cherokee suffered a similar fate for siding with the British. Furthermore, the Native Americans were not permitted to take part in the Paris peace talks, so their concerns were mostly ignored. In addition, certain British protections of indigenous lands, such as those set by the Proclamation of 1763 were disassembled following the Treaty of Paris, further causing the loss of land and influence.

Chapter 5

76. (C) In 1786, Daniel Shays led an uprising of New England farmers and merchants against the government. It helped inspire the Philadelphia convention along with the creation of the U.S. Constitution. The Whiskey Rebellion took place in western Pennsylvania during President Washington's administration. It was a response to Alexander Hamilton's creation of an excise tax on spirits. Gabriel Prosser's Rebellion was an attempted slave uprising in Virginia in 1800.

77. (A) George Washington supported a stronger central government, noting that the current government under the Articles of Confederation was too slow and weak. He states the Articles of Confederation are "not only slow, debilitated, and liable to be thwarted by every breath," but are "defective in that secrecy, which for the accomplishment of many of the most important national purposes." His views on this aligned him with the Federalists, though he avoided political party alignment formally. As noted in the passage, he was unsure what the convention could ultimately accomplish because of strong opposition from groups that supported a weak government and states' rights. He also raises concerns whether such a convention is even legal and therefore stated that "it is not, at this time, my purpose to attend it."

78. (D) George Mason was a strong supporter of state's rights and was deeply suspicious of the 1787 Constitution. He once stated that he would "rather chop off my right hand than put it to the Constitution as it now stands." However, Hamilton, Jay, and Madison supported the 1787 Constitutional Convention, feeling that the current Article of Confederation could not properly meet the challenges that faced the young United States. The three would later publish the Federalist Papers, arguing the need to reform the government.

79. (C) The Articles of Confederation were drafted in 1777 and went into effect at the conclusion of the American Revolution. This document created a loose confederation of the thirteen states under a unicameral legislative body with representatives from each state. It illustrated the antimonarchical sentiment within the colonies. The articles did not give the national government the ability to tax (it had to solicit funds from the states), raise an army (it had to ask the states to draw upon their militias), or regulate trade. The national government under the Articles of Confederation, however, was the only body that could declare war on a foreign power. The articles were replaced with the ratification of the U.S. Constitution.

80. (C) Though the Southern Confederacy, the government of the South during the Civil War, modeled its constitution after the U.S. Constitution, it in actuality more closely resembled the Articles of Confederation, the first government of the United States following the American Revolution. In both the Articles of Confederation and the Confederacy, the states retained most of the political power, leaving a weak central government. Both governments had limited power to raise an army, relying on the states to send troops. Also, both governments had limited abilities to raise revenues or taxes, again relying on the individual states. Furthermore, lawmaking in both governments was extremely slow and cumbersome.

81. (B) The passage is from a series of works known as the Anti-Federalist Papers, which were written in response to the Federalist Papers, which in turn were produced by people such as Alexander Hamilton and John Jay. The author, who used the penname Brutus, remains unknown, but some historians accredit the work to either Melancton Smith of New York or John Williams of Massachusetts.

82. (B) The author was an Anti-Federalist, and the views illustrated the antimonarchial sentiments held by many following the American Revolution. The author feared the Constitution created in 1787 would give too much power to the federal government at the expense of the state governments and the individual. The author was specifically concerned about the possibility of the central government growing too strong with provisions for a strong executive branch, the elastic (or "necessary and proper") clause in the legislative branch, and the idea of the government keeping a standing army in times of peace. Most Anti-Federalists would agree to the Constitution only if provisions were made for the inclusion of a Bill of Rights.

83. (D) Alexander Hamilton was an ardent Federalist and strongly supported a strong national government over states' rights. Hamilton became a leading author of the Federalist Papers, arguing for the ratification of the 1787 Constitution. Patrick Henry, Samuel Adams, and George Mason were well known Anti-Federalists who were greatly concerned about the powers invested in the 1787 Constitution. Mason would ultimately refuse to sign the document and insisted on the inclusion of a Bill of Rights.

84. (A) The Anti-Federalists illustrated the antimonarchical sentiments held by many after the American Revolution. They feared the Constitution created in 1787 would give too much power to the federal government at the expense of the state governments and the individual. They were concerned about the possibility of the central government growing too strong with provisions for a strong executive branch, the elastic (or "necessary and proper") clause in the legislative branch, and the idea of the government keeping a standing army in times of peace. Most Anti-Federalists would agree to the Constitution only if provisions were made for the inclusion of a Bill of Rights.

85. (A) While the Anti-Federalists, including Mason, were advocates for protecting the power of the states because they feared a powerful central government and felt a Bill of Rights was necessary, Mason's statement most closely reflects the notion that the common person should be able to directly participate in the government through the direct election of representatives. Mason would later advocate for the Bill of Rights, which was created on September 25, 1789, and later ratified on December 15, 1791.

86. (D) Many Federalists such as Alexander Hamilton disagreed with the inclusion of a Bill of Rights. They were concerned that a listing of rights could be dangerous: if the government were to protect specific rights, what would become of rights not listed? To persuade nine states to ratify the Constitution, the Federalists conceded to the Anti-Federalists, and a Bill of Rights was added to the document. The Ninth and Tenth Amendments addressed Hamilton's and the Federalists' concerns by giving all rights not noted in the Constitution to the states or to the individual.

87. (A) Both the New Jersey Plan and the Virginia Plan sought to greatly improve upon the overall weaknesses of the Articles of Confederation by creating a stronger central government with three branches including an executive, legislative, and judicial branch. The Virginia Plan, however, called for a bicameral legislative branch, while the New Jersey Plan called for a unicameral legislative branch.

88. (B) The New Jersey Plan was created by William Patterson. Patterson's plan had one legislative house maintained the notion that each state had one vote that was present in the earlier Articles of Confederation. It was created as a response to the Virginia Plan, in which representation was based on population.

89. (A) The Three-Fifths Compromise was an agreement made between the Northern and Southern states at the 1787 Constitutional Convention to deal with the apportionment of seats in the House of Representatives and the distribution of taxes. While delegates who opposed slavery felt that only free citizens should be counted, pro-slavery delegates objected. Roger Sherman and James Wilson introduced the Three-Fifths Compromise to broaden support for the Constitution. Under the proposal, slave populations in each state would be based on three-fifths of the total slave population. The compromise was put in Article I, Section 2, of the Constitution. This was significant because later, in the events leading to the Civil War, it was used to illustrate the constitutionality of slavery as protected by the Constitution. Though the compromise did increase the amount of representation Southern states had in Congress, they still were in the minority with only 47 percent of the seats, and this number declined as the Northern population rapidly expanded over the next 60 years.

90. (A) Judicial review is the power of the courts to strike down laws or actions that violate the Constitution. The only way to overrule judicial review by the legislative body is to amend the Constitution itself. The first use of judicial review was under the *Marbury v. Madison* ruling decided by Chief Justice John Marshall in 1803.

91. (D) While the Democratic-Republicans initially rejected Alexander Hamilton's proposal, following the War of 1812, many of his ideas were implemented in the American System. In both Hamilton's plan and the American System, there were tariffs to further American industry as well as a national bank to help commerce and provide financial stability. Furthermore, both plans called for federal funds to be used to establish infrastructure projects such as roads and canals. Both plans saw the importance of developing an internal economy that would allow profitable markets for agriculture and manufacturing.

92. (C) Alexander Hamilton favored a loose interpretation of the Constitution and a strong central government, mistrusting the common masses. His economic plan often benefited Northern investors and favored manufacturing over agriculture. He also called for the national government to assume the war debts of the states, angering many of the Southern states, which had already paid off their debts.

93. (B) While Hamilton ultimately did support certain notions that could be viewed as mercantilist, including protective tariffs and government support of industry, the quote highlights more free market ideals which serve as a basis for capitalism. Malthusian economics focuses on the scarcity of resources, which Hamilton did not consider; being that he saw the United States having vast untapped resources and land. Physiocracy was a nineteenth-century economic philosophy that saw the wealth of nations coming from agriculture.

94. (C) Alexander Hamilton's plan for paying off the war debt involved the federal government absorbing the state debts, then reissuing bonds at the same value plus interest. Many Southern states had already paid off their debts and felt the reissuing of bonds would benefit mostly Northern investors.

95. (C) In 1793, George Washington issued his Declaration of Neutrality in response to the growing tensions in Europe resulting from the French Revolution. This declaration, however, was undermined by both British and French actions, including the impressment of sailors. Washington, along with Alexander Hamilton, was criticized for using federal troops to crush the Whiskey Rebellion as a way to demonstrate the power of the federal government. In terms of dealing with Native Americans, Washington did use treaties to deal with certain tribes, as illustrated by the 1790 Treaty of New York, but also used military forces, as illustrated by Anthony Wayne's military expedition against the Miami Confederacy, which concluded in 1795 with the Treaty of Greenville.

96. (A) Edmond-Charles Genêt was the ambassador to the United States during the French Revolution. He arrived in 1793. Upon arrival, he began to call on Americans to attack British vessels, as well as Spanish-held New Orleans. These actions were a violation of George Washington's Proclamation of Neutrality. Charles Talleyrand was the French foreign minister at the time of the XYZ Affair. Premier Georges Clemenceau was the leader of France during World War I. Ferdinand Maximilian was instated as the leader of Mexico by France after Mexico defaulted on debts owed to France.

97. (C) This English cartoon provides commentary on American and French relations following the XYZ Affair that took place in the May of 1798. The event began when, in 1796, President John Adams sent Charles Pinckney, John Marshall, and Elbridge Gerry to France to ease tensions in the wake of Jay's Treaty with Britain. Instead of being allowed to meet with the French foreign minister, they were greeted by French agents, who demanded a bribe. This is illustrated by the one sack that has diplomatic prerequisite written on it. The event created an outcry within the United States, leading to an undeclared naval war and helping the passage of the Alien and Sedition Acts.

98. (B) As noted in the previous question, John Bull, the personification of Great Britain, is watching the events unfold with amusement as the United States finds itself in the middle of the diplomatic dispute. Spain, as well as four other nations, are depicted by the group of five individuals at the base of Shakespeare Cliff, who are looking on with curiosity. The Democratic Republicans and their party leader, Thomas Jefferson, tended to support France over Britain in foreign policy. The document itself was created in London in the June of 1798.

99. (D) The Federalist-dominated Congress passed four laws in 1798 that were designed to protect the nation during an undeclared war with France following the XYZ Affair. The four parts of the act consisted of the Naturalization Act, the Alien Act, the Alien Enemies Act, and the Sedition Act. The Sedition Act called for fines or imprisonment of people who criticized the government and the president. The Republicans under Jefferson saw this as a thinly veiled attempt to silence their party. While most of the provisions expired by 1800, the Alien Enemies Act is still in effect. The Non-Intercourse Act was passed in the early nineteenth century as trade tensions existed between the United States, France, and Great Britain during the Napoleonic Wars. The Whiskey Tax and the Declaration of Neutrality both took place during the Washington Administration. The Declaration of Neutrality was Washington's attempt to keep the United States out of the conflicts arising from the French Revolution and would serve as a basis for American foreign policy for much of the nineteenth century. The Whiskey Tax, which was part of Hamilton's economic program, ultimately resulted in the Whiskey Rebellion in 1794.

100. (A) Judicial review is the power of the courts to strike down laws or actions that violate the Constitution. The only way to overrule judicial review by the legislative body is to amend the Constitution itself. The first use of judicial review was in the case described in the transcript, *Marbury v. Madison*. The ruling was decided by Chief Justice John Marshall in 1803. The position of Attorney General and lower federal courts were established by the Judiciary Act of 1789. Using the "necessary and proper" (elastic) clause, Congress created the federal court system beneath the Supreme Court. Many felt that this was an overreach of the federal government, but supporters believed there was a need for a system of federal courts with broader jurisdiction. The act also created the position of attorney general, who heads the U.S. Department of Justice. The attorney general is the top law enforcement official in the federal government, dealing with legal affairs at the national level.

101. (C) The *Marbury v. Madison* case took place after Thomas Jefferson attempted to block John Adams's appointment of William Marbury to the Supreme Court. Marbury attempted to sue, but Chief Justice John Marshall denied his petition. The *Marbury v. Madison* decision established judicial review, allowing the Supreme Court to strike down laws and actions that violated the Constitution. It also further defined the powers of the executive branch.

102. (B) The cartoon was created to criticize Thomas Jefferson for the Louisiana Purchase and plans to build upon the expansion through a further purchase of Western Florida. French Minister Charles-Maurice de Talleyrand is holding maps of the desired territory, while Jefferson, being stung by a hornet (Napoleon), is vomiting $2 million of the national treasury.

103. (B) Though the Federalists began to fall from power following the election of 1800, they remained vocally critical of the Democratic-Republicans and specifically Jefferson, for his support of France. Jefferson, who previously held a strict view of the Constitution and government spending, adopted a more flexible view to allow for the Louisiana Purchase. This angered the Federalists, who worried that westward expansion would further diminish their political influence.

104. (A) Throughout the conflict between France and Britain during the Napoleonic Wars, the British Navy would board American ships and conduct an act known as *impressments*, where they would force sailors to serve on their ships. The most notable instance of this act was the Chesapeake Incident, in which the British Navy attacked an American naval ship in an attempt to impress American sailors. This event brought the United States to the brink of war with Britain. Beyond impressments depicted in the image, the British were accused of funding Native American uprisings in the West. This incensed the western states. In 1810, legislators from the South and West were elected, creating a powerful bloc known as the War Hawks, who called for war against Britain to stop this support and promote American expansion farther into Spanish-held territories.

105. (B) The cartoon depicts the British boarding party overpowering the crew of the Chesapeake and hoisting the British flag. The American sailors are drawn as disorganized and hapless.

106. (C) Prior to the speech, several tribes of the area which is now southern Indiana signed several treaties, including the Treaty of Fort Wayne, the Treaty of Grouseland, and the Treaty of Vincennes. These treaties ceded much of the land of the region to the United States. While certain tribes such as the Miami felt that the treaties would ease tensions between white settlers and the Native Americans, by providing funds and supplies to regional tribes and limiting further encroachment of settlers, Tecumseh rejected the treaties because he was not part of the negotiations.

107. (B) Handsome Lake was a leader of the Allegheny Seneca during the early nineteenth century. Unlike Tecumseh, he advocated the development of peaceful relations with white settlers and called for the adoption of sedentary agriculture. This contrasts the notions put forth in Tecumseh's speech which called for a continuation of traditional Native American practices. Tecumseh's brother, Tenskwatawa (also referred to as the Prophet), preached that Native Americans should reject European American ways. However, like Tecumseh, Handsome Lake was known for his calls for Native Americans to completely reject alcohol, which he referred to as the "great engine" that introduced many "evils amongst Indians."

108. (C) As American settlers began to push west of the Appalachian Mountains, native people grew concerned about the encroachment into places such as Kentucky and southern Indiana, which had been considered a kind of "hunting reserve" and buffer zone between Native Americans and white settlers. Two Shawnee Indian leaders, Tecumseh and his brother Tenskwatawa (also referred to as the Prophet), felt that action needed to be taken to stop U.S. encroachment. They advocated the rejection of western society and argued that land treaties such as the Treaty of Fort Wayne were invalid. They also created a coalition to resist further encroachment onto their land.

109. (C) One of the objectives of the War of 1812 was the attaining of new lands in both British-held Canada and Spanish-held Florida, especially as Congress came under control of the War Hawks, which heralded from the western frontier regions of the growing United States. Madison instead focuses on the actions taken by the British government. Madison directly discusses Britain's interference with American trade, as well as the impressment of American sailors, such as in the Chesapeake Incident. He also discusses the British funding of Native American attacks on western settlers such as those led by Tecumseh and the Shawnee Confederacy.

110. (A) The Hartford Convention took place in 1814 during the War of 1812. New Englanders were strongly against the war and threatened to secede from the Union. However, when the war ended, the Republicans gained even more influence, and the Federalists declined, eventually disappearing as a national party.

111. (A) Following the War of 1812 and the signing of the Treaty of Ghent, relations between the United States and the British were mostly restored. Territorial borders were restored, and impressments by the British ceased, though mainly because the need for sailors lessened with the conclusion of the Napoleonic Wars. While the United States did not gain land in Canada, it did retain land in western Florida that it captured from Spain.

Chapter 6

112. (D) The 1819 case of *McCulloch v. Maryland* concerned Maryland's attempt to challenge the second national bank by imposing a tax on all bank notes not chartered in Maryland. Chief Justice John Marshall wrote the Supreme Court's majority decision in the case, establishing two major principles for the American government: upholding the doctrine of implied powers for the federal government under the "necessary and proper" clause, and asserting the power of the federal government over that of the state governments. Under these measures, the second national bank was deemed constitutional.

113. (C) Congress established the second national bank in 1816. Many states still questioned whether such a bank was constitutional, including Maryland. Maryland attempted to challenge the bank by placing a tax on all banks not chartered directly by the state of Maryland. A federal cashier working for the Baltimore branch of the national bank refused to pay the tax, leading to the court case. Ultimately, the Supreme Court decided that the national bank was constitutional, under the "elastic clause," which states that Congress can make laws deemed "necessary and proper" for carrying out the work of the federal government.

114. (A) The 1832 *Worcester v. Georgia* decision stated that Native Americans have federal protection from state governments that infringe on their tribal sovereignty. The case resulted from the state of Georgia attempting to seize Cherokee land for cotton production. While Chief Justice John Marshall wrote the majority decision deeming the action unconstitutional, the court had no power to enforce the decision. Both Georgia and the federal government under the Jackson administration ignored the ruling, and between 1837 and 1838, the U.S. Army forcibly removed around 15,000 Cherokees. The forced march became known as the Trail of Tears, as nearly one in four Cherokees died during this relocation.

115. (C) As noted in the excerpt, the Missouri Compromise of 1820 outlawed slavery north of latitude 36°30' north (Missouri's southern border) with the exception of Missouri. This upheld the early Northwest Ordinance of 1787, which banned slavery in the Old Northwest Territory but allowed the expansion of slavery in the South. The struggle to maintain a balance of free and slave states helped create the tensions that led to the Civil War.

116. (D) The Missouri Compromise was signed into law in 1820. Missouri was admitted into the Union as a slave state, and Maine (formally part of Massachusetts) entered as a free state. This preserved the balance between free and slave states. It also set the boundary of free and slave states at latitude 36o30' north (Missouri's southern border). The Kansas–Nebraska Act of 1854 effectively repealed the act, and the Dred Scott decision of 1857 deemed the compromise unconstitutional, adding to the tensions that led to the Civil War.

117. (C) Thomas Moore's satiric work "Epistle from a Slave-Lord to a Cotton-Lord" was written in 1833 and appeared in the English publication in the *Times*. Moore offers criticism of what he sees as the oppression found both on American plantations who utilize slave labor and northern factories that employ child labor.

118. (D) Moore argues that public opinion acts as a "general controller of Kings, Lords, and cotton-mills." In the poem, because public opinion has turned on the factory owners and the plantation owners, they are unable to commit the inhumane treatment upon their workers which they once did.

119. (C) Because many immigrants entered the United States through Northern ports, an abundance of unskilled labor was available to work in the emerging textile factories throughout the region. Furthermore, factories such as the Lowell textile mills in Massachusetts employed young, unmarried women from nearby farms to work in the factories. They were seen as ideal labor, since they worked for less money and were considered less likely to organize. They made up a majority of the labor in the New England region until the 1840s, when they were displaced by a large wave of Irish immigrants.

120. (A) At the conclusion of the American Revolution, the market price of tobacco plummeted. Former tobacco farmers began to sell off their slaves and switch to growing wheat and other grains. With the invention of the cotton gin, this trend was quickly reversed, and the number of slaves nearly doubled within twenty years after the gin's invention.

121. (D) As noted by the chart, there were approximately 4,450,000 slaves in the United States producing roughly 3.8 million bales of cotton.

122. (C) Though cotton production in the American South and West played a role in the increase of slavery, many slaves were forced into other forms of non-cotton-related labor based on the economies of the various regions where slavery was common.

123. (A) The cult of domesticity, also referred to as the doctrine of separate spheres, emphasized the role of women in preparing their children for adulthood by acting as a nurturing mother and dutiful wife who exemplified expectations of virtue and morality. The belief was popular in both the United States and Britain during the nineteenth century. Because women were seen as natural nurturers, opportunities as teachers did emerge, but overall, this view became an obstacle for women seeking rights and equality.

124. (C) The National Trades Union was established in 1834 and was the first national union of trades that combined unions from multiple states and boasted nearly 300,000 members. But because of the economic panic of 1839, the union collapsed. It is considered to be an important milestone for the creation of later unions such as the National Labor Union (established in 1866), which grew to nearly 600,000 members, and the Knights of Labor (established in 1869), which incorporated nearly a million diverse members. Both of those unions also eventually collapsed.

125. (A) The 1823 Monroe Doctrine was issued by President Monroe as part of his annual address to Congress. The act closed the Western Hemisphere to further colonization by the European powers. It also was to be a deterrent to keep European nations from interfering with the political development of the newly independent Latin American states. However, while stating European actions in the Western Hemisphere would be seen as a threat, it does not mention military action. In 1904, Theodore Roosevelt greatly expanded the scope of the doctrine by announcing that the United States could intervene in Western Hemisphere states if they became unstable. This has become known as the Roosevelt Corollary.

126. (C) The 1823 Monroe Doctrine was issued as part of James Monroe's seventh State of the Union Address. John Quincy Adams, Monroe's secretary of state, was one of the main authors. The doctrine was partly a response to the creation of the Holy Alliance in Europe, which consisted of Russia, Austria, and Prussia, along with Spain and France. At the conclusion of the Napoleonic Wars, Spain and France wished to reclaim lost lands in the Western Hemisphere, and Russia sought to increase its holdings in the Pacific Northwest extending into Oregon Country. Prior to this, the United States had already recognized the independence of many of the former colonies. Hoping to retain the United States' position as the leading power within the Western Hemisphere, Monroe issued the doctrine as a symbolic closing of the Americas to future European colonization or control. The Monroe Doctrine would be cited by James K. Polk as a reason to annex Texas over twenty years later, after it was discovered Britain might be interested in incorporating the territory. This widened the Monroe Doctrine to allow preemptive measures against perceived threats of European involvement in the Western Hemisphere.

127. (C) Following the Congress of Vienna, the Holy Alliance (including Prussia, Austria, and Russia), Spain, and France agreed to work together to assist Spain in reclaim lost colonies in the Western Hemisphere. In doing so, it was also discussed that Russia would reassert its claims in the Pacific Northwest, including its possession of Alaska down to the area that was referred to as the Oregon Territory. The Oregon Territory at this time was being jointly claimed by the United States and Britain. The United States was concerned that if Russia was successful in asserting its claim in the region, the United States would lose access to the Pacific Ocean.

128. (B) The Monroe Doctrine states that "the political system of the allied powers is essentially different in this respect from that of America." In this regard the United States considered that while European governments were dominated by aristocracy, the Western Hemisphere was to remain free to pursue more democratic means of governing itself. The idea that the United States would be the chief arbitrator in the region was established under the Olney Corollary. The notion that the United States had the obligation to ensure stability within governments of the Western Hemisphere would be part of the later Roosevelt Corollary. While the doctrine reasserts the idea of Washington's 1793 assertion of neutrality in European affairs, it does not explicitly note the idea of isolationism. Furthermore, the Monroe Doctrine notes that the United States would not interfere with European colonies already established within the hemisphere.

129. (A) The American System was introduced following the War of 1812 and was supported by Henry Clay and others, including John Quincy Adams and John Calhoun. It was based on the idea that United States consisted of regions that were complementary to economic development. Raw materials such as agricultural products would be produced in the South and the West, and manufactured goods would be produced in the industrial North. It called for high protective tariffs to protect the United States from Britain dumping cheaper goods on American markets, and thus allowed for new enterprises and industries to emerge. It also called for investment in the nation's infrastructure, such as the construction of roads and canals to promote interstate commerce—for example, the Erie Canal and Cumberland Road. The American System also called for the continuation of the national bank to promote a single currency, establish nationally issued credit, and facilitate trade. It also advocated keeping the prices of public lands high to increase the federal government's revenue from land sales.

130. (A) The Erie Canal opened in 1825 and connected the Hudson River to Lake Erie. The canal ran for nearly 363 miles from Albany on the Hudson to Buffalo on Lake Erie. Over 50 locks were needed to overcome the nearly 600-foot change in elevation. The canal illustrated both the U.S. transportation revolution and Henry Clay's American System.

131. (B) The American Colonization Society was created by Robert Finley in 1816. It had a dual mission: returning freed blacks to Africa in hopes of giving them greater access to freedom, while also alleviating slave owners' fears of an increase in free former slaves living in the United States. Thousands of freedmen and former slaves migrated to Africa through this program, many eventually establishing the independent state of Liberia.

132. (D) When James Monroe was elected in 1816, the United States came under the control of a single party, the Republicans. The Federalist Party had met its demise as a national party in part because of the nation's success in the War of 1812 and the failure of the Hartford Convention. Because the nation was dominated by a single party, political cooperation was common, creating a unifying nationalist spirit.

133. (B) In the election of 1824, four Republican candidates vied for the presidency, since the Federalist Party no longer had a major presence on the national political stage (with the exception of John Marshall in the Supreme Court). The Republican contenders included John Quincy Adams, Andrew Jackson, William Crawford, and Henry Clay. Andrew Jackson won the largest number of both popular and electoral votes but lacked the needed majority of electoral votes. (He won 99 electoral votes but needed 131 for the majority.) The election was then decided in the House of Representatives in what Jackson and his supporters called the "corrupt bargain." John Quincy Adams was declared the winner of the election after Henry Clay put his support behind him.

134. (A) As noted in the chart, John Quincy Adams won the states of New England, including his home state of Massachusetts, Connecticut, Rhode Island, Maine, New Hampshire, and Vermont. The only other state he carried outside of New England was New York.

135. (D) Both Andrew Jackson and Henry Clay carried the western states, with Jackson winning Indiana, Illinois, and Tennessee (which was his home state). Henry Clay only won Missouri, Ohio, and his home state of Kentucky, while Jackson was also able to win southern states such as the Carolinas, Louisiana, Mississippi, and Alabama. Jackson also had victories in the Mid-Atlantic by winning New Jersey, Maryland, and Pennsylvania.

136. (C) Alexis de Tocqueville states that in a system of strict class division, "no one seeks any longer to resist the inevitable law of his destiny" or that an individual's potential becomes limited by their assigned place in a society. However, since the United States does not have an intrinsic social class system, self-improvement and innovation are more natural.

137. (B) Alexis de Tocqueville states, "Aristocratic nations are naturally too apt to narrow the scope of human perfectibility" while contrastingly, "democratic nations, to expand it beyond reason." This continues his argument that democratic nations are more apt at encouraging improvement and innovation.

138. (C) Alexis de Tocqueville traveled throughout the United States in the 1830s and published his most famous book, *Democracy in America*, in 1835. In this work, he describes his observations of American society. He notes the effects of a democratic society in providing equality and opportunity. De Tocqueville discusses the difference between land ownership in Europe and the United States and the impact that access to land ownership has on individual citizens of all classes. The ability to own land and move outward to find new opportunity made Americans unique as a people on the move, which allowed for greater social mobility, causing a break from European traditions of aristocracy. De Tocqueville also discusses other factors of American society, such as the deep role religion had within American society and the inequality found in the treatment of Native Americans and slaves.

139. (B) While de Tocqueville does mention groups such as the inequality found in the treatment of Native Americans and slaves in his work, this passage mostly ignores these factors. He discusses how citizens had access to land and that wealthy farmers, "commingled with the general mass." This highlights the notion that while there was a separation of the poor and wealthy it was less defined then in Europe. He also notes the innovation was found at various levels of society, as noted in the passage about ship building.

140. (A) One of the driving issues of the election of 1832 was the national bank. Jackson strongly opposed its renewal, seeing it as an agent of the aristocracy, benefiting Northern bankers and merchants and not Southerners or common people. He also feared that the bank could use its power to corrupt democratic institutions by bribing officials and buying elections with its economic power.

141. (B) As noted in the passage, $8,405,500 in stock was held by foreign nations, with a majority being held by Great Britain. Jackson argued that this was particularly negative for western states, which held little stock in the bank, meaning that much of their debt was being held by a foreign power.

142. (D) In 1836, Jackson allowed the second national bank to expire. Before the expiration of the national bank, Jackson moved the bank's funds to state banks often referred to as pet banks. Many of these banks were located in New York City, causing the financial capital of the United States to move there from Philadelphia. The Whig Party was created in reaction to the economic panic caused by the ending of the bank, as well as the furthering of executive power in destroying the bank.

143. (A) The creation of a national bank was a major policy introduced by Alexander Hamilton. Both Thomas Jefferson and James Madison initially rejected the idea, similarly to Jackson, on constitutional grounds.

144. **(C)** The Specie Circular was an executive order issued by Andrew Jackson and carried out by his successor, Martin Van Buren. It required that all future lands be purchased using silver and gold. This was done to stop land speculators from purchasing large tracts of land using bank notes that often had little real value, caused in part by the creation of pet banks—small state banks that received the funds of the former national bank.

145. **(C)** Andrew Jackson was nicknamed King Andy because of the way he increased the power and the influence of the presidency and executive branch. This was especially illustrated by his ending of the second national bank. At the same time, he served as a symbol of the common man, increasing the individual's access to the political process. Furthermore, his campaign is seen to have helped usher in a new era of elections with massive rallies and usage of the media.

146. **(A)** Both the Kentucky and Virginia Resolutions and the Ordinance of Nullification asserted the notion of states' rights over that of federal law and authority. The Kentucky and Virginia Resolutions stated that the states had the right to reject the Alien and Sedition Acts passed under the Adam's administration, while the Ordinance of Nullification rejected the 1828 Tariff, which South Carolina referred to as the Tariff of Abominations.

147. **(B)** The 1828 tariff were a continuation of a series of tariffs that had their roots in the War of 1812 and the Napoleonic Wars, when British manufacturers dumped British goods in American Markets at such a low cost that United States manufacturers could not compete. As part of the American System, the United States imposed a series of tariffs to protect American Manufacturing; however these tariffs were specifically unpopular in the South, leading to the 1828 tariff referenced in the passage to become known as the Tariff of Abominations.

148. **(C)** In response to the Nullification Crisis, Congress passed the Force Bill or, formally, "An Act further to provide for the collection of duties on imports." This bill granted the president of the United States the authority to use the armed forces to compel South Carolina to comply with the federal tariffs. The Lodge Force Bill of 1890 was written by Congressman Henry Cabot Lodge, and it allowed the U.S. government to ensure fair. It allowed elections to be monitored for voter fraud and the certifying of the vote count.

149. **(C)** In the cartoon Andrew Jackson is being depicted as a king, illustrating his increase of executive power. In his hand he is wielding a document symbolic of his use of the veto. His feet are shown trampling both the U.S. Constitution and the charter for the second national bank. His legacy toward the Native Americans is, however, not directly addressed. Though Andrew Jackson had gained a reputation as an "Indian fighter" during his early career, as president he instead opted to remove Native Americans to reservations in the West. In 1830, Congress passed and Jackson signed the Indian Removal Act. This legislation forcibly removed thousands of eastern tribes to lands in the West such as the area that is now Oklahoma. Many native people perished in the forced removal, including one in four Cherokees, on what became known as the Trail of Tears.

150. **(D)** The Whig Party formed in 1834 in response to what party members saw as an overextension of presidential authority by Andrew Jackson. The ending of the national bank, as well as infringements upon states' rights, earned Jackson the nickname King Andy. Many supporters of the Whig Party strongly supported term limits to further check the power of the executive branch.

Chapter 7

151. (A) As noted in the passage, three routes to Canada converged in the location where Levi Coffin and his wife lived. While his neighbors were fearful of his actions, over time, he feels they were inspired by his activities and also assisted with the activity, though fugitive slave hunters were extremely active in the region. Word of mouth along the various roots helped spread the word of Levi Coffin and his support grew; however, because the activity was illegal, the message had passed in careful secrecy.

152. (C) Harriet Tubman, born into slavery in Maryland, escaped to freedom in the North in 1849. She returned to the South over 13 times to lead groups of other slaves to freedom on what has become known as the Underground Railroad. Later, Harriet Tubman would assist the abolitionist John Brown in recruiting members for his intended uprising, as well as serve as a Union spy during the Civil War.

153. (D) Transcendentalism emerged during the early nineteenth century as an intellectual, philosophical, and literary movement. Pragmatism was an intellectual movement that focused on practical approaches to understanding of knowledge. It was introduced by C. S. Peirce and William James during the late nineteenth century. The social gospel, an intellectual movement of the late nineteenth and early twentieth centuries, applied Christian ideals to address social problems of the time period. "The Gospel of Wealth" was an essay written by Andrew Carnegie in 1889 describing the role of philanthropy within the new American upper class. Social Darwinism was a theory developed by philosophers such Herbert Spencer in the late nineteenth century. It applied Darwinian theories to human society.

154. (C) The transcendentalist movement emerged as a rejection of what was perceived as the intellectualist doctrine of the institutions of higher learning at the time. Participants in the movement sought understanding beyond empiricism and established ideas, instead trying to rise to a greater level of emotional understanding and a personal and instinctual awareness. Leaders of this movement included Ralph Waldo Emerson and Henry David Thoreau. *Walden*, written by Henry David Thoreau in 1854, serves as a famous example of both transcendentalist and early American literature. While the transcendentalist movement rejected many notions of the prominent religious beliefs of the early nineteenth century, Emerson believed strongly in creating an individual connection to spirituality that transcended established doctrine. His religious views illustrated a connection to many Eastern religions but also strongly supported the notion of divinity within one's life.

155. (A) Nathaniel Hawthorne was a critic of the transcendentalist movement, parodying it in his 1852 work *The Blithedale Romance*. Edger Allan Poe was also known for his criticism and satire of transcendentalism. Ralph Waldo Emerson and Frederick Henry Hedge founded the movement in Massachusetts with the creation of the Transcendental Club in 1836. Thoreau's *Walden* is considered by many to be a hallmark of literature within the movement, as is Fuller's *Woman in the Nineteenth Century*, which also was an early product of the nineteenth-century feminist movement.

156. (A) In 1848, Lucretia Mott and Elizabeth Cady Stanton organized the first convention dealing with women's rights at Seneca Falls, New York. At this convention, they issued the Declaration of Sentiments, outlining the goals and demands they felt were needed for women to achieve equality, as well as the injustices faced by women. The convention lasted for two days and hosted lectures on law and discussions on women's roles in society.

157. (D) During the first half of the nineteenth century, employment opportunities for women were extremely limited. While many young women found employment in textile mills, most worked only until they were married and took on the role of homemakers, as expressed by the cult of domesticity. Other jobs, such as teaching, nursing, and domestic services, were available because they fit into the pattern of what was believed to be the natural sphere of women: nurturers and caregivers with the ability to raise children. Women did not truly begin to enter the field of secretarial work until the invention of the typewriter in the 1880s, and even then, their access was limited. It was not until the First World War that large numbers of females found employment in this area. However, by the 1930s, fewer men entered the field, and women grew to be a majority.

158. (C) In 1837, Mary Lyon established the first women's college in the United States, the Mount Holyoke Female Seminary. Oberlin College in Ohio admitted four female students in 1837, making it the first college in the nation to admit both male and female students.

159. (C) During the first part of the nineteenth century, women began to play a greater role within their households. This change is illustrated by trends such as the smaller size of American families and the greater primary role women played in child rearing. This new role is often credited with helping women establish greater independence while they were being limited by the societal expectations within the cult of domesticity. This domestic feminism was used in the late nineteenth and early twentieth centuries by anti-suffragist movements to attempt to keep women from obtaining the right to vote.

160. (D) William Lloyd Garrison was a prominent leader of the abolitionist movement during the first half of the nineteenth century. Through his publication, *The Liberator*, and as a founding member of the American Anti-Slavery Society, he called for the immediate emancipation of slaves. He also later went on to be a leader in the women's suffrage movement.

161. (B) Both Garrison and the "Declaration of Sentiments" by Lucretia Mott and Elizabeth Caddy Stanton utilize the Declaration of Independence as a foundation for their arguments. Both cite the phrase "that all men are created equal," though Mott and Stanton added "and women" to further their argument.

162. (B) Many workers in the North feared that if slavery were abolished, they would have to compete with African-American workers for factory jobs. It was assumed that the former slaves would be willing to work for lower wages. Many Northern states that outlawed slavery continued to pass laws limiting African-American rights. In some cases, some states would not allow freedmen to take up residency within the state.

163. (A) As the abolitionist movement grew in the United States, divisions began to appear. One major source of contention was the role that women should be allowed to serve. William Lloyd Garrison allowed women to participate actively in his organization, the American Anti-Slavery Society. This alienated some members, including Arthur and

Lewis Tappan, who left the organization and formed their own society, the Liberty Party, in 1840. They felt that female participation went against the appropriate role of women at the time.

164. (D) The temperance movement emerged in the nineteenth and early twentieth centuries in order to reduce and in many cases outlaw the consumption of alcohol. Temperance societies appeared in the United States as early as the 1780s, but the temperance movement began to flourish during the early 1800s, and many leaders linked temperance to other prominent nineteenth-century movements such as women's rights and the abolitionist movement. The temperance societies would eventually inspire the Eighteenth Amendment, outlawing the sale of alcohol in 1918.

165. (B) The Eighteenth Amendment, ratified on January 16, 1919, effectively prohibited of alcoholic beverages in the United States. It made the production, transport, and sale of alcohol illegal. The amendment was in effect for only 13 years, ending in 1933. After that, it was repealed in by the ratification of the Twenty-First Amendment. The Twelfth Amendment to the Constitution was ratified in 1804 and was a response to irregularities during the presidential elections of 1796 and 1800. In 1796, John Adams won the presidency as a Federalist, but the Constitution provided that the candidate who received the second largest number of votes became vice president, and that person was Adams's political rival, Thomas Jefferson. The Nineteenth Amendment gave women the right to vote, while the Thirteenth Amendment ended slavery and involuntary servitude.

166. (A) Horace Mann was a leader in reforming public schools in Massachusetts, and his reforms spread throughout the nation, helping establish the foundation for modern education. He supported the use of taxes to provide public education for all young people and felt education should prepare students to be responsible members of American society. By the 1850s, most Northern states provided free public elementary schools, and the number of free high schools increased, but at a much slower rate. John Dewey also was a noted reformer in public education, helping to bring about a modern approach to schools in the twentieth century.

167. (B) Horace Mann, considered one of the founders of modern public education reform, advocated that schools accept students from diverse backgrounds and would help end poverty. The document talks of expanding education.

168. (B) Educational reformers of the 1800s, such as Horace Mann, felt that schools should move beyond providing simply training in reading, writing, and math. They believed schools should also teach children to be good citizens with self-discipline. Reformers supported taxation to support schools, as well as compulsory attendance until a certain age. Also, many reformers pushed to remove religion from the classrooms. Opposition to this led to an increase in the number of religiously based private schools, especially in the northeastern United States.

169. (B) The Hudson River School emerged in the mid-nineteenth century and began with landscape painters such as Thomas Cole and Frederic Church, who reflected themes of Romanticism. Many of the paintings depicted pastoral settings of the Hudson River

Valley as it was being rapidly developed. They often presented ideal notions of the harmony between humans and their natural surroundings, reflecting the works of transcendentalist authors such as Emerson and Thoreau. The movement illustrated a break with a reliance on the need for European training in artistic development.

170. (D) The Hudson River School focused on the natural beauty in the United States at a time when many began to fear that the encroachment of modern development and industrialization would overtake the untouched wilderness of the Hudson Valley. Many works illustrate idealized pastoral settings, where human beings and nature coexisted peacefully.

171. (B) Like the artists of the Hudson River School, James Fennimore Cooper was one of the first American authors to use the American frontier as a distinct setting in literature. Also similar to Hudson River School artists such as Thomas Cole, his works, which included *The Last of the Mohicans*, illustrate the encroachment of civilization upon the American frontier and, with it, the conflicts that inevitably resulted between nature and progress. Like the Hudson River School movement did in landscapes, in many ways, Cooper's works illustrate a first truly American literary movement, breaking away from Europe and celebrating the American pioneer spirit.

172. (A) During the late 1820s and the 1830s, Joseph Smith created the foundations of the modern Church of Jesus Christ of Latter-Day Saints in western New York during a period known as the Second Great Awakening. According to Smith, he had received a new book of the Bible, which became the foundation of the new Mormon Church. Robert Owen's New Harmony in Indiana and the Shakers in Oneida, New York, served as examples of Utopian communities. They were established in part as a response to the aftereffects of industrialism and the new era of economic capitalism, many reformers of the early 1800s began to question the rapid changes taking place in society. Over the first part of the 1800s, nearly a hundred utopian communities emerged and battled these new trends of societal evils in an effort to create perfect communities.

173. (B) The Second Great Awakening was a Protestant religious movement that took place from the 1790s through the 1850s. It was similar to other movements such as the Hudson River School and the works of authors such as Walt Whitman and James Fennimore Copper in that it was characterized by Romanticism and held common themes such as enthusiasm and emotion. The First Great Awakening, which swept the American Colonies of the 1730s and 1740s, was also a period of Protestant revivals.

174. (D) The 1855 print "The Propagation Society—More Freedom than Welcome" references the nativism fears of the threat posed by the Catholic Church's influence on America especially with increased Irish immigration and the increased presence of Catholic education, which was seen as a threat to American Protestantism and founding principles. This highlighted many American concerns on increased immigration and led to the formation of multiple nativist and anti-immigration organizations.

175. (C) While Spain and Italy are mentioned by the second bishop, during the 1820s through the 1850s, Ireland experienced a massive crop failure. To escape the harsh economic conditions and poverty, many Irish fled their native land for hopes of prosperity in the New World. This led to the rise of nativism, the belief that native-born individuals should be favored over immigrants, within the United States. Also, in response to the Irish, many anti-Catholic leagues formed over fears that the Irish would be more loyal to the pope than to their new country. In the image, one of the bishops is using his crook to anchor the boat to the American shore on a patch of cloverleafs, symbolic of Irish immigration.

176. (D) During the 1850s, many of the nativist groups and anti-Catholic organizations banded together to protect the United States from the perceived threat of Catholics migrating into the country. Originally forming in New York in 1843, the American Republican Party, later called the Know-Nothing Party, emerged. The name Know-Nothing was derived from the various groups' secrecy: when asked about their organization, they would deny knowledge. In 1855, the party officially changed its name to the American Party. The group's anti-Irish and anti-German platform yielded notable support during the 1840s and 1850s, influencing elections as a third party. The party dissolved by 1856, however, after it became divided over the issue of slavery.

177. (B) As illustrated by the patch of clovers (symbolic of the Irish), with the waves of migrants coming to the United States during the 1800s, most migrants established themselves in areas where they had family connections, depending on relatives for support until they could establish themselves. While poorer Irish immigrants created communities within the cities of the Northeast, many German and Scandinavian immigrants established farming communities in the Midwest. In reaction to the large waves of immigrants coming into the United States, nativist societies began to emerge as early as 1830s and held their first national conventions in 1845, as referenced by the young American boy.

178. (A) A majority of the nativist and anti-immigrant groups emerged in the Northeast during the increased waves of immigration during the mid-nineteenth century. Many factory workers feared that they would be forced to compete for jobs and lower wages with the influx of immigrants especially from Ireland. While nativist groups did emerge in the South, they predominantly were formed as a protest of the Democratic Party following the collapse of the Whig Party in 1854. Others also hoped that the formation of parties such as the Know-Nothings or American party would establish a middle ground between pro-slave and abolitionist groups.

179. (B) Commodore Matthew Perry sailed to Edo (modern-day Tokyo), Japan, in the July of 1853, delivering a letter from the president requesting the establishment of trade relations with Tokugawa Japan. In the March of 1854, Perry returned with a larger fleet and the Treaty of Kanagawa was signed between the United States and Japan, which formally opened Japan to U.S. trade. It also had Japan promise to give good treatment to castaways and shipwrecked sailors.

180. (B) In 1853, under orders from Millard Fillmore, Commodore Matthew Perry arrived in Japan with a fleet of ships. He demanded that he be allowed to deliver to the emperor a letter calling on Japan to open trade. Realizing that it could not defend itself against Perry's modern navy, Japan agreed. A year later, Perry returned with an even larger fleet, and the Japanese agreed to U.S. trade terms in the Convention of Kanagawa on March 31, 1854.

Chapter 8

181. (A) In the passage, Travis attempts to cite American ideals such as patriotism and the notions of liberty as reasons the United States should support those fighting for Texas independence. The movement began after increasing numbers of United States citizens flooded across the Mexican border predominantly because of the vast lands suitable for growing cotton from the late 1820s to the early 1830s. However, starting in the 1830s, the Mexican government began to restrict American immigration to Texas, outlawed slavery, and began to pressure settlers to recognize Catholicism and learn Spanish. This led to a series of uprisings which caused the Texas independence movement.

182. (A) While the events of the Alamo and Travis's letter did raise a great deal of sympathy from the United States and even led many to form unofficial militias to support the cause of the independence movement, the United States stayed neutral to honor an earlier pledge of neutrality. Prior to the start of the conflict, the administrations of John Quincy Adams and Andrew Jackson did attempt to purchase the land that is now Texas, though Mexico rejected both offers.

183. (D) The Battle of the Alamo was a siege of a San Antonio chapel and fort held by Americans seeking independence from Mexico. Six thousand Mexican soldiers led by Antonio Lopez Santa Anna held the American position under siege from February 23 to March 6, 1836. In spite of suffering heavy casualties, the Mexican Army eventually took the position, slaughtering all 187 American soldiers within the Alamo. This act of aggression and harsh tactics angered the Americans. The call "Remember the Alamo" inspired more Americans to join up and participate in the fight for Texas independence. Six months after the siege, the Texans soundly defeated the Mexicans at the San Jacinto River, securing Texas's separation from Mexico.

184. (C) David "Davy" Crockett, whose epithet is recalled as "King of the Wild Frontier," represented Tennessee in the U.S. House of Representatives, served in the Texas Revolution, and died at the Battle of the Alamo. James Bowie, who also is credited with the "Bowie" knife, also died during the battle. Andrew Jackson Harrison and George Brown were also defenders of the Alamo.

185. (C) During the conflict for Texas Independence, the U.S. government remained officially neutral. However, in 1829, Mexico outlawed the practice of slavery. By this time, American planters owned roughly 1,500 slaves on their cotton and sugar plantations. Worried about the growth in population of English-speaking, non-Catholic settlers in the region, as well as the inability to fully enforce Mexican law, the government, led by Santa Anna, closed the borders to new immigrants and imposed taxes on American imports. Furthermore, the government increased the number of troops within the region after abolishing regional government. Stephen Austin attempted to protest these developments and advocated for Texas becoming a separate state. His demands were denied, and he was imprisoned for treason. This led to large protests, fueling the calls for independence.

186. (B) The war of Texas's independence ended with the Battle of San Jacinto on April 21, 1836. Sam Houston led an army of Texans to victory over the forces of Santa Anna. The Mexican forces were soundly defeated in a battle that lasted only 18 minutes. President

Santa Anna was captured shortly after the battle and forced to sign the Treaties of Velasco. The 1848 Treaty of Guadalupe Hidalgo concluded the Mexican–American War. The Texans' army was defeated at both the Alamo and Goliad. However, the two battles and the brutal actions committed by the Mexican Army following each helped the Texans gain dramatic support for the cause and became a rallying cry for the Texan army.

187. (A) After the Battle of San Jacinto, President Santa Anna was forced to sign the Treaties of Velasco, recognizing the independence of Mexico and allowing Santa Anna and his army to go free. The treaty called for the end of hostilities between Mexico and Texas, as well as the removal of all Mexican troops in Texas. It also called for the release of prisoners on both sides. The treaty, while signed by Santa Anna, was never ratified by the Mexican government. The major fighting ended with the treaty, but Mexico did not fully recognize Texas independence until the end of the Mexican–American War and the signing of the Treaty of Guadalupe Hidalgo in 1848.

188. (D) John L. O'Sullivan, the author of this passage, is generally credited with being the first to use the expression Manifest Destiny in print. In 1839, he alluded to the ideal in a short essay, but he used the exact phrase in this famous essay "Annexation" in 1845. The term *Manifest Destiny* was used by the loyal Democratic journalist to justify the annexation of Texas and Oregon Territory.

189. (B) In the passage O'Sullivan states that Manifest Destiny is the fulfillment of the United States "to overspread the continent allotted by Providence for the free development of our yearly multiplying millions," or expand its boundaries to the Pacific Ocean. The Monroe Doctrine of 1823 rejected the establishment of new European colonies in the Western Hemisphere, while the ability for states to decide whether they would allow slavery or not was part of the notion of popular sovereignty, established by individuals such as senator Stephen A. Douglas in the 1850s.

190. (B) "Manifest Destiny" expressed the belief that the United States had a mission to expand, spreading its form of democracy and freedom. Inspired in part by the Second Great Awakening, America was once again viewed as a "city on the hill," or a beacon of democracy that had the divine duty of expanding its culture, values, government, and religion across the North American continent. President Polk tied the belief to the Monroe Doctrine, which states that any attempt made by a European power to establish itself in North America would be seen as a threat to U.S. security. The notion of Manifest Destiny was rejected by the Whig Party of the 1830s and 1840s. The Whigs felt that the focus of the United States should continue to be on the ideals of the American system, which stressed development of the economy and internal improvements in existing regions.

191. (C) Though Texas desired to ultimately be annexed by the United States, sectionalism greatly delayed the process. Whigs felt the addition of a new Southern state would further erode their political power. Abolitionists feared that annexing Texas would increase the influence of pro-slavery states. Furthermore, the United States had created a treaty with Mexico, and the annexation of the former Mexican Territory would create grounds for war between the two nations. Ultimately, when British plans to turn Texas into a colony were discovered, Americans became outraged. This eventually helped end the stalemate and allow for congressional approval of the annexation of Texas in December 1845.

192. (B) Throughout the 1840s and 1850s, "Manifest Destiny" was used by Democrats such as President James K. Polk, Democratic journalist John L. O'Sullivan, and many others to justify America's westward expansion, tapping into the nationalistic and religious sentiments of the period. Whigs and manufacturers often resisted the notion of westward expansion, instead wanting the nation's focus to be on economic development. They also saw western expansion as eroding the power and influence of northeastern states. Abolitionists also resisted the concept, fearing that it would increase the number of slave states within the Union. Native Americans feared the expansion would further threaten their traditional land claims.

193. (A) President Polk cited the Monroe Doctrine, initially delivered by James Monroe as part of his seventh State of the Union Address in 1823, in terms of the prevailing spirit of manifest destiny. He used it to justify the annexation of both Texas and the Oregon Territory, to keep other European powers, especially Britain, from laying claims to further lands in North America. Furthermore, Polk extended the doctrine to justify American intervention in the Western Hemisphere, not only against an existing threat, but also against actions that could be perceived as threats.

194. (B) In the passage, President Polk reiterates the initial intention of the Monroe Doctrine by quoting it. He cites, "American continents, by the free and independent condition which they have assumed and maintain, are henceforth not to be considered as subjects for future colonization by any European powers."

195. (B) The slogan "Fifty-Four Forty or Fight!" originated in the 1840s concerning the border dispute between the United States and Britain. The two countries had occupied the territory jointly until 1828. At that time, Britain had offered the United States land south of the 49th Parallel, but Democrats believed the U.S. land claim extended to the southern tip of the Russian claim in America, which is modern-day Alaska. The issue was eventually resolved under President James K. Polk with the 1846 Oregon Treaty, in which the formal boundary was set at the British-proposed 49th Parallel. The final border dispute, dealing with control of San Juan Island, was not settled until 1872.

196. (C) While the debate over the annexation of Texas raged on in the U.S. Congress, Britain began to take an interest in the region. Though Britain opposed slavery, the British saw annexing Texas as an opportunity to curb U.S. expansion in North America, as well as to reduce American authority. Furthermore, they saw it as an economic opportunity, where they could reduce their dependence on U.S. cotton while creating an outlet for manufactured goods without having to deal with high U.S. tariffs. When Britain's plans were discovered, many Americans became outraged. James K. Polk cited this action as a clear violation of the Monroe Doctrine. Furthermore, it ultimately helped President Tyler push through the annexation of Texas on December 29, 1845.

197. (D) During the presidential election of 1844, the Whig Party nominated the well-known Henry Clay as its candidate. The Democrats, however, chose a "dark horse" (relatively unknown candidate) named James K. Polk from Tennessee. Polk made the issue of expansion a focal point of his platform, calling for the annexation of Texas, as well as all of the Oregon Territory. While Polk showed certainty on these issues, Clay seemed to waver. In the end, however, the election was decided by the emergence of a spoiler third party called the Liberty Party. This small abolitionist group split Clay's support, allowing Polk to win the election.

198. (A) Martin Van Buren is being prodded by Andrew Jackson for his avoidance of the annexation question concerning Texas. Democratic candidates James Polk and his vice presidential candidate George Dallas favor annexation, while Senators Thomas Hart Benton and John C. Calhoun present Van Buren with Texas depicted as a hag, whom they carry on a board.

199. (D) The issue of Texas annexation divided the country throughout the 1830s and 1840s. The South quickly supported its annexation for nationalistic reasons (Texas's independence was won by the Americans), as well as the South's desire to incorporate new lands where slavery had already been established. In the cartoon, Texas is illustrated as a violent hag, symbolizing the divisions the debate over annexation caused. Furthermore, the shackles being held in the woman's hand symbolized Texas as a slave territory. The issue was finalized in 1845 when Texas was admitted into the Union as the 28th state. The battle between pro- and anti-slavery groups was exacerbated by the addition of new slave states. Congress attempted to rectify the issue later with the Compromise of 1850 introduced by Henry Clay.

200. (C) During the battle of Palo Alto, it was reported that American soldiers freely shared their water with the wounded Mexican soldiers. The artist exaggerates this through their depiction of the U.S. soldiers, especially in comparison to the depictions of the Mexicans, who are drawn in an exceedingly stereotypically fashion, making them appear slovenly and beast-like.

201. (A) After a successful campaign in Mexico, in which American forces were led by Zachary Taylor and Winfield Scott, most of the larger Mexican cities came under American control. Following the Battle of Chapultepec in September 1847, Winfield Scott occupied the Mexican capital of Mexico City. At this point, Mexico was no longer able to defend itself further and was forced to negotiate peace with the United States with the Treaty of Guadalupe Hidalgo on February 2, 1848. In addition to ending the conflict, the treaty established the U.S.–Mexican border of the Rio Grande, forcing Mexico to cede the land now occupied by the present-day states of California, Nevada, Utah, and parts of Colorado, Arizona, and New Mexico. The treaty also gave the United States undisputed control of Texas, which Mexico refused to officially recognize as independent.

202. (B) Because tensions between Mexico and America were high over the annexation of Texas by the United States in 1845, as well as a border dispute between the two nations, President James K. Polk ordered General Zachary Taylor to the Rio Grande. This eventually sparked the Mexican–American War in 1846. The war was strongly supported by Southern and western states, as well as most Democrats, including John C. Calhoun. Whigs, including Daniel Webster, strongly opposed the war. Many saw the declaration of war as a misuse of executive power. Many also felt that the war was immoral, since it would further extend the practice of slavery. Henry David Thoreau even expressed his opposition by not paying his taxes. He was arrested for this, leading him to write his famous essay "The Duty of Civil Disobedience." Despite the objections, militarily the United States was extremely successful. Stephen Kearney took control of Mexico, and Taylor successfully captured lands as far south as Mexico City.

203. (A) The Gadsden Purchase by President Franklin Pierce on June 24, 1853, was the last major territorial purchase of the contiguous continental United States. The land was purchased from Mexico and now makes up the southern borders of New Mexico and Arizona. One of the main reasons for the purchase, besides settling border disputes remaining from the Mexican–American War, was for a planned route of a transcontinental railroad. The purchase sparked further debates over the issue of slavery, and the plans for the railroad were suspended with the outbreak of the Civil War.

204. (C) The Compromise of 1850 was introduced by Henry Clay after tensions arose with the acquisition of new territories from Mexico. Under the Compromise of 1850, Texas gave up its claims to the land that is now New Mexico. The state was compensated with $10 million, which it could use to pay off debts it still owed from its separation from Mexico. Furthermore, the territories of New Mexico, Nevada, Arizona, and Utah would decide on slavery through popular sovereignty. The compromise also outlawed the slave trade in the District of Colombia, and California was admitted into the Union as a free state. The Fugitive Slave Act was also enacted as part of the legislation forcing citizens to assist in the return of runaway slaves seeking freedom in the North.

205. (B) In the wake of the Mexican–American War, the United States gained vast territories in the West. This raised concerns over the expansion of slavery. To find a middle ground between those who supported slavery and those who were opposed, Congress opted to leave the decision to the individual territory as each applied for statehood. This, however, often led to bitter struggles within the territories, as illustrated in Kansas. As Kansas applied for statehood, violence between abolitionists and supporters of slavery broke out, leading to an event described as Bleeding Kansas.

206. (C) The Dred Scott decision of 1857 declared that blacks were not guaranteed citizenship under the Constitution and therefore did not have political or legal rights. It also stipulated that an African American's residence in a state or territory where slavery was illegal did not in any way grant emancipation. Combined, these principles further guaranteed the protection of slave owners' property rights while stripping even freedmen of any legal protection. This made the Fugitive Slave Act even more repressive, since those charged as fugitives had little legal protection or recourse. In essence, this made it easier to kidnap freemen and allowed for cruel treatment of slaves who were captured.

207. (C) The personal liberty laws were established by several Northern states to help free blacks in the face of the Fugitive Slave Act, which was passed as part of the Compromise of 1850. The laws limited use of prisons to hold accused fugitives, forcing bounty hunters to provide evidence that their captives were in fact fugitives, as well as providing for the rights of the accused. This was done so the Northern states would not have to invoke the notion of nullification.

208. (B) Though Stephen Douglas played a large role in brokering and helping its eventual passage, Henry Clay of Kentucky is generally credited with authoring the Compromise of 1850. Millard Fillmore, who was vice president and president of the Senate at the time, and Senator Thomas Benton of Missouri found themselves in such a heated debate over the legislation that Senator Henry S. Foote, who was serving as floor leader, drew a pistol on Senator Benton.

Chapter 9

209. (C) *Uncle Tom's Cabin*, written by Harriet Beecher Stowe, was well received in the Northern states, selling an estimated 300,000 copies in its first year published. In the South, however, it did not receive such a warm welcome. Many declared it slanderous. The author and bookstores that attempted to sell the novel received numerous threats. Authors of the South began to produce works to counter Stowe's attacks. These works included *The Sword and the Distaff* by the famous Southern novelist William Gilmore Simms and Mary Henderson Eastman's *Aunt Phillis's Cabin*. John Brown led his famous uprising at Harpers Ferry almost seven years later, and the Know-Nothing Party represented the views of the nativist groups, taking a platform on restricting the influx of immigrants.

210. (C) The passage is referring to the Compromise of 1850, which was created by Henry Clay with input from Stephen Douglas to address tensions dealing with the expansion of slavery and newly acquired lands. The author of the passage argues that Harriet Beecher Stowe's work (*Uncle Tom's Cabin*) restarted these tensions. The Three-Fifths Compromise dealt with how slaves would be counted in the census for apportioning congressional seats in the United States Constitution. The Great Compromise is also based on the creation of the Constitution, merging the New Jersey Plan and Virginia Plan, leading to the creation of the House of Representatives and the Senate. The Missouri Compromise was an earlier attempt to balance the concerns of free and slave states.

211. (B) The author of the passage states, "It will operate heavily upon the colored class of the South, both slave and free—it will cause laws to be enacted and enforced which will cut up their few remaining privileges by the roots—it will not advance emancipation one iota." The other feels that not only slaves, but freeman living in the South as well will lose the few freedoms they have been granted. Furthermore, the author sees this book doing nothing to further the cause of the abolitionist movement.

212. (C) The Kansas and Nebraska Act uses the Compromise of 1850, referred to as the Compromise Measures, to argue that the Missouri Compromise of 1820 was now void. This allowed the decision of slavery to be decided by popular sovereignty. The Fugitive Slave Act was part of the Compromise of 1850, which was being used to justify the decision.

213. (A) The Dred Scott decision was the first time since the *Marbury v. Madison* case that the Supreme Court struck down a law passed by Congress. In Dred Scott, the court deemed that the Missouri Compromise was unconstitutional because it violated slave owners' rights to property. This upheld Stephen Douglas's proposed Kansas–Nebraska Act of 1854 insofar as slavery could not be automatically outlawed in the territories, but at the same time, it also made it illegal to outlaw the practice outright through popular sovereignty. Instead, the state would have to practice the Freeport Doctrine, also introduced by Douglas, which would involve creating laws that were so unfriendly to slavery that they would in effect keep the practice out of the state.

214. (B) The Kansas–Nebraska Act was introduced by Senator Stephen Douglas of Illinois in 1854. Its proposed purpose was to admit Kansas and Nebraska as states in order to build a connecting railroad from Chicago to the West. However, the act repealed the Missouri Compromise of 1820, which prohibited slavery north of Missouri, and allowed settlers in those territories to instead decide the issue through popular sovereignty. This led to a series of events in 1854 event known as Bleeding Kansas, in which pro-slavery groups and abolitionists gathered in Kansas to influence the territories' stance on the issue. John Brown gained national attention during this time by killing multiple pro-slavery supporters with a sword, and this period in its entirety caused further political separation between the North and South.

215. (A) The Free-Soil Party mostly consisted of former members of the Whig Party and Democratic Party who strongly opposed the expansion of slavery. They existed as a third party during the 1848 and 1852 elections, with their strongest support being in New York. By 1854, most of the Free-Soil Party was absorbed into the newly emerging Republican Party.

216. (B) "Bleeding Kansas" was the name given to the outbreak of violence in the Kansas Territory in 1854 as pro- and anti-slavery groups (including the abolitionist John Brown) battled over the issue of slavery. This was a response in part to the passage of the Kansas–Nebraska Act, which stated the decision over slavery would be left to popular sovereignty. "Bleeding Sumner" refers to the assault on the abolitionist senator Charles Sumner from Massachusetts, who was severely beaten by Congressman Preston S. Brooks of South Carolina in 1856. Brooks attacked Sumner after Sumner made an anti-slavery speech, "The Crime Against Kansas," which directly insulted Senator Andrew Butler of South Carolina. John Brown, a militant abolitionist, led a raid on the military arsenal at Harpers Ferry in 1859, hoping to use the weapons stored there to arm future slave uprisings. Prior to these three events, in August 1831, Nat Turner led a slave rebellion in Virginia. It resulted in 56 deaths, the largest number in such an uprising during the antebellum period. Southern states responded with stricter slave laws and Black Codes.

217. (C) From 1845 to 1849, immigration increased from 114,371 people to 369,980, or a total increase of 255,609, which marks the largest growth. Immigration will peak at 427,833 in the 1850s but then begin to decline.

218. (D) The Irish Potato Famine, which lasted from 1845 to 1852, led to a mass migration of Irish immigrants to come to the United States. In fact, roughly 75 percent of immigrants who came to the United States during the nineteenth century arrived during the period of the famine. The German March Revolution, also known as the German Revolutions, took place in the 1840s and promoted pan-Germanics and rejected the autocratic state that existed. The Free-Soiler movement existed from 1848 to 1852 and led to the creation of a single-issue party that sought to oppose the expansion of slavery into the Western territories.

219. (C) Starting in the early 1800s, immigrants to the United States began leaving Europe in hopes of better opportunity and wages. Furthermore, crop failures throughout Europe, especially in Ireland, and politically repressive governments increased the number of people coming into the United States. The Industrial Revolution offered many factory jobs. Since the new arrivals to the country were often willing to work for lower wages, tensions began to grow with established workers. Nativist groups began to form and eventually formed a national party called the Know-Nothings.

220. (D) Prior to the Civil War, in the period from 1845 until 1855, immigration increased more than 500 percent. However, these numbers dropped by nearly 36 percent by 1862. Immigration did still occur albeit in smaller numbers. It is important to note that a majority of these immigrants came to the Northern states and played a vital role in the Union's efforts during the Civil War.

221. (C) In 1846, a slave named Dred Scott attempted to sue his owner for freedom. He argued that his master took him to the Wisconsin Territory, where slavery was illegal; Scott maintained that if he lived in a free state, he should gain the status of a free man. The court had to consider two key points: whether Scott was a citizen in the first place and whether residence in a free territory would gain Scott his freedom. The decision, written by Chief Justice Roger Taney, stated that blacks were not considered citizens and therefore did not have legal protection, including the right to sue. The ruling also stated that being in a free territory did not make a slave free, because it would violate the owner's right to property, causing the Missouri Compromise to be deemed unconstitutional.

222. (D) The Dred Scott decision, which was handed down in 1857 by Chief Justice Roger Taney, stated that African Americans were not considered citizens under the Constitution and therefore did not have legal protection.

223. (A) The Supreme Court noted that the Fifth Amendment made any law that limited a slave owner in personal property, such as slaves, from migration into free territory was unconstitutional. The Sixth and Seventh Amendments deal with rights in trial, while the Fourteenth Amendment would supersede the Dred Scott decision upon its ratification in 1868.

224. (C) The Freeport Doctrine was part of the Lincoln–Douglas debates during the 1858 Illinois Senate race. In the debates, Abraham Lincoln tried to make Stephen Douglas look like a defender of slavery, while Douglas attempted to defend himself by citing the notion of popular sovereignty. The earlier Dred Scott decision stated that territories were not allowed to outlaw slavery, making Douglas's position look weak. Douglas developed a position, which became known as the Freeport Doctrine, that while states could not outlaw the practice of slavery, they could still pass laws unfriendly to the practice that would prevent slavery from taking hold. Douglas's position was well received by the people of Illinois, and Douglas went on to win the Senate seat. At the same time, it alienated much of his Southern support, hurting his future presidential bid. The Lincoln–Douglas debates gave Lincoln nation recognition, enabling him to become the Republican candidate in 1860.

225. (A) In the passage, the *Democratic Enquirer* argues that Virginia has not changed its stance on slavery since the American War for independence and it is the North's radical stance on slavery which is causing divisions within the United States. It also notes that the North is complicit in John Brown's actions at Harpers Ferry.

226. (B) While both articles discuss the specific actions of John Brown, they frame the event in terms of generalizing the views of the opposing region. The Democratic paper states, "But what a great wrong has been inflicted on Virginia by her brethren of the North," while the Republican paper states in reference to the South and the execution of Brown that it was a "plain admission on the part of Slavery that they dare not spare a brave man's life."

227. (A) After leading the 1856 Pottawatomie Massacre in Kansas, the abolitionist John Brown in 1859 led an attempted attack on the federal arsenal at Harpers Ferry, Virginia (now West Virginia). His goal was to capture the weapons held at the arsenal and use them to start an armed slave revolt. Initially, he asked Harriet Tubman to join him, though she had fallen ill prior. Brown's raid was defeated by a military detachment led by Colonel Robert E. Lee. John Brown's actions in Bleeding Kansas and Harpers Ferry represented a militant approach within the abolitionist movement. They furthermore illustrated the growing division and increasing tensions concerning slavery. Some saw Brown as a brave martyr, while many others viewed him as a terrorist. The raid itself furthered the tensions between the North and South, helping to usher in the Civil War.

228. (A) Bo Peep exclaims, "I wish poor old Hickory was alive. He'd bring 'em back in no time," in reference to Andrew Jackson. During his time as president he was known as a strong executive leader. In the face of the southern nullification crisis, where South Carolina threatened to secede from the union over tariffs, Jackson responded strongly, encouraging Congress to pass the Force Bill.

229. (C) The wolves are emerging from the forest of palmetto trees, the symbol of South Carolina, which was leading the calls for succession. They represent the European powers that could take advantage of the weakened United States as each state fell away from the Union. The wolves state, "If we can only get them separated from the flock, we can pick their bones at our leisure," meaning that Europe will be able to take advantage of the individual states if the Union failed.

230. (B) In the cartoon Buchanan, or "old Buck," is running away, despite Bo Peep's pleas. The presidency of James Buchanan is difficult to summarize fully and has been debated by historians since his presidency. He is often blamed for his inaction as Southern states began to secede from the Union, limited in his actions by his strict constitutionalist views. He was also a supporter of slavery and strongly opposed the abolitionist movement embodied by the Republican Party. He has also been criticized for his dealings with the financial crisis of 1857, which in part resulted from the Democratic Party's push for lower tariffs that led to deficit spending under his administration. During the 1860 election, the Democratic Party split between the North and the South.

Chapter 10

231. (B) Going into the war, the Union had several clear advantages over the Confederacy. It had a larger population with a more industrialized base, so it could create a larger and better supplied military. It also had a more balanced economy containing both factories and farms. It furthermore had more money in its treasury and banks. The Confederacy also had advantages. Seven of the eight military colleges in the United States were located in the South, giving the Confederacy more experienced leadership. Also, many Confederates considered this a war to save their way of life, boosting Southern morale early in the conflict.

232. (D) While the Confederacy suffered disadvantages such as a smaller population than the North and lacked the level of developed infrastructure of railroads found in the North, it was prepared in military leadership. A majority of the U.S. military colleges were located in the South, and many of the United States' most experienced military leaders, such as Robert

E. Lee, chose to fight for their home states in the South instead of staying with the Union Army. The South's insistence on state independence hurt its cause, however, because the independence of each state limited the power of the Confederate government. Furthermore, the South failed to receive the support of the powerful industrial European states of Britain and France, giving it little recourse against the North's industrial might.

233. **(C)** Abraham Lincoln and Jefferson Davis were in many ways opposites. When Davis became president of the Confederacy in 1861, he had much more political experience than Lincoln. He had served as a U.S. senator and as secretary of war under Franklin Pierce. He also was a West Point graduate with military experience in the Mexican–American War. As president, however, he was ineffective. Lincoln, while lacking in political and military experience, better understood the importance of public opinion. This allowed him to connect better with voters and maintain the support of the various leaders in Congress and the states. Moreover, Lincoln surrounded himself with skilled advisors, while Davis often refused to delegate authority, causing tensions within his cabinet and with other officials.

234. **(D)** During the Civil War, life for many slaves remained relatively unchanged. Many were taken from fieldwork to do manual labor for the Confederate Army. As the Union began to penetrate the South, many slaves did attempt to escape or seek refuge with the Union Army. Others remained in their homes and on their masters' plantations through the war. Slave uprisings did not drastically increase during the period. The South did suffer from a lack of industrial development compared with its Northern counterpart. The North had factories for the production of clothing, rifles, and ammunition. Much of the war materials in the South were produced through cottage industries or through smuggling. Food shortages also plagued the South, as evidenced by the bread riots that occurred in Richmond, Virginia, in 1863. Furthermore, the Confederate government printed currency in such large quantities that it was devalued, making it hard for Southerners to purchase the few necessities that were available.

235. **(C)** The First Battle of Bull Run took place on July 21, 1861. It is considered to be the first major land battle of the Civil War. The battle took place near the town of Manassas in Virginia, so it is also referred to as the First Battle of Manassas. (The Union often labeled battles based on physical features, such as the Bull Run River, while the Confederates named the battles after nearby towns.) The Union Army, numbering roughly 28,000, was led by Brigadier General McDowell, while the Confederate Army, consisting of roughly 32,000 men, was led by Brigadier General Johnston. The Union Army, which was ill-trained and inexperienced, failed to resist a Confederate counterattack and was forced to retreat, marking a Confederate victory. The Union suffered nearly 3,000 casualties, while the Confederate Army suffered roughly 2,000. The battle foreshadowed that the Civil War was going to be long and hard-fought for both sides. McDowell was removed from command and replaced by George B. McClellan. Meanwhile, because of his stoic nature during the conflict, a previously unknown colonel by the name of Thomas Jackson earned the nickname "Stonewall" after he refused to yield during a Union advance. The Battle of Fredericksburg occurred in December 1862 near Fredericksburg, Virginia. The Battle of Chancellorsville was fought from April 30 to May 6, 1863, near Spotsylvania, Virginia, and the Battle of Antietam took place on September 17, 1862, near Sharpsburg on the Antietam Creek in Maryland.

236. (C) The *Merrimac*, constructed by the Confederacy, and the *Monitor*, constructed by the Union, illustrated an advancement of naval technology: the creation of ironclad ships. Ironclad ships were wooden steamships plated with iron. The traditional wooden ships were no match for these new vessels. The Confederacy was the first to employ this invention in naval warfare, but the Union quickly responded. The *Merrimac* and *Monitor* finally met in battle at Hampton Roads, off the coast of Virginia in March 1862. The battle itself was indecisive, with both sides declaring victory, but at the same time, the battle received much attention from the world's naval powers. The era of wooden navies had come to an end because ironclad ships had made them obsolete.

237. (A) The Border States were important as a buffer zone, and if Maryland joined the Confederacy, Washington, D.C., would be engulfed by the Confederacy. These states were far from impenetrable; they became the sites of many of the war's most notorious battles and were crossed on numerous occasions by the Confederate Army. Moreover, they were home to numerous factories, especially in Maryland and Delaware, which would have greatly benefited the industry-weak Confederacy. Many of these states had slavery already, so when President Lincoln issued the Emancipation Proclamation, these states were exempt.

238. (D) Initially, the Confederate government planned to set up defensive positions and wait. Leaders hoped that by using a war of attrition, they would be able to inflict heavy Union casualties with limited losses on their own side. By consistently repelling Union offensive strikes, they hoped to wear down their opponents' morale and will. This strategy failed because the Union had tremendous advantages by way of resources and in many ways was able to conduct a war of attrition of its own, despite its continual heavy losses. The South also failed to achieve the support of European powers such as Britain and France, although the two nations relied on Southern cotton. Instead of supporting the South, they found sources elsewhere, such as in India and Egypt.

239. (B) As noted in the previous question, the South initially planned for a war of attrition against the Union. However, after General Lee's army was able to adequately protect Richmond following the Second Battle of Bull Run, he attempted to launch an attack on Union soil at the Battle of Antietam in Maryland, which was a Border State in the Union. He believed a victory on Union soil would help the Confederate states win the support of European powers and turn Northern opinion against the war. Though a Union victory, the Battle of Antietam was the bloodiest day of the Civil War, with the Union losing over 12,000 soldiers and Lee losing 14,000 soldiers, or nearly a third of his army.

240. (C) The Battle of Gettysburg was a three-day battle that took place in July 1863. More men died in this battle than any other battle on American soil. After the failed attack at Antietam, General Lee once again attempted to win a battle in the North. The Army of the Potomac, this time led by General Meade, engaged the Confederate Army of Northern Virginia at Gettysburg. On the third day, following heavy Confederate artillery assaults on Union lines, Lee ordered a massive Confederate charge to be led by General George E. Pickett. Because of the failure of the earlier artillery strikes, the charge was met by a strong Union defense, crushing the Confederate forces. Lee was forced to retreat, and his army was never able to recover from the losses or stage another Northern offensive.

241. (B) The cartoon map illustrates General Winfield Scott's "Anaconda plan," which was designed to crush the Confederate economy by establishing a naval blockade of the Confederate ports and then dividing the Confederacy in half by taking control of the Mississippi River through both naval and ground forces.

242. (D) The Anaconda Plan, devised by General Winfield Scott, called for a naval blockade of Southern ports while leading a military force down the Mississippi River, cutting the Confederacy in half. Scott felt that cutting off the Southern economy through the blockade and then dividing the Confederacy would leave the South little choice but to seek peace, avoiding the need for the Union to engage in a bloody war.

243. (C) At almost the same time of the major battle at Gettysburg, which was a turning point for the Eastern Theater of the Civil War, Grant successfully laid siege to Vicksburg in the West ending with a Union victory on July 4. By taking this Confederate position, the Union was able to take control of the Mississippi River, dividing the Confederacy in half.

244. (B) The Emancipation Proclamation was issued by President Lincoln in 1863 following the Battle of Antietam. While it was meant to emancipate (free) the slaves, it was applied only to the Confederate States. This limited the proclamation's immediate impact, since the Confederate States saw themselves as not bound to the Union or Lincoln.

245. (B) The proclamation directly tied the issue of slavery to the Civil War, making the conflict about something beyond simply reunifying the United States. While many Northern Democrats were upset by the action, it proved to be successful politically, and President Lincoln was able to win the election in the following year with 55 percent of the popular vote, defeating George McClellan.

246. (D) Initially the Union Army refused to enlist African-American volunteers. Congress eventually opened the military to African Americans in 1862 after McClellan's defeats in Virginia. After the issuance of the Emancipation Proclamation, the number of African Americans increased rapidly, though volunteers served in segregated units under mostly white supervision. Regardless, by war's end, they made up roughly 10 percent of the Union Army. They were not initially placed in combat units, but instead were forced to perform menial jobs and manual labor. Also, until 1864, they received less pay. Over time, black regiments such as the 54th of Massachusetts gained recognition for their abilities in combat. After 1863, the Confederacy also began to create African-American units. The black soldiers faced strong racism and harsh treatment, however, and were often given insufficient supplies and arms.

247. (C) In this pro-Democrat cartoon, presidential candidate General George McClellan is portrayed as the intermediary between the current Union Abraham Lincoln and Confederate president Jefferson Davis. Davis and Lincoln are committed to tearing the nation apart in order fulfill their unyielding beliefs, while McClellan is attempting to hold the nation together. General McClellan, who was the presidential candidate in the election of 1864, did serve as Lincoln's general in the Peninsular campaign, but was criticized for being overly cautious and too slow moving.

248. (C) After his failed Peninsula Campaign, which culminated with the bloody Battle of Antietam, George McClellan was removed from command in 1862. In 1864, however, Northern Democrats nominated him in the presidential election against President Lincoln. He tried to appeal to a war-weary Union public with an antiwar platform that called for ending the conflict and negotiating with the Confederacy. The Democrats found themselves split, while the Republicans, calling themselves the National Union Party, stayed strongly united. Furthermore, a series of military successes bolstered support for Lincoln, who easily won the election with 55 percent of the popular vote.

249. (A) During the Civil War, "Copperheads" referred to Northern Democrats and others who openly expressed their sympathies with and support for the Confederacy. They were given the label by Republicans who saw their actions as poisonous to the Union— dangerous as the venomous copperhead snake. Lincoln suspended the writ of habeas corpus to suppress the Copperheads during the Civil War. Copperheads were also referred to as Peace Democrats. The groups created several large societies, including the Knights of the Golden Circle in Ohio, which was led by Harrison H. Dodd. The organization called for armed uprisings in several Northern states. Copperheads also supported former general George B. McClellan in the 1864 election, but because of the negative press surrounding the organizations and recent Union military success, McClellan lost the election.

Chapter 11

250. (C) The Thirteenth Amendment, adopted on December 6, 1865, was the first of the Reconstruction Amendments. It officially abolished slavery and involuntary servitude, except as punishment for a crime. While the Emancipation Proclamation, announced by Lincoln in 1863, was intended to free slaves, it only did so in areas controlled by the Confederacy and did not address the Border States. The Twelfth Amendment, ratified in 1804, did not deal with slavery or the rights of African Americans at all. Its intention was to correct problems within the presidential electoral process.

251. (D) The Fourteenth Amendment, ratified on July 9, 1868, overturned the 1857 Dred Scott decision, which declared that African Americans were not citizens and therefore were not protected under the Constitution. The amendment opened citizenship to all people regardless of race or color and guaranteed due process and equal protection to all citizens. It also extended protections under the Bill of Rights to the state government. Before the Fourteenth Amendment, it was deemed that these protections applied only to the federal government.

252. (C) The Fifteenth Amendment was ratified in February 1869 and stated that no citizen could be denied the right to vote because of race or color. Furthermore, citizens could not be denied the right to vote because they had been slaves. Even though the Fifteenth Amendment was not ratified until 1869, as early as 1867 the military had begun to register African Americans in the South following the passage of the Reconstruction Act. The Sixteenth Amendment did not deal with Reconstruction, but instead with Congress's ability to levy an income tax.

253. (B) While the Thirteenth Amendment outlaws practices such as slavery (including states with gradual emancipation laws), it does allow for involuntary servitude as part of punishment for crime, with due process within the legal system. Past Supreme Court cases have defended the Constitutionality of the draft and have drawn distinction between involuntary servitude and the draft. While not specifically applying to the draft, the 1916 *Butler v. Perry* case is one example of this.

254. (A) Article 2 of the Fourteenth Amendment introduces gender-specific language into the Constitution, stating that all male citizens over twenty-one years old should be able to vote. This will pose a strong obstacle to the suffragist movement of the later nineteenth and early twentieth century, as individuals such as Elizabeth Cady Stanton who once said of the amendment, "If that word 'male' be inserted, it will take us a century at least to get it out."

255. (B) The insistence that Southern states ratify the Fourteenth Amendment was an integral part of the Radical Republican's Reconstruction Act of 1867. The 1864 Wade–Davis Bill was introduced by Radical Republicans in response to President Lincoln's Reconstruction plan, which the Republicans saw as too lenient. The Fifteenth Amendment was ratified in 1869 during the Grant administration.

256. (B) Lincoln's plan for Reconstruction was considered lenient by many Radical Republicans. Many felt that the South needed to be punished for seceding from the Union and starting the war. Lincoln, however, felt it was more important to reunify the nation, and his plan illustrated this in many ways. He did not require any state to give former slaves the right to vote. Lincoln's leniency was also illustrated by his rejection of the 1864 Wade–Davis Bill. Fearing that Southern states would reinstitute slavery after being readmitted to the Union, Radical Republicans introduced the legislation to increase the percentage of voters required to take a pledge. This illustrated the clashing of opposing viewpoints that would define the Reconstruction Era.

257. (B) In the opening of Lincoln's plan, he cites Article II, Section 2 of the U.S. Constitution directly, which gives the president the power to pardon and grant clemency.

258. (B) The 1864 Wade–Davis Bill was introduced by Radical Republicans in response to President Lincoln's Reconstruction plan, which the Republicans saw as too lenient. In Lincoln's plan, only 10 percent of the voting population needed to take a loyalty pledge to the Union before the state could reenter the Union politically. The Wade–Davis Bill attempted to increase this number to 50 percent.

259. (C) Both Lincoln's Plan and the Wade–Davis Bill upheld the Thirteenth Amendment and required that all slaves be freed and that their continued freedom be guaranteed. The Radical Republican's plan for Reconstruction went further and required that states also adopt the Fourteenth Amendment. Neither plan granted full amnesty to Confederate politicians and soldiers, but Lincoln's plan was more lenient. Furthermore, both plans had a list of requirements that had to be met by each state to be reinstated into the Union and have occupying forces removed, though Lincoln's plan was considered by Radical Republicans to be too lenient.

260. (A) Both Lincoln and Johnson supported what Radical Republicans saw as lenient plans for Reconstruction. But both insisted on what became known as the Ten-Percent Plan. Once 10 percent of a Southern state's 1860 voters had taken an oath of loyalty, the state could rejoin the Union. This was after it had established a new state government that would ratify and adhere to the Thirteenth Amendment, which outlawed the practice of slavery. Neither plan called for the redistribution of land, an act supported by many former slaves as well as Radical Republicans. Lincoln's plan for states to reenter the Union, which was in many ways similar to Johnson's, was relatively simple. This was because Lincoln believed that the Southern states had never legally seceded in the first place. After Lincoln's death, Johnson initiated his own Reconstruction plan. It continued Lincoln's pardons of former Confederates. It also called on Southern states to repudiate their war debts.

261. (B) The Freedman's Bureau, or the Bureau of Refugees, Freedmen, and Abandoned Lands, was created in 1865 to provide aid to freed people and help them make the adjustment to freedom. It was created under the U.S. Department of War and headed by General Oliver O. Howard. While the bureau was short-lived (it was dismantled by 1872), it played an important role in providing for the basic needs of millions of war refugees. It, along with other programs established using Reconstruction funds, created a public school system similar to the ones found in the North.

262. (B) During the 1866 congressional elections, Radical Republicans were elected in large numbers. This was, in part, a response to Andrew Johnson's resistance to the Fourteenth Amendment, which would give African Americans citizenship and, with it, legal status and constitutional protections. The Radical Republicans began to institute their own plans for Reconstruction. In 1867, they passed the Reconstruction Act, which implanted six sweeping provisions. One measure divided the South into five districts and put it under military rule. It also forced states to create new constitutions and allow both white and African American males to vote. It also called on all Southern states to guarantee equal rights to all citizens and ratify the Fourteenth Amendment.

263. (A) This image most likely represents the views of the Radical Republicans, as it is highly critical of President Andrew Johnson and the former Confederacy. The image shows an African American man cast his vote for the Republican candidate while the Democratic box remains empty. Meanwhile, President Andrew Johnson is seen holding a "Suffrage Veto," with additional "Veto[es]" of measures by the Radical Reconstruction. Furthermore, Johnson is talking with a person labeled "Ex. C.S.A.," referencing the Confederacy.

264. (B) American political history was made in February 1868 when Andrew Johnson became the first president to be officially impeached. In an impeachment, the House of Representatives officially charges an official with committing an illegal act. Though the main reason Congress moved to impeach Johnson was political and partisan disagreements, the main justification was that he had violated the Tenure of Office Act, which was passed in 1867. In 1868, President Johnson attempted to fire Secretary of War Edwin Stanton, who had been appointed under Lincoln. This action violated the 1867 act. Ten other charges were made against Johnson, but after his trial in the Senate, Johnson escaped removal from office by one vote.

265. (C) The 1869 *Texas v. White* decision strengthened the federal government's actions during Reconstruction. It announced that states did not possess the legal right to secede and that attempts to separate from the Union were in fact illegal, which reiterated both Lincoln and Johnson's view stated in their plans for Reconstruction. It also upheld the federal government's right to restructure Southern states' governments. This act further affirmed the power of the national government over the state governments. The notion of "separate but equal" was upheld by the Supreme Court decision in the 1896 case of *Plessy v. Ferguson*. The 1969 decision in *Brandenburg v. Ohio* protected the First Amendment right of the Ku Klux Klan and other inflammatory groups to hold rallies. The Fourteenth Amendment protected citizens' rights regardless of race or color.

266. (C) In the two part cartoon showing: woman, representing the South is seeing being forced to carry president Grant in a bag marked "carpet bag and bayonet rule." Meanwhile, Rutherford B. Hayes is depicted plowing under the carpet bag and bayonets with a plow. The plow is labeled "Let 'em alone policy." Meanwhile, in the background the military encampment of the first image is gone and now replaced with farmers growing crops and rebuilding destroyed structures, illustrating that the South is more prosperous with Hayes's more lenient actions.

267. (D) Ulysses S. Grant became a national hero because of his leadership during the Civil War. In 1868, he received an overwhelming majority of the electoral votes, though the popular vote remained relatively close against his Democratic opponent, Horatio Seymour. Many credit Grant's win to the support of African Americans who were exercising their newly established suffrage for the very first time. While Grant's administration is often remembered for being marred by corruption, he did oversee several important actions under Reconstruction. He passed legislation promoting black voting rights and oversaw the passage of the Fifteenth Amendment. He also signed the Civil Rights Act of 1875, giving African Americans equal treatment in jury selection and public accommodations. He also oversaw legislation including the Ku Klux Klan Act and the Enforcement Act to weaken the Klan, effectively wiping it out of existence until it reemerged in the twentieth century. He wanted to better unify the nation. This was illustrated by his signing of the Amnesty Act of 1872, which provided pardons to former Confederates. He favored limiting the number of troops to be stationed in the South, worried that too large a number would create resentment. At the same time, he tried to maintain enough to protect African Americans and suppress groups such as the Ku Klux Klan.

268. (B) While Reconstruction did extend many new rights and freedoms to former slaves, the idea of redistributing land was never put into action. Private property was seen as a vital right, so provisions for giving land to former slaves never were carried out. In the South, many plantation owners found themselves with their land but without labor and a means to pay hired hands. Meanwhile, former slaves and poor farmers found themselves with no land to support themselves. This led to the arrangement of sharecropping and tenant farming in the South. The plantation owners divided their land and gave it to the landless farmers to grow crops. At the end of the season, the sharecroppers would give a portion of the harvest to the landowner. This system often became corrupt. After failed harvests, the farmers often found themselves in debt to the landowners and would have to borrow against the following year's harvest. This cycle of debt often led to situations similar to that under slavery, creating a cycle of poverty for many poor planters.

269. (D) In 1873, a major Northern banking firm went bankrupt, triggering a long series of financial failures that included banks, railroads, and numerous other companies. As a result, millions of people lost their jobs. This depression lasted for five years, and many began to blame the Grant administration, which was plagued with charges of corruption during the two terms of Grant's presidency. Though the Republicans retained control of the presidency with the election of Rutherford B. Hayes, through what is often called a *corrupt bargain*, and maintained the Senate, they lost control of the House of Representatives.

270. (A) The 1875 Whiskey Ring Scandal was one of several scandals to plague the Grant administration. In 1875, it was discovered that officials in the administration were pocketing money collected from whiskey taxes. This was one of several corruption cases that emerged during the Grant administration. In 1872, it was discovered that shares of stock in the Crédit Mobilier, a railroad construction company, were being sold to members of Congress at a discounted rate well below market value. It was also discovered that congressmen accepted numerous bribes from both the Union Pacific Railroad and the Crédit Mobilier. Grant's administration was also found to be connected with the 1869 Black Friday Scandal, which involved illegal gold speculation. The Star Route Scandal of 1881 plagued the Garfield administration and involved corruption within the postal service. The Teapot Dome Scandal was one of multiple scandals to plague the Harding administration, while Whitewater marred the Clinton administration during the 1990s.

271. (B) In the 1876 election, the Republicans nominated Rutherford B. Hayes, while the Democrats nominated Samuel Tilden of New York. In the election, Tilden won the popular vote, but neither candidate received the necessary electoral votes after the elections were contested in four states, including three in the South: Florida, Louisiana, and South Carolina. The election was placed in the hands of a bipartisan committee consisting of members from both houses, as well as members of the Supreme Court.

272. (C) The Compromise of 1877 was the deal struck within the bipartisan electoral committee created to decide the outcome of the 1876 election. The Democrats agreed to give the presidency to the Republican candidate, Rutherford B. Hayes. Meanwhile, the Republicans agreed to remove federal troops from the South, construct another transcontinental railroad through Southern states, and end Reconstruction. With the removal of federal troops, many Southern states introduced various codes that greatly limited the rights and freedoms of African Americans, as well as institutionalizing segregationist policies. While laws such as the Force Acts continued, the army was no longer there to offer protection, and the decision of *United States v. Cruikshank* stated that the federal government could not enforce acts of discrimination made by individuals, further disenfranchising African Americans.

273. (B) In 1866, a group of former Confederate soldiers in Tennessee created a secret society they called the Ku Klux Klan. Membership in the society spread throughout the South, encouraged by Southern whites' fears of African Americans' newly found rights and freedoms. Much of the membership consisted of former Confederate leaders, who were excluded from pardons and therefore politics. As Reconstruction progressed, the violent acts of the Klan increased. Raids were conducted on black communities as well as on those who supported Republican reforms. Fear and intimidation were used to keep black communities from voting, as well as to force African Americans into a subordinate role in society. Congress responded by passing the Enforcement Acts in 1870 and 1871. These acts outlawed the use of terror and force to keep people from exercising their right to vote.

The military was also used to suppress the Klan's activities, helping to wipe out the Klan. The organization later reemerged in the post-Reconstruction years, however, and began to play a major role in politics in various regions throughout the nation.

274. (A) In response to the emergence of the Ku Klux Klan during the years following the Civil War, the federal government instituted laws to protect the rights of freedmen. One of these laws was the Force Acts of 1870. The Tenure Act of 1867 required the president to seek the approval of the Senate to remove officials the president had appointed. The act became the basis of Andrew Johnson's impeachment in 1868. The Reconstruction Act of 1867 divided the South into military districts.

275. (C) As Southern states met the demands of the Reconstruction Plans and were restored into the Union, many began to pass laws that restricted African Americans' rights. These laws were known as Black Codes. These codes were intended to keep newly freed slaves in their subordinate position, deny them political empowerment, and keep them out of certain sectors of the economy. Black Codes took the form of strict curfews, vagrancy laws, forced-labor contracts, and restrictions of property ownership. The Radical Republicans attempted to combat these actions through stricter Reconstruction measures, passage of equal-rights laws, and the use of the military. When Reconstruction ended, these codes continued and grew even more severe.

276. (D) The 1876 decision of *United States v. Cruikshank* was rooted in an 1873 conflict between a white militia and freedmen gathered in front of a Louisiana courthouse. The event became known as the Colfax Massacre. In the aftermath, several of the white militia members were tried under the Enforcement Act of 1870, which made it a felony for a group to conspire to deprive anyone of his or her constitutional rights. The Cruikshank decision found, however, that only the state governments, not the federal government, could try individuals under the act. This decision, as well as the 1873 Slaughterhouse Cases and the Civil Rights Cases of 1883, ruled that the Fourteenth Amendment protects citizens from rights infringements only on a federal level, not to the states. These actions effectively ended Reconstruction reforms intended to bring about equality and let the states begin to create further Black Codes and institute Jim Crow laws.

277. (B) After decisions such as the Cruikshank decision, Slaughterhouse Cases, and Civil Right Cases, states began to create laws segregating facilities and public accommodations. This notion of "separate but equal" was upheld by the 1896 *Plessy v. Ferguson* decision. This allowed segregated conditions to continue constitutionally until they were eventually overturned in the 1954 *Brown v. Board of Education* decision. The remaining Jim Crow laws were overruled by the Civil Rights Act of 1964 and the 1965 Voting Rights Act under the Lyndon B. Johnson administration.

Chapter 12

278. (C) The Civil Service Commission was created by the Pendleton Civil Service Reform Act in 1883 in the wake of James Garfield's assassination. It ended the spoils system by instituting a merit-based system, which required those seeking certain government jobs to take the civil service exam. It furthermore kept elected officials and appointees from firing public employees. This helped remove patronage from federal public employment.

279. (D) The Pendleton Act was passed on January 16, 1883, under the administration of Chester A. Arthur, in response to the assassination of President James Garfield by Charles Guiteau in 1881. Guiteau was a disgruntled Stalwart (member of the political faction within the Republican Party against civil service reform) who was hoping to receive a political appointment under the spoils system. The spoils system, also known as the patronage system, involved elected officials rewarding supporters with jobs or promoting public employees for political support. While the practice existed long before his administration, Andrew Jackson's administration is most associated with the term. It was derived in 1828 from the saying "To the victor belong the spoils." The Pendleton Civil Service Reform Act ended the spoils system and instituted a merit-based system. This law initially applied only to the federal government, allowing political machines to thrive at the state and local levels.

280. (C) Oliver Kelley, a former employee of the U.S. Department of Agriculture, established the National Grange of the Patrons of Husbandry in 1867. The Grange, as it became known, spread rapidly through the Midwestern farm belts following the economic Panic of 1873. Because of the panic, farmers began to suffer from the low prices of crops, increased amounts of debt, and unfair railroad shipping practices. The Grange soon evolved from a social fraternity into a political organization. During the 1870s, the Grange helped farmers establish cooperatives to bring down the price of farm equipment and supplies, cooperatively run grain elevators, and cooperatively run credit unions and banks. Eventually, the political wing of the movement was absorbed into the Farmers' Alliances of the 1880s and later the Populist Party in the 1890s.

281. (B) Farmers of the post–Civil War period experienced the rapid mechanization of agriculture. Improved plows, seed spreaders, and mechanical reapers, as well as steam-powered threshers and bailers, helped farmers cultivate larger amounts of land and reap larger harvests. This increased the supply of agricultural goods, lowering prices, and buying the new equipment, often caused the smaller farmers to accumulate debt. Often these smaller farms were absorbed by larger farms, increasing the average size of farms. Also, many poorer farmers called for the coinage of silver and the removal from the gold standard. This action would cause inflation, which would benefit farmers burdened with debt. Though farming was hard on the Great Plains, the continuation of homestead acts continued to draw settlers to the open lands of the West through the late nineteenth century.

282. (C) As the mechanization of farming began to increase following the Civil War, more land in the West was tilled, and production of agricultural goods increased rapidly. This drove down the price of these goods. To maintain a profit, farmers were forced to produce even more. This constant production of excessive surplus continually kept prices lower. Following the Panic of 1873, many farmers found themselves in severe debt from low prices as well as the cost of new equipment. This, in part, led to the emergence of the Grange and Farmers' Alliances.

283. (C) The McKinley Tariff, which was passed in 1890, harmed farmers because it increased the prices of farm equipment and failed to address the falling prices of agricultural goods. Furthermore, it helped lead to the Panic of 1893. Interestingly, the economic panic caused by the tariff in many ways helped its author, William McKinley, get elected to the presidency over William Jennings Bryan in 1896, after many voters blamed the Democrats for the continuing economic downturn. The Grange, Farmers' Alliances, and the Populist

Party were political organizations that strongly represented the interests of farmers, especially in the Midwest. The Homestead Acts helped people obtain free public land in the West.

284. (D) The Homestead Act of 1862 was signed into law by President Abraham Lincoln. Several subsequent homestead laws were created following this initial act. The act gave 160 acres of land to any citizen for free after payment of a registration fee. The homesteader then had to live on the land for five years, cultivating it, and build a permanent dwelling. Initially, the act was open to all white citizens, as well as immigrants who intended to become citizens. After the passage of the Fourteenth Amendment, African Americans also became eligible under the act. The system had many critics, and many complained that the best lands were often taken by land speculators, who would later sell the land for a profit.

285. (A) As the American railroad systems expanded following the Civil War, previously inaccessible regions throughout the United States became easily reached. This made farming in the West more profitable, and many people began to move to the West to become private landowners and farmers. Furthermore, homestead acts made land affordable to poor people from the United States as well as immigrants. This resulted in the forced removal of Native American tribes who occupied these western lands. The increase of farming and the introduction of new mechanized tools led to greater surpluses of agricultural goods, driving down their prices. The prices were further lowered as the European demand for American agricultural goods declined.

286. (A) The Morrill Land-Grant Act was passed in 1862 during the Lincoln administration, though an earlier version of the bill was passed by Congress in 1859 but vetoed by President Buchanan. The legislation was created to increase the number of colleges in the newly forming states in the West. It reflected the intentions described in the earlier Ordinance of 1785 and Northwest Ordinance of 1787, which called for land to be set aside for education purposes. Each state was given a certain amount of federal land, which the state would sell, using the profits to set up an endowment to create an institute of higher learning—a major boost for higher learning in the United States. Michigan State University, which was established in 1855 through a state-run land grant program, became the model for the Morrill Land-Grant Act.

287. (C) In the wake of the ending of Reconstruction in the late 1870s, many Southern states began to impose severe Jim Crow laws, which institutionalized racism and discrimination. Furthermore, with the withdrawal of federal troops, the African-American population had little protection from supremacy groups, such as the White League, which could freely terrorize black communities. With the passage of the Fourteenth Amendment, African Americans became eligible for free lands under the Homestead Act. Many families took advantage of this and began to move to the open lands of the Great Plains, especially after the 1879 Louisiana Constitutional Convention declared the right to vote could be decided only by the state and not the federal government. Nearly 6,000 African Americans moved to Kansas in what has been called the Kansas exodus or exoduster movement.

288. (C) The Dawes Severalty Act was passed in 1887 to deal with the distribution of Native American lands in what is now Oklahoma. The act divided the lands in the reservations into individual, privately owned plots in hopes of forcing the Native Americans to adopt Western cultural practices of farming and the nuclear family, forcing them to abandon communal ownership. This action also interfered with traditional religious and tribal government practices. In addition, the size of the land parcels distributed was often not large enough to sustain a living, furthering poverty on the reservations. In 1936, Congress issued the Meriam Report, which illustrated the fraud and mismanagement of Native Americans by the Department of Indian Affairs, which enforced the Dawes Act. The report also found that the Dawes Act illegally deprived Native Americans of their land rights, and further use of the act was ended.

289. (C) In 1874, General Oliver Howard, who earlier served as commissioner of the Freedman's Bureau, was sent to Idaho to fight in what are now called the Indian Wars. In 1877, he ordered that the Nez Percé tribe be relocated to a reservation despite an earlier treaty negotiated by Chief Joseph that ensured the tribe's right to the Wallowa Valley. When the Nez Percé resisted removal, Howard's troops used force, declaring their disobedience an act of war. After the American forces began to attack the Nez Percé, Joseph began to lead his tribe to Canada. Before they could reach the border, however, they were stopped by the army and were forced to surrender and relocate to Oklahoma.

290. (B) While historians debate the true origins of the Ghost Dance, it became prominent among numerous Native American groups in the 1880s. The ritual called for the peaceful end of the violence inflicted by the white settlers that continually stripped the Native Americans of their land. It also was believed that it would bring the tribes back to their traditional roots. After 1890, the Sioux Nation was forced onto reservations. In response to the hardships, the Sioux began to practice the Ghost Dance, even though it was outlawed by the Bureau of Indian Affairs (BIA). The BIA blamed Chief Sitting Bull for letting his people continue the ritual and sent federal troops to the reservation to arrest him, leading to the Battle of Wounded Knee, or the Wounded Knee Massacre. This event marked the end of the Indian Wars. The Ghost Dance was similar to that of Tenskwatawa's movement prior to the War of 1812 in that it also called for a rejection of white culture and technology and a return to traditionalism.

291. (B) Frederick Jackson Turner published what has become known as the Frontier Thesis in 1893. He argued that the United States' continual expansion into its westward frontier was important in defining the growth of the American character, as well as American democracy. He stated that the harshness of the wilderness stripped settlers of many of their European elements and allowed for more truly American traits such as individualism and egalitarianism to take root.

292. (B) Historian Frederick Jackson Turner released his Frontier Thesis in 1893, as the western frontier was deemed closed after the completion of the Transcontinental Railroad and the increase of population in the western states. He argued the West and expansionism during the nineteenth century positively affected American government and society. He noted that the frontier made Americans different from Europeans by helping them develop a truly unique culture.

293. (A) "Robber baron" was the nickname given by critics to the heads of industry during the period following the Civil War. Also known as captains of industry, these men dominated their particular area of business and amassed enormous fortunes. Examples include Andrew Carnegie in the steel industry, Cornelius Vanderbilt in railroads, and J. P. Morgan in banking and investment. By the 1890s, 90 percent of the nation's wealth was held by less than 10 percent of the population. The term robber baron was derived from what was seen by many as nefarious business practices, such as the use of monopolies and trusts, ill treatment of labor, and price fixing.

294. (A) In a monopoly, a business has dominant control over a product or service so it can limit competition or make itself a nearly sole provider. In the image, this is illustrated by the images of the stages of steel production on the blocks Carnegie has stacked. Early legislation such as the 1890 Sherman Anti-Trust Act attempted to limit this practice and promote fairer competition, though the law was rarely used against business until the early twentieth century under Theodore Roosevelt's administration. Monopolies that defined the post–Civil War period included John D. Rockefeller's Standard Oil Company. Another example of an early American monopoly was U.S. Steel. It was created by investor J. P. Morgan when he combined Andrew Carnegie's steel company with two other steel companies. The end result was the world's first billion-dollar industry.

295. (B) Vertical integration is a management strategy where a business controls all aspects of a commodity's production from start to finish. As depicted in the image of Andrew Carnegie, his steel company controlled the mines that produced the ore as well as the coal needed to process it, the mills that produced the steel, and the ships and trains needed for transportation. By controlling every aspect of production, the company could manage prices better and beat out competition, allowing Carnegie to obtain a near monopoly on American steel production.

296. (A) John D. Rockefeller's Standard Oil serves as an example of horizontal integration as a business practice. Beginning as a corporation in Ohio in 1870, the company acquired or put out of business almost all competing refineries. It soon expanded internationally, becoming one of the world's first international companies, controlling a majority of the world's refineries. This allowed it to control production as well as prices. Rockefeller's monopoly was eventually broken up into 34 separate companies in 1911 under U.S. antitrust laws.

297. (C) The Sherman Anti-Trust Act, passed in 1890, marked the federal government's first true attempt to limit trusts, cartels, and monopolies. A trust is a business formed with intent to control an area of commerce. A cartel is a group of independent businesses formed to regulate production and prices of goods among members. A monopoly is a business with such dominant control over a product or service that it can limit competition or make itself nearly a sole provider. While the law was intended to create a fairer playing field for businesses and industry, it was not truly pursued until Theodore Roosevelt's administration. In fact, one of its earliest direct applications was against unions involved in the 1894 Pullman strike.

298. (B) As illustrated in the cartoon, the Sherman Act is depicted as fog which limits the view of the individual standing on the boat labeled American Business. Businesses are being presented as navigating into unclear territory, as the Justice Department, symbolized by the buoy, is also obscured, further adding to the climate of uncertainty.

299. (C) The Pullman strike of 1894 occurred after George Pullman cut wages in response to the depression in 1893. A union leader of the American Railway Union named Eugene V. Debs responded by organizing more than 120,000 workers to strike. It was announced that railroad workers would not run any trains that used Pullman cars. Though the strike was based in Chicago, the strike shut down rail lines across the nation. Eventually, the federal government, citing the Sherman Act, intervened by passing an injunction against the union, making the boycott illegal, and employing federal troops to break up the striking workers. The injunction, which was upheld in the courts, served as a major setback for labor, though the strike did lead to investigations of Pullman's business practices.

300. (C) The U.S. Supreme Court's 1886 decision in the case of *Wabash, St. Louis and Pacific Railway Company v. Illinois* ruled that only the federal government can regulate commerce that extends beyond state boundaries. The decision led to the creation of the Interstate Commerce Commission in 1887. The Hepburn and Elkins Acts of 1903 were passed during Theodore Roosevelt's administration. The acts strengthened the Interstate Commerce Commission by increasing the agency's enforcement powers. The Comstock Law, enacted in 1873, banned the shipment of obscene or lewd mail through the postal service. While the law was originally used to limit pornography, it was later used to limit the shipment of contraceptives.

301. (A) The Interstate Commerce Act, which was passed in 1887 under the administration of Grover Cleveland, created the Interstate Commerce Commission (ICC). The ICC was a federal agency created to address public concerns over unfair railroad practices such as rate fixing and rebate programs that hurt small farmers and interfered with fair business competition. It also was to address railroad companies' influence over politics, especially in railroad towns. The government was to have the power to determine maximum rates and to stop discriminatory practices. The act and the agency were initially unsuccessful, since the ICC was not given any real enforcement powers. This was later addressed under Theodore Roosevelt's administration with the passage of the Elkins and Hepburn Acts of 1903, which increased the agency's regulatory power.

302. (C) Both the Knights of Labor and the American Federation of Labor (AFL) directly discuss the negative impact of emerging monopolies and trusts had on the American Worker. The Knights of Labor declaration states, "Development and aggressiveness of great capitalists and corporations" were leading to the "pauperization" of workers. Samuel Gompers, the president of the AFL, discusses "the power of wealth and concentration of industry" could potentially lead to conditions similar to slavery for the American worker.

303. (B) The Knights of Labor was established in 1869, and unlike the earlier National Labor Union, it organized individuals instead of just unions. It allowed a diverse membership of skilled and unskilled labor, with the exception of professional gamblers, lawyers, bankers, and people who sold liquor. Besides these exceptions, it did not discriminate, making it one of the first labor organizations that allowed membership regardless of gender, race, or ethnicity. The union collapsed in response to the Haymarket riot, and the American Federation of Labor (AFL) emerged in its place. Led by Samuel Gompers, the AFL initially allowed only white, male, skilled laborers to join.

304. (A) In May 1886, workers at the McCormick Harvester plant in Chicago and other protesters gathered outside to argue for an eight-hour workday. Tensions between protesters and law-enforcement officers were high after four workers were killed by police on a previous day. At one point, someone in the crowd threw a bomb at the police, who then opened fire. In the resulting chaos, seven police officers and four protesters were killed, and more than sixty others were injured. Ultimately, the Knights of Labor, which was heavily involved with the strike, became associated with anarchists and soon collapsed. Public opinion became critical of unions, and the movement for an eight-hour workday was greatly delayed.

305. (B) The quotation is an excerpt from William Jennings Bryan's "Cross of Gold" speech given in 1896 at the Democratic nominating convention in Chicago. The speech was extremely well received at the time; Bryan was reportedly carried out on the shoulders of cheering supporters after he completed it. Election historians still consider it to be a quintessential piece of American oration. The speech was given in response to the debate of bimetallism, after the Coinage Act of 1873 placed the nation on a strictly gold standard. This directly hurt western farmers, and a push for a return of bimetallism or the silver standard became a focus of the Populist Party, which supported Bryan in the 1896 election.

306. (D) In the election of 1896, the Republicans recaptured the White House with William McKinley's defeat of the Democratic candidate, William Jennings Bryan. Bryan was able to capture the support of both the Populist Party and Democrats. He also earned the support of western farmers through his support of bimetallism. Though he met previous elections with limited success, he was praised as a master orator and was seen as the spokesman of the western farmers still suffering from the Panic of 1893. However, Bryan failed to win the support of the pro-business wing of the Democratic Party, which occupied many of the eastern states. The eastern states were also weary of Bryan's mostly Populist platform, which was seen as anti-business and anti-railroad. The passage's opening even alludes to the Eastern states wariness of Bryan's positions. Furthermore, McKinley's campaign outspent Bryan's by a considerable margin. The election was close; McKinley sealed the election with 51 percent of the popular vote.

307. (B) The Populist Party emerged out of the earlier Farmers' Alliances of the 1870s and 1880s. It first appeared in 1887 as a national third party. It was created in response to industrialism and the concentration of wealth in the hands of large banks and big business. The party called for banking reform, blaming the Panic of 1873 and the following economic downturn on unfair banking practices. The Populists called for the end of the national banking system, which never happened; instead, the Federal Reserve was created in 1913. Furthermore, they called for the nationalization of the railroads. This platform emerged mainly from the farmers who made up a major constituency of the party. They were against the unfair rate and rebate systems, which hurt small farms. These ideas led to accusations of socialism within the party. Rejecting the concentration of wealth, the Populists also called for a graduated income tax. This meant one's tax rates would increase as his or her income increased. Steps to institute this policy began in 1894 with the Wilson–Gorman Tariff, which imposed a uniform tax. The Populists' major focus was ending the gold standard and instead opting for "free coinage of silver." The Populists' 1896 presidential nominee, William Jennings Bryan, gave his famous "Cross of Gold" speech calling upon the nation to move away from the gold standard.

308. (B) Tammany Hall was the Democratic political machine that dominated New York City politics through the mid-twentieth century. The machine gained most of its strength by providing services such as finding jobs and housing for the numerous immigrants who flooded into the city. In return for these services, the machine obtained the ability to control the immigrants' votes and get its candidates into elected offices. The machine then used these elected officials to provide it with services and sometimes just illegal public funds. One of the most notable leaders of Tammany Hall was William Marcy Tweed, better known as Boss Tweed. Tweed's ring became notorious for municipal graft and overcharging for services and contracts. The famous American cartoonist Thomas Nast began to use his political cartoons to bring attention to the illegal actions of the Tweed Ring, and it was eventually brought down in 1871. Tammany, however, continued into the next century.

Chapter 13

309. (B) Seward's Folly refers to the U.S. purchase of Alaska from Russia in 1867. The purchase was engineered by Secretary of State William H. Seward and Tsar Alexander II for the cost of $7.2 million. At the time, Alaska was seen as a barren wasteland, and the purchase of the nearly 600,000 square miles of northern land was called Seward's Folly or Seward's Ice Box. Later, Alaska was found to possess mineral resources of gold and oil that were worth many times what the United States had spent on the purchase. This action was one of several taken by Seward that greatly expanded the international influence of the United States. In 1865, Seward reaffirmed the Monroe Doctrine by arranging to have 50,000 American troops sent to the Texas–Mexico border to resolve the Maximilian Affair, where France tried to instate its own puppet regime in Mexico. Furthermore, in 1867, the year in which the Alaska territory was purchased, he arranged for the annexation of the Midway Islands. This new territory in the Pacific provided an important military base and coaling station, further fostering trade with Asia.

310. (D) While Guam, the Philippines, and Puerto Rico were all acquired with the 1898 signing of the Treaty of Paris, Hawaii was annexed several years after a coup overthrew the ruling monarchy of Hawaii. American missionaries began to arrive in Hawaii in the 1820s, and by the 1850s, American sugar plantations began to dominate the islands' economy. By 1872, native Hawaiians were only a minority population on the island, and American business interests began to dominate the island's government. In 1893, the American business interests staged a revolution backed by the U.S. military, forcing Hawaii's last queen, Liliuokalani, to relinquish control and recognize the new government. While calls for the United States to formally annex the island began as early as 1894, they were rejected until 1898, when the administration of William McKinley formally annexed the territory.

311. (C) The Hay–Bunau Treaty was signed on November 18, 1903, by John Hay, the secretary of state under Theodore Roosevelt, and Philippe Bunau-Varilla, who was serving as minister to the United States for the new nation of Panama. The treaty gave the United States complete control of the 10-mile-wide Canal Zone, allowing for the construction of the Panama Canal to begin in May 1904. Philippe Bunau-Varilla, who was born in France, was the chief engineer of France's attempt to construct a canal through the Isthmus of Panama in the 1880s. He also convinced the United States to choose Panama (which at the time was part of Colombia) as the location for its attempt to build a canal linking the Atlantic and Pacific.

312. (D) In 1895, Richard Olney, the secretary of state under President Cleveland, ordered Britain to settle a boundary dispute it had with Venezuela through U.S. arbitration. This expanded the Monroe Doctrine beyond merely closing the Western Hemisphere to Europe and established the United States as the lead arbitrator in the Western Hemisphere. While Perry's opening of trade with Japan in 1854, as well as John Hay's 1899 Open Door Policy, were important expansions of American foreign policy, they dealt more with Asia, which is beyond the Monroe Doctrine's focus on the Western Hemisphere.

313. (C) The "insular cases" were the subject of a Supreme Court decision in response to the acquisition of the new territories of Hawaii and the land gained after the Spanish–American War. With these new lands, people began to debate whether new territories received full constitutional protections and rights. From 1901 to 1905, the Supreme Court made a series of rulings stating that the Constitution fully applied only in incorporated territories (Alaska and Hawaii), but not in unincorporated territories (Guam and the Philippines). This allowed Congress to make the final call on whether new U.S. possessions gained constitutional privileges or not.

314. (B) In 1890, Alfred T. Mahan published *The Influence of Sea Power upon History*, arguing the importance of a strong, modern navy to maintain national strength. He argued that history illustrated that a highly developed modern navy and use of blockades could overpower a well-established land army. He also argued that the United States needed to accomplish several goals to maintain a modern navy, as illustrated by Britain throughout the nineteenth century. He argued for a canal through the isthmus of Central America, as well as numerous bases and coaling stations throughout the Pacific to promote trade with Asia. Mahan's work directly influenced the foreign policy of President Theodore Roosevelt, as illustrated by his leadership in the construction of the Great White Fleet, the completion of the Panama Canal, and his support for the Open Door Policy in China. Even the Roosevelt Corollary to the Monroe Doctrine can be seen as an extension of Mahan's arguments for the importance of naval power.

315. (A) Mahan states, "We have not the navy, and, what is worse, we are not willing to have the navy." During the late nineteenth century, American production, both agriculturally and industrial, produced a surplus of goods, which caused the United States to look for markets overseas. Mahan argued that a strong navy was needed to obtain and protect these new markets and trade routes.

316. (A) Because of improved technologies in the post–Civil War period, U.S. industry and agriculture had grown beyond the nation's rate of consumption. Business and political leaders believed that foreign markets were essential to further economic growth, so they promoted a more proactive foreign policy. This was one of numerous factors that promoted American overseas expansion. Other factors included ideas such as social Darwinism and Rudyard Kipling's "White Man's Burden," which promoted the idea that the superiority of Western culture should be spread to underdeveloped regions. Frederick Jackson Turner's Frontier Thesis, which stated that the American frontier was the source of culture, further inspired expansion into new frontiers to maintain the American spirit. Naval strategist Alfred T. Mahan's *The Influence of Sea Power upon History* (1890) advocated expansion as crucial for the United States to become a world power.

317. (B) In 1899, Secretary of State John Hay sent notes to France, Germany, Britain, Italy, Japan, and Russia, stating no country would extend its sphere of influence over China that would close Chinese markets to other Western powers. This would keep Chinese markets open to all of the major powers, especially the United States. While none of the nations agreed to the Open Door Policy, Hay announced in March 1900 that all of the countries had accepted the terms. The Open Door Policy showed little success early on, but the principles were reasserted in the Nine Powers Treaty signed in February 1922. The policy officially ended with the Japanese invasion of China during World War II. Still, the foreign policies of Theodore Roosevelt, William Taft, and Woodrow Wilson focused on maintaining an open door to trade with the abundant Chinese markets.

318. (B) The Anti-Imperialist Leagues began in New England following the start of the Spanish–American War in 1898. The leagues grew in size and included prominent Americans such as Mark Twain and William Jennings Bryan. The leagues' views were mixed between pragmatism (belief that an overseas empire would be too costly to maintain and require an expensive, enlarged military) and racism (worries that an overseas empire would lead to an influx of nonwhite immigrants). Other beliefs of anti-imperialists reflected more sentimental notions that American imperialism violated the self-determination of distant lands. In the end, however, America's business interests, with their need for new raw materials and expanded markets, won out, and the United States continued to expand its overseas possessions.

319. (A) Valeriano Weyler was sent to Cuba in 1888 to quell the disorder caused by the insurrectos, revolutionaries fighting for Cuban independence under the leadership of José Martí. Weyler set up concentration camps to crush the rebellion. Conditions in the camps were extremely harsh; prisoners lacked proper food, water, and other necessities. Nearly 30 percent of those interred within the camps died because of this. Reports of these actions were sent back to the United States, and American newspapers nicknamed Weyler "Butcher Weyler." Stories of atrocities at the camps and other sensationalized reports, known as yellow journalism, helped convince the United States to declare war on Spain in 1898. Victoriano Huerta was a dictator during the Mexican Revolution. Wilson attempted to overthrow Huerta after he staged a coup and murdered Mexico's elected president, Francisco Madero, in 1912.

320. (B) On February 15, 1898, the USS *Maine* exploded in Havana Harbor, Cuba. While the actual cause of the explosion was debated, the United States blamed the Spanish military and used the action as a pretense for war. On April 25, 1898, President McKinley formally issued a declaration of war. In 1976, nearly a century after the fact, another investigation found that the cause of the explosion was most likely not a Spanish mine. The *Constitution* is one the United States' oldest naval vessels, commissioned in 1797. The *Maddox* was the U.S. ship involved in the Gulf of Tonkin incident that led to the escalation of the Vietnam War. The *Chesapeake* helped spark the War of 1812 after it was attacked by the British ship *Leopard* and four members of its crew were impressed.

321. (D) On April 19, 1898, both houses of Congress adopted the Teller Amendment to the declaration of war issued against Spain. The amendment stated that the United States would not annex the island nation of Cuba, but instead leave it in the hands of the Cuban people. The Teller Amendment was replaced in 1901 by the Platt Amendment, which extended the U.S. sphere of influence over Cuba. Under the Platt Amendment, the United States had the right to override decisions made by the Cuban government and directly intervene if Cuba became unstable. It also granted the United States territorial rights in the Guantanamo Bay Naval Base. The 1898 Treaty of Paris ended the Spanish–American War, causing Spain to relinquish its claims to most of its remaining colonial possessions. It gave Cuba its independence and gave the United States control of the Philippines, Puerto Rico, and Guam. The Hay–Bunau Treaty gave the United States control over the Panama Canal Zone.

322. (B) Publisher and newspaper tycoon William Randolph Hearst issued the famous quote to artist Frederic Remington, who was stationed in Cuba with the goal of reporting on atrocities taking place there. This served as an example of yellow journalism, sensationalized news reporting used by the major newspapers to compete for readers. Hearst and Joseph Pulitzer, who controlled the press at the time, attempted to outdo each other's papers as a part of the fierce competition to attract each other's readers. The stories concerning Cuba helped the revolutionaries in Cuba gain American sympathies and eventually push for war to free Cuba from Spanish control. Muckraking journalism was another prominent form of journalism during the period.

323. (C) The Roosevelt Corollary was issued in 1904 by President Theodore Roosevelt. It was announced in response to the Dominican Republic's government going bankrupt earlier that year. Attempting to keep European powers, such as Germany, from interfering with Latin American and Caribbean nations that had fallen into debt, Roosevelt created this addition to the Monroe Doctrine. In the corollary, the United States asserted the right to intervene within these states to "stabilize" their economic affairs. This notion was extended to include not only economic instability, but also political unrest. In addition to justifying involvement in the Dominican Republic, the corollary was cited as justification for the United States to act in Cuba, Nicaragua, Mexico, and Haiti. In this manner, the doctrine is often said to have allowed the United States to act as an international police force in the Western Hemisphere.

324. (A) Roosevelt, Taft, and Wilson continue the initial notion of the Monroe Doctrine of keeping the Western Hemisphere closed to colonization by European powers. While Roosevelt noted that the United States would act as an international policing presence, and would use military forces to protect United States interest (which was not an initial part of the Monroe Doctrine), both Taft and Wilson deviate from these ideas. While the United States did continue some aspects of Washington's call for neutrality with regards to Europe, which was part of the initial Monroe Doctrine, all three policies did call for greater involvement in international affairs within the western hemisphere.

325. (C) Dollar diplomacy is associated with the foreign policy of William Howard Taft. It described the efforts under President Taft to further the U.S. policy aims in Latin America and East Asia through economic power. Unlike McKinley's Gun Boat diplomacy or Theodore Roosevelt's Big Stick diplomacy, Taft's approach advocated exchanging "dollars for bullets." In other words, his administration encouraged U.S. bankers to invest in foreign areas of strategic concern to the United States, such as East Asia and Latin America. Much of this effort was led by Secretary of State Philander C. Knox, who regarded the State Department as effectively an agent of the corporate community. This policy was clearly illustrated in Costa Rica and Honduras, where the United Fruit Company had a tight grip on just about every sector of the economy, so these nations came to be referred to as "banana republics." Taft's Dollar diplomacy is also illustrated by the 1909 revolt in Nicaragua. The United States quickly backed the insurgents, who were supported by U.S. mining interests. Following this, Knox encouraged U.S. bankers to invest in Nicaragua and offer substantial loans to the new regime, giving the United States increased financial leverage over the country. President Wilson attempted to move away from both Big Stick diplomacy and Dollar diplomacy with his Moral or Missionary diplomacy. Later, Hoover would introduce the Good Neighbor Policy in Latin America, though the policy itself is generally credited to Franklin Roosevelt. This policy called for the withdrawal of American troops and treatment of Latin American nations more as equals.

326. (D) Unlike Theodore Roosevelt's Big Stick diplomacy and Taft's Dollar diplomacy, Wilson's policy was based on a belief that the United States needed to use the promotion of American values and democratic institutions to promote international security. The practice became known as Moral or Missionary diplomacy. Wilson moved from an era of diplomacy focused on force or finance to a policy committed to justice, democracy, and Christian values. This policy was illustrated when Victoriano Huerta seized power in Mexico, killing the elected president, Francisco Madero. Despite the urging from many in the United States, Wilson refused to recognize the government, calling it a "government of butchers." Wilson's policy of Moral diplomacy was not always successful. In 1914, he ordered the U.S. Marines to invade Veracruz after American sailors had been detained in what was called the Tampico Incident. William Taft's urging of U.S. banks to refinance Haiti's national debt serves as an example of Dollar diplomacy, and Herbert Hoover's removal of troops from Nicaragua illustrates the later Good Neighbor Policy.

327. (B) While Wilson's policy was a rejection of Big Stick Diplomacy, as noted in both the speeches of Roosevelt and Wilson, the two presidents discuss the importance of the completion of the Panama Canal. However, as noted in his speech, Wilson rejected the methods used to obtain the canal, stating, "the United States will never again seek one additional foot of territory by conquest." The goal of the 1907 Gentlemen's Agreement was to reduce tensions between the United States and Japan, the two most powerful nations of the Pacific. The agreement was made between President Theodore Roosevelt and the emperor of Japan. In the agreement, the United States agreed not to place restrictions on Japanese immigrants or students, provided Japan limited further emigration to the United States. The policy was based on the nativist and anti-Japanese sentiments emerging in California during the late nineteenth and early twentieth centuries. As a result of the policy, the number of Japanese coming to the United States was reduced, and in return, California allowed Japanese students to attend public schools.

328. (C) Vice President Theodore Roosevelt stated the now-famous words "Speak softly and carry a big stick" at the Minnesota State Fair in September 1901, 12 days before the assassination of President William McKinley put him into the presidency. He also had used the slogan earlier in personal correspondence. Roosevelt borrowed the expression from an African proverb, implying that power was available to retaliate if necessary. He felt that the United States should actively pursue a policy of peace while at the same time brandishing military might. This sentiment became the basis of President Theodore Roosevelt's foreign policy, often referred to as Big Stick diplomacy, which placed a strong focus on the U.S. commercial interests in Latin America. It was also further illustrated in his issuing of the Roosevelt Corollary to the Monroe Doctrine, asserting the right of the United States to intervene in troubled states in the Western Hemisphere to promote stability. Some illustrations of Big Stick diplomacy can be seen in the creation of the Great White Fleet (a modern navy that traveled the globe to display American naval might), Roosevelt's involvement in the Venezuelan dispute with Great Britain, and the construction of the Panama Canal. Roosevelt's diplomacy is further illustrated by his use of military force as justification for U.S. intervention in Cuba and Nicaragua. Roosevelt's Square Deal was his election platform in 1904, dealing with domestic policy.

329. (A) Booker T. Washington and W. E. B. Du Bois were two influential leaders of the fight to obtain social equality for America's disenfranchised African Americans. While they shared the same fight, they differed greatly in their envisioned methods. Washington called for accommodation, where African Americans would "cast their bucket where they stood." While assimilation both socially and economically was his eventual goal, he focused first on social equality earned through the hard work of African Americans. He believed that their primary focus should be in vocational education, and over time, future generations would rise up politically and economically. Dubois rejected this notion, which he referred to as the acceptance of "alleged inferiority of the Negro." He instead believed African Americans should obtain a liberal arts education and pursue skilled professions, seeking immediate political and economic equality alongside social equality. This belief would later lead Dubois in his role in founding the Niagara movement in 1905, when he stated, "We want to pull down nothing but we don't propose to be pulled down." He also later joined the NAACP and worked as the editor of its chief publication, *The Crisis*.

330. (A) From 1793 to 1803, Toussaint L'Ouverture led the island of Haiti to independence. In doing so he made Haiti the first independent state in the Western Hemisphere to outlaw slavery. Gabriel, Vesey, and Turner all refer to leaders of slave uprisings in the United States during the first half of the nineteenth century. In 1870, Joseph Rainey of South Carolina became the first African American elected to Congress. Also in that year Hiram Revels was elected the first African-American senator.

331. (C) W. E. B. Du Bois and William Monroe Trotter began the Niagara movement in 1905 to push for the end of the racial segregation and disenfranchisement of African Americans. The organization also rejected the calls for accommodation made by black leaders such as Booker T. Washington. The Niagara movement was eventually absorbed by the National Association for the Advancement of Colored People (NAACP) in 1911.

332. (A) The establishment of the NAACP in 1909 was probably the greatest achievement by African Americans during the Progressive Era. The NAACP consisted of African-American leaders and white social justice reformers and was created in response to the 1908 race riots in Springfield, Illinois. The organization established the mission to fight racial segregation and disenfranchisement of African Americans in the courts. As the organization grew, it directly fought against Jim Crow laws. The NAACP's success was highlighted by the 1915 Supreme Court ruling in *Guinn v. United States*, which overturned practices that had kept African Americans from being eligible to vote because of the Grandfather Clause, as well as the 1954 Supreme Court decision in *Brown v. Board of Education*, which helped overturn *Plessey v. Ferguson*, which had legalized the notion of "separate but equal."

333. (B) The 1896 Supreme Court decision in *Plessy v. Ferguson* upheld the constitutionality of racial segregation in public accommodations in what became known as the doctrine of "separate but equal." This allowed Southern state governments to pass Jim Crow laws, which further disenfranchised African Americans. The basis of *Plessy v. Ferguson* began when Homer Plessy, who was one-eighth black, challenged a Louisiana law that segregated railroad cars. Plessy argued that the segregated railroad cars violated his Thirteenth and Fourteenth Amendment rights. The Supreme Court disagreed, stating that segregation was acceptable as long as equal accommodations were provided.

334. (B) Muckraking journalism refers to an early twentieth-century reform and expose writing. The writers in this movement attempted to create detailed accounts of social and economic hardships, as well as political corruption, which was at the focus of Progressive Period reforms. The term itself originated with Theodore Roosevelt, during a 1906, where he referenced a section of John Bunyan's *The Pilgrim's Progress. Yellow journalism* is generally defined as late-nineteenth-century journalism revolving around the two publishing magnets of the period, Joseph Pulitzer and William Randolph Hearst. While this type of journalism is often associated with the beginning of the Spanish–American War, the name actually has its origin in the fact that both publishers featured the period popular comic *Hogan's Alley* and its featured character, the Yellow Kid.

335. (C) As depicted in the image, the witch's plume is labeled "Scandal monger" and the caption makes a play on a nursery rhyme, describing the absurd action of sweeping cobwebs from the sky. Furthermore, the witch is seen flying on a muckrake. These illustrate the pejorative use of the term *muckraker journalism*, where writers were criticized for their overly critical reports on what they saw as societal problems. Critics of these journalists saw this as sensational journalism to bolster sales through creating fake controversy.

336. (A) Progressive Period journalists, known as muckrakers, included Ida Tarbell, whose "History of the Standard Oil Company" (1904) exposed the cutthroat business practices used by the Standard Oil Company to eliminate competition. Lincoln Steffens wrote *The Shame of Our Cities* (1904), which exposed municipal corruption and the ties between government and big business. Upton Sinclair's *The Jungle* (1906), besides being in part a manifesto for socialism, helped inspire the Food and Drug Act by illustrating the dangerous and unsanitary conditions in the meatpacking industry. Samuel Hopkins Adams's work "Drugs That Make Victims," published in *Collier's Weekly* in 1905, was an exposé on fraudulent medicines that often contained dangerous and addictive chemicals. His work helped inspire stricter regulation of pharmaceuticals.

337. (B) During the 1836 presidential election, the Anti-Mason Party held the first nominating convention. Party supporters elected delegates who would attend the party convention and vote for the party candidate the electors supported. Soon after, the other major parties adopted the practice. During the Progressive Era, numerous additional reforms were made to the political system, giving the common person more access to government. Many states began to instate the initiative, which allowed average citizens to put bills before state legislatures. Furthermore, referendums, which gave citizens the right to vote directly on bills, became more common within state governments. Citizens were also given the power to remove elected officials from office with the recall. Finally, in 1904, Oregon began to elect its senators directly, rather than having them chosen by the state legislature. In 1913, this practice became constitutional law with the ratification of the Seventeenth Amendment, which required all states to choose their senators through direct elections.

338. (C) Socialists sought to end or reduce private ownership of the means of production, while progressives felt change could be achieved by making government more responsive and reforming the current system.

339. (A) Florence Kelley, the daughter of an influential Pennsylvania congressman, gained her own prominence as a leading reformer for workplace safety and against unsafe working conditions and child labor. In 1893, the governor of Illinois made Kelley the chief factory inspector for the state of Illinois, where she fought against child labor. In 1899, she joined the National Consumers' League, which fought to address the harsh conditions found in sweatshops. Furthermore, in 1907, she worked to sway opinion in the Supreme Court case *Muller v. Oregon*, which limited the maximum workday for female employees.

340. (B) The 1911 fire at the Triangle Shirtwaist factory was one of the largest industrial disasters in New York City history. Nearly a 150 men and women died in the fire. This high number was due to the common practice of locking factory workers inside the building during the workday to avoid theft and unnecessary breaks. In response to the fire, progressive reformers such as Frances Perkins pushed for increased workplace safety laws as well as the passage of workers' compensation laws. The fire also caused the International Ladies' Garment Workers' Union to increase in size and prominence as the union joined the fight for reform. Political machine bosses such as Al Smith, who was the Democratic presidential candidate in 1928, also joined the call to reform labor conditions in New York City factories.

341. (C) The 1908 case of *Muller v. Oregon* led to a landmark decision in labor history because it upheld the right of states to enforce limits on the hours a woman was required to work because of health-related reasons. The case was argued by future Supreme Court justice Louis Brandeis. Interestingly, a state law limiting working hours in New York was struck down in the 1905 *Lochner v. New York* decision. The 1917 *Bunting v. Oregon* decision extended *Muller v. Oregon* by allowing the state to limit the hours men worked as well.

342. (D) While Roosevelt did expand America's international influence through his corollary to the Monroe Doctrine and his mediation of the conflict between Russia and Japan, the Square Deal dealt only with his domestic program. Theodore Roosevelt announced his Square Deal in 1904. In the Square Deal, Roosevelt would pursue antitrust suits. Over the course of his presidency, he broke up nearly 44 trusts and monopolies. At the same time, Roosevelt wanted to protect business from extreme union demands. This was illustrated by his dealings with the United Mine Workers strike, where he addressed both the miners' and owners' concerns. By way of promoting consumer protection, Congress passed the Pure Food and Drug Act, creating the Food and Drug Administration (FDA), which allowed for the government to inspect meat products and outlawed the production, sale, or shipment of dangerous medicines. The Antiquities Act of 1906 and the expansion of national parks and monuments helped establish the precedent for future conservation activities.

343. (B) Though predating the official platform of the Square Deal, during the Roosevelt administration, Congress passed both the Elkins Act (1903) and the Hepburn Act (1906), increasing the federal government's ability to regulate the railroad industry. The Elkins Act forced railroads to notify the public if they changed their rates, and it made it illegal for railroads to offer or receive rebates. The Hepburn Act allowed the Interstate Commerce Commission (created under the Interstate Commerce Act of 1887) to set maximum rates for the railroads. It also limited the railroads' ability to give out free passes and forced them to adopt a uniform method of accounting.

344. **(B)** In 1908, Theodore Roosevelt handpicked William Taft to be his successor and continue his policies. One area in which Taft was successful in continuing Roosevelt's policies was in breaking up trusts. While Roosevelt distinguished good trusts from bad trusts, Taft actively went after all trusts that were in violation of the law. This created tensions when he pursued U.S. Steel, a trust allowed by Roosevelt. Overall, while Taft had many character traits that would make him ideal for his later role on the Supreme Court as a justice, he fell short of many of Roosevelt's expectations. His secretary of the interior, Richard Ballinger, sold many of the lands protected under Roosevelt's conservation program and fired Gifford Pinchot as head of the U.S. Forest Service. In foreign policy, Taft adopted what was called Dollar diplomacy instead of Roosevelt's Big Stick diplomacy. While Taft did not support women's suffrage, Roosevelt did not truly make it part of his platform either until he ran for president again (this time against Taft) in 1912 under his New Nationalism platform.

345. **(A)** While Roosevelt's platform of New Nationalism shared many similar ideas with Wilson's New Freedom, the two platforms differed in their views of how trusts should be dealt with. Wilson did not believe that trusts should be regulated; instead, they should be broken up. He argued that businesses should be made smaller, but government should not be made bigger in the process. However, both Roosevelt and Wilson believed in the importance of a strong president, as illustrated by the progressive reforms instituted by both Roosevelt and Wilson domestically, as well as their actions in foreign policy. Also, both Roosevelt and Wilson believed in lowering the tariffs, especially after Taft's poor dealing with the Payne Aldrich Tariff of 1909, which further increased tariffs, hurting western farmers. Wilson's 1913 Underwood Tariff was the greatest lowering of federal tariffs since the Civil War.

346. **(A)** The Clayton Antitrust Act was passed in 1914 during the Wilson administration. The act gave the federal government greater strength in regulating business and controlling the formation of monopolies and trusts. The act directly defined illegal business conduct and practices such as companies issuing noncompetitive rebates and directors sitting on multiple boards of competing companies. It also gave the federal government the power to regulate mergers. Furthermore, unlike the earlier Sherman Anti-Trust Act, this law did not make labor unions and farm organizations subject to antitrust laws, so workers' rights to strike, boycott, and picket were made legal. Furthermore, injunctions were deemed illegal. This law marked a major step forward for organized labor, though World War I limited unions' further progress.

347. **(C)** The Federal Reserve was created under the 1913 Federal Reserve Act, which was passed to reorganize American banking by creating a decentralized private banking system under federal control. This new system addressed the pressing financial needs of the country at the time, which included moving credit out of eastern banking centers to make it more widely available, as well as better controlling the amount of money in circulation. Wilson did address the needs of farmers by signing the 1916 Farm Loan Act, which set up regional banks that could offer loans to farms at low interest. He also signed the Clayton Antitrust Act in 1914 to give the Federal Trade Commission (created under the Federal Trade Act) more power to enforce antitrust laws. The 1913 Underwood Tariff was significant because it marked the first substantial lowering of U.S. tariffs since the Civil War. From this point, the U.S. government's main source of revenue shifted from tariffs to money received through the federal income tax. The income tax had just been established as legal under the Sixteenth Amendment.

Chapter 14

348. (C) Wilson's statement illustrates the core of Moral diplomacy, which was the foreign policy of the Wilson administration. Gunboat or Big Stick diplomacy was the policy of Theodore Roosevelt; Dollar diplomacy was the foreign policy of Taft; and the Good Neighbor Policy was initiated by President Hoover and expanded under the presidency of Franklin Roosevelt.

349. (A) When the war began in Europe in 1914, the U.S. population was very much divided amongst religious and ethnic lines. Many Catholics, along with those of German and Austrian ancestry, supported the Triple Alliance (Germany, Austro-Hungarian Empire, and for a time Italy). The Irish objected to any support of Britain. However, those of French and English descent supported the Triple Entente of the United Kingdom, France, and the Russian Empire.

350. (D) Fascism is a political ideology that places the nation and its often autocratic leader above the individual citizen. It is often accompanied by fanatical nationalism and rejection of the socialist political ideology. In the wake of World War I, numerous European states began to adopt fascist regimes. After Italy received what it believed was an unfair deal with the Treaty of Versailles, Benito Mussolini rose to power and installed a fascist regime. It forcefully destroyed the socialist party and created a single-party authoritarian state. Hitler's rise to power through his Nazi Party in Germany also illustrates the creation of the fascist state in the years following the First World War. While the assassination of the Archduke Franz Ferdinand by Serbian nationalists in 1914 ultimately led to the first shots of the First World War, numerous underpinnings served as the "long fuse" that created the environment for the largest military conflict in history to that point. The rise of imperialism during the nineteenth century, as illustrated by the race to Africa and the partitioning of Asian markets, created tensions among European nations. One expression of these tensions was the First and Second Moroccan Crisis, in which Germany attempted to intervene in French-held Morocco. To better control and protect their empires, nations created large armies and navies. These large militaries were made possible by an increase in populations as well as by factories, which made mass production possible. Furthermore, nations began to create interconnected secret alliances for military protection, as well as to isolate rival powers. After the assassination of the Austrian archduke, other nations were brought into a conflict that did not directly concern them. Finally, jingoism, or extreme nationalism, created immense patriotism that fueled popular support for wars.

351. (B) Interwoven treaties brought the major nations of Europe into the First World War, while the U.S. policy in the early twentieth century still in many ways followed George

Washington's call to avoid creation of intertwining treaties. Wilson was elected in 1916 in part because of the notion that he had kept the nation out of war. In doing so, he hoped he could lead the peace following the conflict. This is illustrated through Wilson's Fourteen Points, which laid out his plans for maintaining international peace. Neutrality was also initially important because the U.S. population consisted of people from all nations. Ethnic Germans and Irish supported the Central Powers (Germany, Austria, and the Ottoman Empire), while Slavic peoples supported the Allies (Great Britain, Russia, and France). Furthermore, the connection of a common language caused others to support Britain and its allies. Businesses also found it profitable to maintain neutrality because it allowed them to openly trade with both sides of the conflict.

352. (B) On January 22, 1917, President Wilson made one last attempt to call for the end of the First World War with a "peace without victory." Germany had recently begun to make considerable gains in the fighting in Europe, and on January 31, 1917, Germany announced it would resume unrestricted submarine warfare. The announcement led Italy to join the Allied forces, because it was worried that it would lose access to the Adriatic Sea. This use of unrestricted submarine warfare would also challenge the naval blockade Britain had in place since 1915. For the United States, the use of unrestricted submarine warfare gave the nation little choice but to go to war, but Wilson waited for an "actual overt act" to take place. This act occurred when German submarines sunk seven unarmed American merchant ships and British intelligence agents intercepted the Zimmerman telegraph, which called for Mexico to ally with Germany against the United States.

353. (D) On January 8, 1918, Woodrow Wilson issued his Fourteen Points, which illustrated the president's vision for sustained peace following the First World War. The Fourteen Points addressed what Wilson believed to be the causes of the war, promoted self-determination among nations, and created the League of Nations to help maintain peace and security in the postwar world. The league would prevent future conflicts through disarmament agreements, peacefully resolving disputes between members and working for the common defense of member states. The league was ultimately rejected by the United States over concerns that it would interfere with American independence in its foreign policy and possibly drag the nation unwillingly into future European conflicts. While the league ultimately failed, it served as a prototype for the future United Nations.

354. (D) Over 300,000 African Americans served in the First World War, albeit in segregated units. However, most were not able to serve in combat and instead were assigned to manual labor. The U.S. Marine Corp refused to accept African Americans altogether. Yet those who did see combat often served with distinction. An example of this was the 369th Infantry Regiment, also known as the Harlem Hell Fighters who earned Frances Croix de Guerre, the country's highest combat medal.

355. (C) The Great Migration during the First World War refers to the mass migration of African Americans from the South to cities in the North and Midwest. Between 1910 and 1920, nearly 1.75 million individuals relocated. The reason for this migration was the increased demand for factory workers, especially in war industries. An example of new access to industrial jobs was Ford's opening of his factories to African-American employees in 1914. Furthermore, the Southern agricultural economy was experiencing an extended period of agricultural decline. Matters were made worse by the boll weevil, an insect that decimated Southern crops. Finally, many African Americans had become fed up with the continued discrimination and segregation that had become institutionalized in the Southern states. However, these new immigrants in the North were often faced with extreme prejudice in their new homes as well. The competition with white workers for jobs created tensions that often erupted into violence, as illustrated by the 1919 Chicago race riot, in which 38 people were killed and 520 injured. This migration did help the formation of cultural movements such as the Harlem Renaissance and allowed the early civil rights moment to expand.

356. (D) In the text, Wilson states, "Every power and resource we possess, whether of men, of money, or of materials, is being devoted and will continue to be devoted to that purpose until it is achieved." The War Industry Board was created on July 28, 1917, after the United States had declared war on Germany and its allies. In January 1918, it was reorganized under the direction of Bernard M. Baruch. The major focus of the board was to coordinate the purchase of war supplies, set price controls at wholesale levels, and mediate between labor and business to avoid strikes. Another agency set up during the war was the Food Administration, which was created under the Lever Food and Control Act and led by Herbert Hoover. His task was to ensure the production of food. He fixed the price of American grains, which greatly bolstered the income of American farmers. His work in this agency gained him national prominence as a great pragmatist, which eventually won him the presidency. The Lever Food and Control Act also created the Fuel Administration, which instituted daylight saving time to reduce the use of lamp oil during the summer months. The government also created the Committee of Public Information (CPI), which was headed by the journalist George Creel. The CPI had the job of ensuring public support for the war through films, speeches, radios, and other uses of media. The CPI also held massive rallies to promote the sale of war bonds, which helped finance the war. In 1917 and 1918, the government also passed the Espionage and Sedition Acts, which were designed to quell vocal opposition to the war.

357. (D) In May 1917, the U.S. government passed the Selective Service Act, authorizing a draft of young men to fill the shortage of soldiers needed for military service. After the United States initially declared war on Germany, the U.S. military was still relatively small, and only roughly 32,000 new soldiers had enlisted. When General Pershing arrived in Europe with America's initial force, he quickly realized that many more soldiers would be required. The Selective Service Act required that all men ages 21 to 30 register for military service, and the following year, the requirement was extended to include all men ages 18 to 45. In a departure from earlier uses of the draft, such as during the Civil War, the men called to service could not hire a substitute. Furthermore, while the Civil War draft led to massive riots, the World War I draft met with relatively little resistance; it generally had great support.

358. (B) The Espionage Act, passed in 1917, made it a crime to interfere with military operations and recruitment. It also outlawed acts that promoted insubordination within the military or any other action that might support America's enemies during the war. In 1918, this law was amended to include the Sedition Act, which prohibited many forms of speech that were considered derogatory toward the government or the military. Eugene V. Debs, a labor organizer and perennial socialist presidential candidate, was arrested for violating this act in 1918 by giving a fiery speech against the draft. He was sentenced to ten years in prison but was pardoned after three years by President Harding.

359. (B) The Wilson administration was blamed for problems left from the First World War, which included abuses of civil liberties under the Espionage and Sedition Acts, the League of Nations controversy, and the strikes and inflation that followed the war. Warren G. Harding was nominated as the Republican candidate for president, and Governor Calvin Coolidge of Massachusetts was the vice presidential nominee. Their platform opposed the League of Nations and promised low taxes and high protective tariffs. They also called for restrictions on immigration to achieve what Harding called a return to normalcy. The actions illustrated the move toward isolationism and the pro-business environment that would define the three Republican administrations of the 1920s.

360. (C) Under the Harding and Coolidge administrations, much of the strong push for increased government regulation of the progressive movement declined and many industries benefited from the lack of regulation, which allowed for a trend of consolidation. Furthermore, the practice of buying stock on margin would lead to a growth of the investment industry.

361. (C) During his inauguration address in the January of 1961, John F. Kennedy closed with his now famous line, "And so, my fellow Americans ask not what your country can do for you, ask what you can do for your country." This line echoes the statement made in Warren G. Harding's address to the Home Market Club in Boston during his presidential campaign.

362. (C) On November 11, 1918, the fighting in World War I officially ceased. Yet the challenges created by the conflict were by no means over. By 1919, nearly 4,000 American servicemen were returning home per day, yet the government had made no plans to help them merge back into society. With wartime production slowing, government regulation of industries ending, and the job positions filled during the war, the nation faced massive job shortages. Women, who had played a major role in the war industries during the conflict, were pressured to resign or were fired to free up positions for returning men. Returning white soldiers found they had been replaced in their civilian jobs by African Americans. The resulting economic recession marred the first part of the 1920s and further fueled racial tensions within the United States.

363. (B) From November 1919 through January 1920, the U.S. Department of Justice attempted to capture and deport whoever they saw as leftist radicals and anarchists. These raids, led by Attorney General Mitchell Palmer, were in the context of the greater Red Scare (fear of communist and socialist subversion) taking place within the nation. This Red Scare was triggered in part by the Russian Revolution of 1917, as well as by tensions with organized labor following the First World War, as illustrated by the strike and bombing plots in Seattle during 1919. Palmer set up a special force to monitor and arrest those suspected of being against the U.S. government, especially those accused of being communists, socialists, or anarchists. On January 2, 1920, federal agents stationed in more than 33 cities arrested several thousand people suspected of having radical or leftist beliefs. The Red Scare and the Palmer raids began to lose momentum by May 1920, and many of those arrested were ordered to be released.

364. (C) The 1920s were a period when the ideas of isolationism and nativism became once again prominent. Though the Ku Klux Klan had been mostly wiped out during Reconstruction, it began to reemerge starting in 1915. Yet unlike the organization of the late nineteenth century, the new Klan used modern recruitment and funding techniques and expanded greatly in size. Also, it was no longer isolated to the South but dominated politics in Northern states such as Indiana. Furthermore, the targets of this hate group were no longer just African Americans. The group also began terrorizing Catholic and Jewish communities, along with immigrant populations. The activities of the Klan began to decline after the leader of the Indiana Klan was found guilty of raping a minor in 1925. The National Origins Act further illustrated nativist feelings during the 1920s. The law, passed in 1924, established the first permanent limitation on immigration into the United States and established the first quota system based on national origin. While many of the American policies during the 1920s illustrated isolationism and nativism, other actions, such as the Washington Naval Conference and the Kellogg–Briand Pact, were attempts to maintain peace through international agreements. The Volstead Act of 1918 and the Eighteenth Amendment, ratified in 1919, illustrated the final success of the temperance movement to outlaw the general consumption of alcohol.

365. (A) The Supreme Court's *Schenk v. United States* decision of 1919 upheld the constitutionality of the 1917 Espionage Act, stating in an opinion written by Oliver Wendell Holmes Jr. that speech presenting a "clear and present danger" is not protected under the First Amendment. The case was in response to the arrest of Charles Schenk, who violated the Espionage Act by mailing leaflets to people in an attempt to interfere with the government's efforts under the Selective Service Act. Holmes argued that Congress has a right to protect society from words that could cause needless endangerment of the greater population, such as falsely shouting "Fire!" in a crowded theater. The Schenk decision was modified by the 1969 *Brandenburg v. Ohio* decision, which stated that the government cannot punish subversive speech unless it directly incites a lawless act or crime. The Brandenburg decision also states that First Amendment rights also protect the rights of subversive groups such as the Ku Klux Klan. "Separate but equal" was found constitutional in the *Plessy v. Ferguson* decision in 1896, but that decision was repudiated by the 1954 decision in *Brown v. Board of Education*.

366. (C) Sacco and Vanzetti were immigrants from Italy who were also believed to be anarchists. In 1920, they were convicted of killing two men during an armed robbery in Massachusetts. In 1927, they were executed for the crime. Many critics at the time believed that the authorities and the decisions in the trial were strongly influenced by prejudice against immigrants and fears of subversives brought about by the Red Scare. The execution of the two men was protested internationally as well as within the United States.

367. (A) The Kellogg–Briand Pact, signed in 1928, prohibited the use of war except in matters of self-defense. The idea was originally drafted by Secretary of State Frank B. Kellogg and French foreign minister Aristide Briand. Fifteen nations initially signed the pact, and later they were joined by sixty additional countries. The pact's assertion of outlawing war was idealistic, and it eventually proved ineffective as the underpinnings to the Second World War emerged in the late 1930s. The 1921 Washington Conference resulted in three disarmament treaties (the Four-Power Treaty, the Five-Power Treaty or Washington Naval Treaty, and the Nine-Power Treaty), which limited the size of the world's largest navies. Starting with Herbert Hoover, but most notably championed by Franklin Roosevelt, America adopted the Good Neighbor Policy toward Latin America. Under the Good Neighbor Policy, the United States would promote security and peace within the Western Hemisphere through nonmilitary means.

368. (B) As part of Wilson's Fourteen Points for creating peace after World War I, he called for the creation of the League of Nations. The league was to be an organization that would represent the countries of the world and help ensure security and peace among its member states. Many in the United States rejected the idea of the league, feeling it would interfere with the independence of America's foreign policy. Article X in particular became a sticking point, especially for many Republican senators. The article stated that an attack on one member state would be considered an attack on all other members. The senators felt that this type of agreement could potentially drag the nation into another world war. Ultimately, the United States rejected membership in the League of Nations. Without the United States, and given Russia's rejection of membership, the league's success was greatly limited. Most notably, it was unable to prevent the Second World War. It did, however, serve as a working model for the later creation of the United Nations following World War II.

369. (A) During the nineteenth century, colonization societies formed and encouraged free Americans of African descent to return to Africa. The American Colonization Society, which was founded in 1816, included notable members such as Thomas Jefferson and James Monroe. Liberia was founded in 1821 in part due to these societies. During the 1920s, Marcus Garvey and his organization, the Universal Negro Improvement Association (UNIA), launched its own Back to Africa movement and negotiated settlement with the Liberian government. However, the Liberian president ultimately rejected the organization's proposal and would not allow its members to enter.

370. (D) During the 1920s, Harlem became the epicenter for an artistic and literary awakening among the African-American population that has become known as the Harlem Renaissance. In the decades from 1914 to 1929, the population of African Americans living in the Harlem area of New York City grew to nearly 200,000. Jazz musicians such as Duke Ellington and Louis Armstrong, poets such as Langston Hughes, and writers such as Alain Locke created works that celebrated the African-American culture and greatly influenced American society as a whole.

371. (B) The 1925 Scopes Trial illustrated the debate over conservative and fundamentalist religious beliefs verses modern scientific notions of human evolution and natural selection. The trial occurred after a teacher named John Scopes challenged a Tennessee law that banned the teaching of evolution in public schools. The nationally acclaimed lawyer Clarence Darrow defended Scopes against the state's representation by the famous politician William Jennings Bryan. Though Scopes lost the case, the media circus surrounding it brought the struggle between traditional values and modern beliefs to the national level.

372. (C) In 1928, the Republican candidate, Herbert Hoover, easily won the election against the Democratic candidate, Al Smith. Many Americans were suspicious of Smith, the former governor of New York, because he was Catholic and spoke with a distinct New York accent. Many feared that because Smith was Catholic, he would take orders from the pope, which would hurt American sovereignty. Smith also called for the repeal of Prohibition, a view that was unpopular to many conservatives. Hoover, in contrast, was extremely popular and nationally known as a great pragmatist for his role in providing aid to Europe following the First World War. Hoover campaigned on the notion of continued prosperity based on the Republican platforms that defined the decade.

Chapter 15

373. (B) As illustrated in the graph as well as in history, during the period noted on the chart, Republican presidents including Taft, who supported the Payne–Aldrich Tariff, Harding, who supported the 1924 Fordney–McCumber Tariff, and Hoover who supported the 1930 Hawley–Smoot Tariff saw increases in tariffs. Conversely, Democratic president Wilson oversaw the implementation of the 1913 Underwood Tariff, which was the greatest lowering of federal tariffs since the Civil War.

374. (B) In 1924, Congress passed the Fordney–McCumber Tariff, which raised America's protective tariffs on imports from other nations to historically high levels. The 1930 Hawley–Smoot Tariff increased these levels further. This hurt Europe's ability to pay off its debts, because it became nearly impossible to raise money by exporting goods to the United States. Furthermore, many European nations responded by passing retaliatory tariffs that made it difficult to sell American goods abroad. As a result, international trade declined drastically, leading to the economic instability that resulted in the prolonged global depression of the 1930s. The tariffs further hurt farmers because prices of manufactured goods increased at the same time it became harder for them to sell agricultural products to foreign markets. Consequently, much of the financial prosperity of the 1920s would never be realized by Midwestern farmers.

375. (D) October 29, 1929, has become known as Black Tuesday because nearly 16.5 million shares of stock investments were hurriedly sold, causing the market to plummet. Prior to that day, bankers attempted to pool their money to buy enough stock to stabilize the increasingly volatile markets. Despite their efforts, the market continued to crash. Numerous factors are blamed for the crash. Some economists see high tariffs of the 1920s and failed policies of the Federal Reserve as major catalysts of the crash. Others blame the practice of buying on margin (buying stocks with loaned money) as a major cause because it artificially inflated stock prices. Still others blame irresponsible banking practices mixed with a decline in consumer spending.

376. (B) The practice of buying on margin was a system where investors could purchase a stock at a fraction of its actual price and borrow money to cover the rest of the stock's cost. Brokers could charge high rates of interest and at any time could demand full payment for the remainder of the money owed. If the stock price rose, the investor could sell the stock, repay the money, and still make a profit. If the stock price declined, however, investors were still responsible to repay the broker.

377. (C) "Buying on margin" was a popular practice of buying stocks in the 1920s. A consumer could buy a stock with only roughly 10 percent of its cost by taking a loan for the rest of its value. By the end of the 1920s, up to 90 percent of the purchase price of stocks was being made with loaned money. This inflated the price of stocks, while at the same time increasing demand. However, when the market declined, the investors with stocks purchased on margin could not repay their loans which had a rippling effect that also negatively affected banks, which could not regain the loaned money.

378. (A) From 1937 to 1938 the United States faced a recession that lasted for nearly 13 months. Prior to the downturn, production, wages, and profits were on a considerable rise, though unemployment remained high. This had negative repercussions for President Roosevelt, who claimed previous economic improvement was a direct result of his New Deal programs. With the recession, business groups and conservatives used the recession as evidence that the same New Deal programs were in fact negative for business growth.

379. (D) As noted in the document, when the market crashed in 1929, Hoover believed the key to recovery was a renewal of confidence in the economy. He felt the best way to address the economic conditions was through the voluntary controls put into place by private businesses. He organized a meeting of the nation's economic leaders at which they promised to maintain wages and employment. However, as the economy worsened, this plan failed. Hoover also attempted to protect American businesses by signing the Hawley–Smoot Tariff into law in 1930. This protective tariff, the highest in the nation's history, ended up further stifling international trade, which worsened the Depression. He also established the Reconstruction Finance Corporation in 1932 to prop up large corporations and banks. Despite these efforts, banks continued to fail, and unemployment rose.

380. (B) The Reconstruction Finance Corporation (RFC) was established by Herbert Hoover in 1932 to provide credit to banks, railroads, farm mortgage associations, and other businesses to prevent further failures and collapse in these areas of the economy. The other goals refer to programs that were part of Franklin Roosevelt's First and Second New Deal. The program that provided relief to homeowners facing foreclosure was the 1933 Homeowners Loan Corporation (HOLC), which offered low-cost mortgage refinancing. The program that attempted to increase the prices of agricultural goods by paying farmers to produce less was the Agricultural Adjustment Administration, also created in 1933. Several programs provided work relief for the unemployed by hiring them to complete public works projects such as roads and buildings and by funding arts programs; these programs included the Civilian Works Administration, Public Works Administration, and Works Progress Administration. To provide old-age pensions, disability payments, and unemployment benefits, the government established the Social Security Administration in 1935.

381. (A) During the 1920s and 1930s, the famous British economist John Maynard Keynes argued that the government could best address economic crises such as the Depression through spending. He felt that if the government gave money to consumers, either with direct government payments or indirectly through government jobs, people would purchase more consumer goods, and the economy would begin to grow. This idea is the basis for what is called Keynesian economics and also has been referred to as pump priming. Later, during Ronald Reagan's presidency, this theory was rejected, and the idea of supply-side economics was adopted. Under this theory, also known as trickle-down economics, the government should cut taxes to businesses and investors, allowing the businesses to expand and hire more workers, thereby allowing the economy to grow.

382. (A) In some ways, those participating in the Bonus Army protest rejected the notion that, "No governmental action . . . can replace that God-imposed responsibility of the individual." During the summer of 1932, nearly 20,000 veterans of the First World War and their families gathered in Washington, D.C., to ask for the immediate payment of a pension bonus they had been promised. The pension was not to become available until 1945, but the marchers found themselves unemployed and penniless following the stock market crash and ongoing Depression. The House of Representatives agreed to their request, but the Senate firmly stood against it. While some of the marchers left, many stayed and established "Hoovervilles," shacks constructed of cardboard and scrap metal. General Douglas MacArthur was ordered by Hoover to remove the Bonus Army. MacArthur used force to do so, and many of the veterans were injured. This image of excessive force being used against downtrodden veterans of the U.S. military contributed to Franklin Roosevelt's landslide election in 1932.

383. (D) The election of 1932 marked a significant change in the way Americans viewed the role of government and the individual citizen. Hoover himself stated in 1932 that the election would be a "contest between two philosophies in government": Hoover's belief that the federal government could not and should not try to fix the average citizen's problems, versus Roosevelt's view that the Great Depression could be solved only through direct government action in the form of far-reaching programs and direct relief. Hoover's attempt to address the Depression through limited assistance and voluntary self-regulation of business seemed to fail, so Roosevelt was elected in a landslide, promising the nation a New Deal. The New Deal consisted of a wide range of government relief programs, new regulations, and recovery acts that affected all aspects of American business and society.

384. (A) Al Smith, a conservative former Democratic presidential candidate, helped established the American Liberty League to oppose the New Deal. The group stated its mission as to uphold the Constitution and fight Roosevelt's program, which it felt illustrated socialist tendencies. Huey Long was initially a strong supporter of Roosevelt. Additionally he often criticized banking houses such as Morgan and Rockefeller. Upton Sinclair also initially supported FDR; however, like Long, Sinclair eventually became critical of the president because they felt his reforms did not go far enough. Wallace served on Roosevelt's cabinet.

385. (D) Established in 1933, the Civilian Conservation Corps provided government works jobs to young single men, primarily in the area of conservation. The Emergency Banking Act, also known as the Glass–Steagall Act, was set up to regulate bank transactions, the Agricultural Adjustment Act regulated crop production, and the National Recovery Administration attempted to set up codes of fair competition and assist workers in collective bargaining. The Securities and Exchange Commission was set up to monitor the stock exchange.

386. (C) Established in 1934, the Security and Exchange Commission is charged with supervising the stock exchange and the securities industry. The National Labor Relations Board, created under the Wagner Act, dealt with labor practices, while the Social Security Act provided pensions for the elderly and aid to people with disabilities. The Federal Emergency Relief Act helped states provide aid for the unemployed, and the Federal Deposit Insurance Corporation helped insure bank deposits.

387. (C) The National Recovery Administration (NRA) was established in June 1933 as part of the National Industrial Recovery Act (NIRA). The purpose of this New Deal agency was to respond to the decline of industrial prices, the failure of many businesses, and the corresponding unemployment. The agency established industry codes to ensure fair business practices and regulated wages, working conditions, and working hours. The agency's symbol was the Blue Eagle, and businesses that participated with the NRA placed

Blue Eagle posters in their storefronts. However, the Supreme Court's 1935 decision in *Schechter v. United States* declared the program unconstitutional, and NIRA was replaced by the National Labor Relations Act, which shifted government support to unions. The Civilian Conservation Corps and the Works Progress Administration provided direct relief to America's unemployed by offering government jobs in federal works projects. The Home Owners' Loan Corporation offered relief to home owners by allowing them to refinance their mortgages at a lower cost to avoid foreclosure. The Tennessee Valley Authority developed the Tennessee Valley and brought electricity into the region.

388. (B) The "Brain Trust" was the nickname given to President Roosevelt's unofficial advisors, whom he assembled during his campaign. They included prominent academics and leaders of business such as economist Rexford Tugwell and political scientist Raymond Moley.

389. (C) In 1935, President Franklin Roosevelt launched what has become known as his Second New Deal, or Second Hundred Days, in part to respond to his critics who stated he had not done enough for the average citizen's welfare. This was clearly illustrated through the 1935 Social Security Act, which established the Social Security system. Under this system, the government would provide support to those unable to support themselves. It included old-age pensions, unemployment insurance, and aid for the disabled. Furthermore, programs under the Second New Deal imposed tighter controls on business and gave more support to unions, as illustrated by the 1935 Wagner Act. This legislation protected union practices such as collective bargaining while outlawing spying on union activity and blacklisting union members. The Second New Deal also offered further job relief for the poor, such as the Works Progress Administration, which provided government jobs to nearly eight million adults, and the National Youth Administration, which offered education, recreation, employment, and counseling for young adults (ages sixteen to twenty-five).

390. (D) Upton Sinclair, the muckraking author of *The Jungle*, and Huey "Kingfish" Long, a senator from Louisiana, initially supported Roosevelt's rise to the presidency. Yet they soon began to rally against the president because they felt he did too little to address the needs of the poor or address the imbalance of wealth in the nation. Sinclair, in his bid for the governorship of California, called for higher inheritance and income taxes as well as pensions for the elderly. Huey Long called for a minimum income for all families of $5,000, paid for by dividing up the wealth of millionaires. Long was considered a possible challenger for the presidency in 1936 but was shot and killed at the Louisiana statehouse in 1935.

391. (B) Another notable critic of Roosevelt's New Deal was Father Charles Coughlin, a radio evangelist, who used his weekly broadcasts to openly criticize the president's policies. He held a strong stance against international banking and called for nationalizing banks, utilities, and natural resources.

392. (A) Not all critics supported nationalization and redistribution of wealth. William Randolph Hearst, a onetime supporter of the Democratic Party, criticized Roosevelt's heavy taxes on the wealthy and the inheritance tax. Other politicians, including Robert Taft, the Republican senator from Ohio, saw the New Deal as creeping socialism. The American Liberty League, which emerged in 1934, spearheaded much of the New Deal opposition. The league was headed by Alfred Smith, the former Democratic challenger to Herbert

Hoover. It included numerous heads of business and politicians, who argued that the New Deal violated the Constitution and was leading the nation to Bolshevism.

393. (C) The Dust Bowl occurred in the Midwest from 1931 to 1940. It resulted from intensive farming practices that stripped the ground of the prairie grasses. When a massive drought hit and crops failed to grow, high winds sweeping over the plains carried off much of the remaining soil into massive dust clouds. These storms became known as "black blizzards" that reached as far as the East Coast. Nearly 60 percent of Midwestern farmers lost their farms during this period, many migrating to California to find work as agricultural laborers. John Steinbeck captured the plight of these displaced farm families in his celebrated novel *The Grapes of Wrath*.

394. (C) The Agricultural Adjustment Act of 1933 was designed to provide direct aid to farmers by providing direct government assistance to farmers who agreed to cut production of certain crops. It was believed that by lower production, the price of the crops would increase. The act was being paid for in part by placing a tax on companies that processed the crops. The Home Owners Loan Corporation did often some indirect assistance to farmers and others by helping individuals refinance mortgages and avoid foreclosure. The Wagner Act, on the other hand, was designed to define unfair labor practices and mediate differences between employers and workers. The Civil Works Administration was a program designed to reduce unemployment by creating federal jobs.

395. (A) While the New Deal programs were often discriminatory, not allowing African Americans into professional or skilled-labor opportunities, Roosevelt often sought the advice of African-American public policy advisors, often called the "Black Cabinet" or the Federal Council of Negro Affairs. The cabinet focused on civil rights and racial inequality. However, Roosevelt, not wanting to alienate Southern Democrats, declined to support anti-lynching legislation or bans of the poll tax in the South. Members of the Black Cabinet included Dr. Robert Weaver, a Harvard economist who advised on race relations. In 1966, Weaver became the first black cabinet member, serving under Lyndon Johnson as secretary of housing and urban development.

396. (B) Many of the federal relief programs developed during the Depression furthered racial segregation in the country. African Americans often found themselves barred from professional and skilled-labor job opportunities. The Social Security Act, passed in 1935, excluded farmers and domestic workers, an area of employment that contained a majority of African-American workers. Furthermore, policies during the Depression did little to address discrimination in private businesses. White businesses would often fire minority workers to open job opportunities for whites. Roosevelt, who appointed numerous African Americans to midlevel government posts and created an unofficial "Black Cabinet," rejected anti-lynching laws and the banning of poll taxes. A. Philip Randolph, an influential civil rights leader, did convince Roosevelt to create the Fair Employment Practices Committee, which enforced a ban on discriminatory hiring in the federal government and in corporations that received federal contracts.

397. (B) Founded in 1940, the America First Committee (AFC) was one of the largest antiwar movements in American history. The committee used its massive membership to create a petition to force President Roosevelt to maintain neutrality. The group staunchly fought against the Lend–Lease program and rejected the Atlantic Charter. Other goals of the organization further illustrate its isolationist ideals: the AFC supported heavily fortifying the United States by pursuing an impregnable system of defense, as well as ending all aid to warring nations. The AFC contained many notable members, including future president Charles Lindbergh, but the organization fell apart after the Japanese surprise attack at Pearl Harbor.

398. (D) The Lend–Lease program began in March 1941 with the passage of the Lend–Lease Act. Its intent was to allow the U.S. government to lend, lease, or sell military supplies and defense aids to any nation that the United States deemed vital for the defense of America. Roosevelt compared the policy to lending a hose to a neighbor if one saw that the neighbor's house was on fire. During the war, nearly $50 billion in goods were appropriated to this program. Aid was initially offered to Britain and France. Later, the Soviet Union was also permitted to take part in the program after it entered the war following Hitler's June 22, 1941, invasion of nearly three million men crossing the German–Soviet border. While economic recovery was not initially the program's intent, the increased wartime production that was in part due to the Lend-Lease program helped pull the United States out of the Great Depression. In September 1939, prior to the start of the Second World War, the United States was already providing aid to protect democratic governments on the European continent. During the Spanish Civil War, the United States provided non-weapon goods to the republican government's Loyalists against Franco's fascist uprising on what was called a cash-and-carry basis. This was done with the passage of the Third Neutrality Act in May of 1937.

399. (D) From early in Roosevelt's presidency, he and his use of executive power were greatly criticized by such groups as the American Liberty League. Programs such as the NRI were directly challenged in court, and later Roosevelt's attempt to change the composition of the Supreme Court further fueled concerns of executive overreach.

400. (D) In response to the 1931 Japanese invasion of the iron- and coal-rich Chinese province of Manchuria, the United States issued the Stimson Doctrine. The doctrine stated that the United States would not recognize any territorial gains taken by force. The doctrine had little effect on Japanese policy. The Japanese proceeded to set up a puppet government in Manchuria. When the League of Nations protested, Japan withdrew from the organization. Japan then violated the 1922 Five Powers Treaty and began to enlarge its navy. After Japan forced the Vichy government (the puppet government established in France by Germany) to allow it to construct military bases in southern Indochina (modern-day Vietnam) in 1941, Roosevelt froze all Japanese assets within the United States. Japan responded by doing the same to U.S. assets in Japan. This brought trade between the two nations to a halt. The United States ultimately declared war on the Japanese on December 7, 1941, after Japan's planes bombed the U.S. naval base at Pearl Harbor. This action brought the United States into the Second World War. The Good Neighbor Policy refers to a program started by Coolidge and Hoover but most notably continued by Roosevelt. The Good Neighbor Policy, as announced at the conference of Latin American nations in 1933, aimed to end American armed intervention in the region. The United States instituted this policy in 1934 by ending the Platt Amendment and withdrawing U.S. forces from Haiti. The first Neutrality Act, passed in 1935, was one of three neutrality acts passed before the United States' entrance into the Second World War. The act was written in response to the Italian invasion of Ethiopia. The first Neutrality Act stated that the United States would not sell or ship arms to nations involved in a conflict and warned U.S. citizens traveling to such regions that they did so at their own risk. The 1936 second Neutrality Act expanded the first to include prohibitions on loaning money or credit to warring nations. The third Neutrality Act, passed in 1937, gave the government more flexibility by allowing the president to permit the sale of non-war-related materials on a cash-and-carry basis. This was in response to the civil war in Spain, where fascist forces under General Francisco Franco overthrew the republican government in the summer of 1936.

401. (A) The Nine-Power Treaty was created in 1922 and signed on February 6th that year at the Washington Naval Conference. The signatories of the treaty included the United States, Belgium, Great Britain, China, France, Italy, Japan, the Netherlands, and Portugal. The purpose of the treaty was to maintain the Open Door Policy, which was established by John Hay between 1899 and 1900, by protecting Chinese sovereignty by maintaining its independence and territorial integrity.

402. (A) After Japan's successful attack on Pearl Harbor on December 7, 1941, the Japanese military began to absorb the islands of Guam, British-held Hong Kong, and Singapore. In the spring of 1942, the Japanese military defeated a combined force of American and Filipino troops. General Douglas McArthur was forced to retreat from the island on March 10, 1942. At that point, he delivered his immortal promise, "I shall return," and escaped with his troops to Australia. MacArthur was true to his promise and launched his Philippines campaign in October 1944, securing the island nation with the conclusion of the war.

403. (B) The Atlantic Charter was an agreement signed by President Franklin Roosevelt and the British prime minister on August 14, 1941, off the coast of Newfoundland on a battleship. The document was drafted secretly and contained several main principles that outlined the two nations' war aims. Within 15 months after the Atlantic Charter's release, 15 other nations endorsed the document.

404. (C) The Nazi Party, which took control of Germany in 1933 under the leadership of Adolf Hitler, illustrates an extreme form of fascism. Though the party's full name was the National Socialist Workers' Party, it rejected the ideologies of socialism and communism. During the practice of genocide known as the Holocaust, the Nazi Party targeted known communists and socialists along with Jewish people and other groups Hitler deemed to be impure. Fascism is a political ideology characterized by the belief that the state is more important than the individual, and fascists usually support a strong, centralized government run by a dictator with absolute power. Benito Mussolini of Italy and Francisco Franco are other examples of fascist leaders during this period.

405. (A) The terms of the Atlantic Charter included that neither nation would pursue territorial expansion during the conflict, no territorial changes would be made without the agreement of the region's inhabitants, and that both nations would promote self-determination for all people, free trade, promotion of better future cooperation between nations to avoid aggression, and the disarmament of the aggressor nations.

406. (A) The Atlantic Charter is similar in many ways to the principles of the Fourteen Points issued by Woodrow Wilson as the United States entered the First World War.

Wilson's Fourteen Points were announced in a speech on January 8, 1918, that outlined the U.S. war aims and peace terms. These included promoting free trade, self-determination, and outlined the underpinnings of the League of Nations. Similarly, the Atlantic Charter later served as the basis for the formation of the United Nations after the Second World War. The Platt Amendment of 1901 allowed the United States to expand its sphere of influence in Cuba following the Spanish–American War. The Roosevelt Corollary to the Monroe Doctrine was created formally in 1904 and stated the United States would police the Western Hemisphere in conflicts between European Powers and nations of the Western Hemisphere. The Gentlemen's Agreement of 1907 was created during the administration of Theodore Roosevelt to reduce tensions between the United States and Japan by the United States not imposing restrictions on Japanese immigration and Japan not allowing further emigration to the United States.

407. (B) The Office of War Mobilization was established to oversee and coordinate the nation's industrial production of war goods. This agency, headed by former Supreme Court justice James Byrnes, oversaw other government agencies such as the War Production Board, which decided what raw materials would be received by what industries. It limited the amount of gasoline and rubber that could be used, as well as organized nationwide drives to collect scrap metals and even fats, which were used to make soap and lubricants. The government also established the Office of Price Administration (OPA) to prevent inflation. The OPA rationed consumer goods such as meats, shoes, butter, and coffee. The Selective Training and Service Act was passed in 1940 to recruit men into the military. This action was taken more than a year prior to Pearl Harbor in response to the expansion of the global war. This made it the first U.S. peacetime draft.

408. (B) Tehran, Yalta, and Potsdam were the sites of conferences where the Big Three— Roosevelt of the United States, Churchill of Britain, and Stalin of the Soviet Union—met to discuss the Allied strategy in World War II. Tehran, the earliest meeting of the three leaders, began in November 1943. At this conference, it was decided that the Allies would work together to defeat Hitler in Europe first and then concentrate on Japan. After this conference, the Soviet Union agreed to officially declare war on Japan, which it did on August 8, 1945. The Yalta Conference took place in February 1945. At Yalta, the Big Three laid out plans for postwar Europe, which included free general elections and the creation of the United Nations, where the United States, France, the Soviet Union, and China would be given permanent seats on the Security Council. The Soviet Union also furthered its pledge to support the Allies against Japan after Germany was defeated. The Allies also made plans to divide Germany into occupied zones. The Potsdam Conference began in July 1945. Stalin was the only member of the original Big Three to attend. Roosevelt had died of a stroke earlier, and Harry Truman succeeded him. Churchill was replaced by Clement Atlee as prime minister of Britain. During this conference, Truman ordered the use of the atomic bomb on Hiroshima and Nagasaki in Japan. This conference was fraught with disagreement. Stalin stated that he would not support free elections in Eastern Europe, and Poland's boundaries remained disputed. In many ways, this conference hinted at the tensions that would define the Cold War.

409. (A) Roosevelt's Executive Order 9066, dated February 19, 1942, gave the military the authority to relocate citizens of Japanese, German, and Italian descent to internment camps established within the United States. Japanese-Americans received the harshest treatment under this order; nearly 120,000 Japanese citizens and many Nisei (second-generation American-born U.S. citizens of Japanese descent) were taken from their homes and put into camps that lacked adequate resources and sanitation. The prohibition of wartime strikes was a result of Congress passing the Smith Connelly Act over Roosevelt's veto in 1943. The act stated that unions had to give 30 days' notice before striking and made it a federal crime to strike in an industry being run by the government. A. Philip Randolph convinced President Roosevelt to create the Fair Employment Practices Committee (FEPC), which banned discriminatory hiring in the federal government and in corporations that received federal contracts.

410. (A) While both German Americans and Italian Americans were targeted by Franklin Roosevelt's Executive Order No. 9066, Japanese Americans faced the harshest treatment due to the act. Nearly 3,200 individuals of Italian background were arrested and nearly 300 of individuals of Italian heritage were forced into camps. Additionally, roughly 11,000 people of German heritage were arrested and over 5,000 were interned. Even still, the Japanese in the United States were even more negatively impacted by the executive order. Entire communities were relocated and denied constitutional protections and basic civil liberties. This was especially true for people of Japanese heritage living on the U.S. West Coast.

411. (D) In 1976, President Gerald Ford formally rescinded the executive order and in 1980, President Jimmy Carter led the creation of the Commission on Wartime Relocation and Internment of Civilians to study the impact of the order on Japanese Americans. Later, President Ronald Reagan signed the Civil Liberties Act of 1988, based on the commission's recommendations. However, it was not until November 21, 1989, the President George H. W. Bush signed an appropriation bill to make payments surviving internees and issue a formal letter of apology.

412. (C) Following a coordinated Soviet offensive into Eastern Europe, the Allied forces on June 6, 1944, launched the largest amphibious assault in history, code-named Operation Overlord, on the beaches of Normandy, France. The planning for the assault began with the meeting of Roosevelt, Churchill, and Stalin during the 1943 Tehran Conference, which was commanded by the supreme allied commander, Dwight Eisenhower. The beaches were stormed by 176,000 troops with the support of 4,000 landing craft, 600 warships, and nearly 11,000 planes. By July 4, nearly four million men had landed on the beachhead. To avoid German detection, the Allies set up a decoy invasion under the code name Operation Quicksilver, which was an attempt to trick the Germans into thinking the invasion would take place farther north in the French region of Pas-de-Calais. Operation Barbarossa was the code name of Germany's invasion of the Soviet Union in 1941. Over 4.5 million Axis troops stormed the Soviet border, making it the largest military operation in military history in both number of troops and total casualties. Over 1.5 million men died in the campaign. Operation Torch was the code name for the Allied invasion of North Africa that began on November 8, 1942. Operation Cartwheel was the military strategy developed by General Douglas Macarthur in the Pacific Theater during the Second World War.

413. (B) Early in the war, the Allies decided that their forces would primarily focus on defeating Hitler in Europe and then use their combined military strength to crush the Japanese in the Pacific. The reason for this decision was concerns that Germany might be able to defeat the Soviet Union while simultaneously isolating Britain from the United States. After Germany was defeated, the Allied forces would use their combined strength to fight the Japanese to an unconditional surrender. The 1943 Tehran Conference held between the Big Three (Roosevelt, Stalin, and Churchill) formalized this agreement. During the conference, Stalin, the premier of the Soviet Union, agreed to formally declare war on Japan and coordinate the Soviet offensive alongside the British and American invasion of France.

414. (C) As the emperor states in the document, Japan declared war to "insure Japan's self-preservation and the stabilization of East Asia." During the period prior, Japan had continually expanded into regions of China and Korea, and later into southeast Asia and the Pacific. In doing so, it was able to access raw resources for its expanding industrial economy.

415. (C) In his speech, the emperor praises the fighting ability and the valiant efforts of the Japanese military, as well as the efforts of the Japanese society as a whole. However, he notes that the Allied forces had created a difficult scenario for the Japanese effort, stating, "the general trends of the world have all turned against her interest." The emperor further note discussed the use of the atomic bomb on Hiroshima and Nagasaki, stating, "the enemy has begun to employ a new and most cruel bomb, the power of which to do damage is, indeed, incalculable." This quote also illustrates later concerns of future damage and losses continued fighting would cause for the Japanese civilization.

416. (D) The Battle of Midway, which took place between June 4 and 7, 1942, is considered to be one of the most important battles in the Pacific Theater and a turning point in the campaign. The U.S. Navy inflicted massive damage on the Japanese Navy, decisively defeating it. During the battle, the Japanese lost four aircraft carriers, over 250 fighter planes, and a battleship that they were unable to replace in the duration of the war.

417. (C) The Manhattan Project was the code name given to the U.S. development of an atomic bomb, which took three years and relied on the work of over 120,000 people, making it one of the largest government-funded research projects of all time. The idea was first set into motion in 1939, when physicist Albert Einstein wrote a letter describing the possibility of a new type of weapon that could be created by splitting uranium atoms. The first atomic bomb was tested on July 16, 1945, near Alamogordo, New Mexico, ushering in the Atomic Age. Later, two atomic bombs were used against Japan, one in Hiroshima (August 6, 1945) and the other in Nagasaki three days later. The bombs were used to force Japan into an unconditional surrender without an American-led invasion of the island nation. This marks the only time nuclear weapons have been used in direct warfare, and many people still debate the morality of the attack. Over 110,000 people were killed in the initial attack, and countless other survivors suffered from radiation poisoning.

418. (A) On August 14, 1945, Emperor Hirohito contradicted key Japanese military leaders and agreed to an unconditional surrender. The formal surrender was signed on September 2, 1945, on the U.S. battleship *Missouri*. Japan at this time had experienced two devastating attacks on Hiroshima and Nagasaki, the deployment by the United States of the first and only atomic weapons ever used directly in combat. The terms of the surrender included the total disarmament of Japan, limitation of Japan's size to four main islands, and the occupation of the island nation until Japan proved it had fully adhered to the terms of the treaty.

419. (A) Being that the document is a speech by the Japanese Emperor Hirohito, it addresses the Japanese perspective on the war and the war's conclusion. The emperor does give the Japanese perspective of why the war began and justified why it declared war on both the United States and Great Britain. It furthermore illustrates the emperor's views on how the conflict ultimately impacted the nation of Japan. However, the document does not take into account the viewpoint of the United States and its criticism of the use of atomic weapons, and referral to the United States as the enemy illustrates its continued bias against the United States.

Chapter 16

420. (C) In 1947, the British government announced to the United States that it would no longer be able to provide aid to the crumbling economies of Greece and Turkey. This worried the United States because it knew that the Soviet Union had strong interests in exerting its interests into the Dardanelle Straits. The United States was concerned that this would allow for the Soviet Union to not only bring Turkey and Greece under its sphere of influence, but could open up other nations in the region, such as Iran to Soviet influence. As a result, Truman was able to secure $400 million in military and economic assistance for the two nations.

421. (B) Following the Second World War, the United States adopted policies that were intended to help rebuild war-torn Europe, promote self-determination, and contain the spread of Soviet influence. After Great Britain announced in 1947 that it could no longer afford to aid the Greek government's fight against the communist insurgents, President Truman asked Congress for nearly $400 million in military and economic aid for Greece and Turkey. Truman stated that it was the duty of the United States to support free nations that were fighting to resist communist domination. The Marshall Plan, also known as the European Recovery Program, was instituted in 1947 in response to fears that communist organizations were gaining strength in democratic nations across Europe. The Marshall Plan illustrated the U.S. belief that American aid in reconstruction would allow for economic recovery and create strong democracies. The Soviet Union openly rejected the Marshall Plan and pressured its satellite nations to not participate in the program.

422. (A) George F. Kennan was a diplomat, stationed in Moscow, who wrote what has become known as the Long Telegram in 1946. In this telegram and a later essay entitled "The Sources of Soviet Conduct" (1947), he argued that the Soviet Union was expansionist and its influence needed to be contained. He especially stressed the containment of Soviet influence in areas that were of strategic importance to the United States. Kennan's idea of containment became the basis for the Truman Doctrine, issued in February 1947, and the Marshall Plan, announced in June of the same year. His notion of containment also influenced the formation of NATO in 1949, American military activities during the Korean and Vietnam Wars, U.S. policy toward Cuba after the rise of Castro, and other defining aspects of U.S. diplomacy throughout the Cold War.

423. (C) Like the Truman Doctrine, which called for supplying aid to countries while stemming the spread of Soviet influence, the Berlin Airlift describes the delivery of nearly 13,000 tons of supply aid by British and American aircraft following a Soviet blockade of the portions of Berlin controlled by the western allies. Following the end of the Second

World War, Germany was divided into four occupied zones. The three western zones were controlled by the United States, Britain, and France, while the eastern zone was occupied by the Soviet Union. In 1948, the western allies agreed to merge their occupied territories into one democratic German state called the Federal Republic of Germany (West Germany). The Soviet Union responded in 1949 by creating a communist state called the Democratic Republic of Germany (East Germany). A problem arose, however, because the western allies also had claim to the western part of the German capital of Berlin. After East Germany was created as a communist state, many East Germans fled the nation by traveling to western Berlin and flying to a free state such as the United States or Canada. Stalin responded by creating a blockade around the city to stop the western allies' access to the capital. The people of West Berlin would quickly run out of food and other necessities without western support, but Truman decided to avoid war by forgoing the use of military force. Instead, the United States and Britain began an airlift of these supplies. It lasted until 1949, when the Soviet Union agreed to end its blockade.

424. (A) In 1945, President Truman outlined a twenty-one-point plan for domestic policy that, by 1948, developed into what Truman called his Fair Deal. It continued, strengthened, and expanded many of the programs that defined Franklin Roosevelt's New Deal, which had defined presidential public policy during the Great Depression. Initially, Truman's Fair Deal continued to push for progressive policies such as universal health care coverage and government-provided incomes for working farmers. Both of these measures were defeated by members of both parties in Congress. Truman did achieve some notable goals under the Fair Deal. He increased the national minimum wage, expanded Social Security coverage to more Americans, increased government works projects involving flood control and irrigation, and provided financial support to poor urban communities. The New Frontier was the name of the program announced by President Kennedy upon winning the presidential election in 1960. Like Truman's Fair Deal, it called for far-reaching progressive reforms. These reforms included greater federal aid to education and urban renewal, health care for the elderly, and the creation of a Department of Urban Affairs. Like Truman's plan, these far-reaching reforms were rejected by Congress. Kennedy did manage to increase the minimum wage and provided some increased support through the Area Redevelopment Act and the Housing Act, both signed in 1961 and providing funds to depressed urban areas. The Great Society was introduced by Lyndon B. Johnson in 1964. In many ways, the Great Society included and expanded upon ideas of the Fair Deal and New Frontier, but unlike the two earlier presidents, Johnson experienced much greater success in turning his planned policy into law. The Great Society included the 1965 Medicare Act, which provided health care for the elderly through the Medicare program and care for the impoverished through Medicaid, a policy that it shared with the goals of the New Frontier. Johnson also created the Department of Housing and Urban Affairs, which also had been a proposed part of the New Frontier.

425. (A) From 1945 to 1960, the American gross national product increased from around $212 billion to over $500 billion. This economic prosperity was also reflected in the homes of Americans, as the per capita income of the American family rapidly increased. Corporate expansion was also consistently growing during this time period. Combined, these types of growth contributed to a strong consumer economy. To avoid the risky investment practices that had led to the Depression, companies began to form conglomerates—corporations that owned diversified businesses. Franchises, or businesses contracted from a larger company, also began to emerge. Together, they helped fuel the consumer economy that defined the postwar years in the United States.

426. (B) The United States adopted the containment policy that was central to the Truman Doctrine in Asia, as well as Europe. This would also later be seen in the U.S. involvement in Vietnam. During the onset of the conflict, instead of acting unilaterally, the United States went to the U.N. Security Council. Since China was excluded and the Soviet Union was absent in protest, the United Nations was able to formally declare North Korea the aggressor and passing a resolution for member states to assist.

427. (D) The escalation of the war was limited to a certain extent as Truman had hoped, but it was fought to a stalemate. In 1953, a truce was signed, dividing the peninsula at the 38th parallel. The United States lost over 54,000 soldiers, and many questioned whether the loss of life and capital was worth such limited success.

428. (C) General Douglas MacArthur, who had been a hero in the Pacific war in World War II and the military governor of Japan after the war's conclusion, was removed as Commander in 1951 after he sent a letter to House Minority Leader Joseph W. Martin criticizing the president. This was the last straw in a conflict between MacArthur and Truman over a difference in view of how far the conflict should have been escalated.

429. (B) The Montgomery GI Bill preceded the Korean War. It was signed into law in 1944 to provide funds for soldiers returning from the Second World War so they could pursue an education after they finished their service. The Korean War began in June 1950 with the invasion of the communist North Korean army into the democratic nation of South Korea. The Korean peninsula had been divided at the 38th Parallel following the conclusion of the Second World War. Though President Truman had desegregated the military in 1948, this war marked the first time that African-American and white soldiers fought side by side in combat. The war was fought until 1953, when an armistice was signed, and the peninsula remained divided at the 38th Parallel. Because of the conflict, the United States adopted a policy of permanent mobilization, which led to the creation of a military-industrial complex. This was a powerful partnership between the military, the scientific community, and private industry. Furthermore, the Korean War directly affected the U.S. relationship with Japan. The once bitter enemy of the United States during the Second World War officially became its partner against the spread of communism with the signing of a formal treaty in 1951.

430. (C) Issued in 1957, the Eisenhower Doctrine was a response to fears that the Suez Canal could fall under Soviet control with the absence of a British or French presence in the region. This threat was intensified by the U.S. economy's growing dependence on petroleum, which made the Middle East more vital in the nation's foreign policy and economy. This policy continued the ideas of the Truman Doctrine and Marshall Plan in that it promised military and economic support to countries that might become targets of communist states. Eisenhower's fears of the spread of communism in Asia were illustrated by his domino theory, first described in a speech delivered in 1954. He stated that if one nation in the region fell to communism, that event could spark a chain reaction. This theory helped fuel the U.S. involvement in Vietnam.

431. (C) As noted, the Eisenhower Doctrine placed new importance on fossil fuels. In 1956, President Eisenhower signed the Federal-Aid Highway Act, creating the U.S. interstate highway system. With over 41,000 miles of roads, this project was the largest public works program in American history. Ninety percent of the funds for the project were provided by the federal government, with the remaining 10 percent coming from state governments. Eisenhower was inspired to construct the system after seeing the German highway system during the Second World War. The completion of the interstate highway system further fueled suburban sprawl and marked the decline of the nation's railroad system. Eisenhower, like the earlier Republican administrations of Harding, Coolidge, and Hoover, supported the deregulation of business and smaller government and opposed the expansion of the Tennessee Valley Authority, created as part of the New Deal. Medicare (health care insurance for the elderly) and the Department of Housing and Urban Development, while first introduced as part of the New Frontier under Kennedy, were passed into law under Johnson as part of his Great Society.

432. (A) The House Un-American Activities Committee (HUAC) was originally established in 1938 to investigate German-American involvement with the Ku Klux Klan and the Nazi Party, but it is better remembered for its postwar activities in trying to probe for communist infiltration of the government and Hollywood. This was illustrated in 1947 when leading writers, directors, and actors were called before a House committee meeting to address the perceived communist infiltration into the film industry. A group of ten participants, who later became known as the Hollywood Ten, refused to participate and were held in contempt by the committee, jailed, and later blacklisted within the film industry. The actions of HUAC are often confused with the actions taken by Senator Joseph McCarthy. While both HUAC and McCarthy's committee sought to root out communist infiltration, HUAC was run by the House of Representatives, and McCarthy operated exclusively through his Senate committee.

433. (A) In 1950, Senator Joseph McCarthy headed a Senate subcommittee investigating un-American Activities and possible communist infiltration into the government. One of the people McCarthy attacked was John Stewart Service. Service was accused of disloyal activities. Secretary of State Dean Acheson ultimately fired Service, but he was reinstated in 1957 by the U.S. Supreme Court. Alan K. Simpson became an outspoken critic of McCarthy's actions, as was news anchor Edward R. Murrow.

434. (B) The action of invoking the Fifth Amendment implies that a people cannot be forced to offer information that may indict in possible wrongdoing or as noted in the Fifth Amendment, "nor shall any person . . . be compelled . . . to be witness against himself."

435. (B) The American author and playwright wrote *The Crucible* in early 1950s in response to the actions taken by a Senate investigative committee led by Joseph McCarthy. Miller compared the witch hunts of Salem, Massachusetts, during the colonial period with McCarthy's actions toward American citizens during the nation's second Red Scare. Like Arthur Miller's victims of the Salem witch hunt, the victims of McCarthyism were forcefully submitted to interrogation where they had little option but to confess, regardless of their guilt, and release the names of coconspirators. McCarthyism quickly declined in 1954 after Senator McCarthy attempted to investigate the U.S. Army for communist infiltration.

This alienated even his staunchest supporters, and in December 1954, the Senate censured McCarthy for the remainder of his term.

436. (C) President John F. Kennedy introduced his "flexible response" doctrine in 1961 as a skeptical response to Eisenhower's New Look Policy, because the introduction of intercontinental ballistic missiles (ICBMs) made Eisenhower's policy obsolete. Eisenhower's approach was limited to a policy of deterrence, stockpiling a large quantity of nuclear weapons that could be deployed through conventional means. Flexible response was created to address what Kennedy saw as a "missile gap" created by Eisenhower's strategy and opted for a more diverse and flexible approach to a Soviet threat that extended beyond just deterrence. The policy was created to introduce variable options other than the threat of nuclear weapons to respond to enemy aggression. The three main stages provided for in this policy included the use of direct defense of a Soviet attack using conventional military force, deliberate escalation in cases where a Soviet attack might possess an advantage in a strike against a NATO nation, and a general nuclear response, which reflected the policy of mutually assured destruction.

437. (B) On April 17, 1961, the United States supported a paramilitary group consisting of 1,400 Cuban exiles. The group attempted to launch an invasion of Cuba to overthrow Fidel Castro, who had been in power since 1959. The action was a terrible failure for the Kennedy administration. The Cuban Missile Crisis followed shortly after in the October of 1962. The Soviet Union attempted to build nuclear missile bases in Cuba to counter similar bases established in places such as Turkey by the United States. The Vienna Summit of 1962 was between Kennedy and Soviet Premier Nikita Khrushchev. The two leaders attempted to address numerous tensions of the Cold War including Berlin. The Peace Corps were established during the Kennedy administration in 1961 to provide social and economic development to underdeveloped regions of the world.

438. (D) In April 1961, the U.S. government, led by President John F. Kennedy, attempted to overthrow Cuba's communist government of Fidel Castro by launching the failed Bay of Pigs invasion. In response, beginning in 1962, Castro agreed to allow the Soviet Union to construct missile bases on the island nation in order to ensure trade with the Soviet Union and create a deterrent for possible future U.S. attacks. This led to military escalation between the United States and the Soviet Union that became known as the Cuban Missile Crisis. For 14 days, the world waited as it seemed that nuclear war had become a real possibility as the two superpowers faced off against each other. Finally, on October 28, 1962, the world breathed a sigh of relief when the United States and the Soviet Union created an agreement to resolve the confrontation peacefully. Unlike the Flexible Response Policy, Kennedy agreed to the removal of strategic nuclear missiles from Turkey, and Nikita Khrushchev withdrew the Soviet missiles from Cuba. The two nations also established a Moscow–Washington hot line, also known as the "red phones," to provide direct communications between the two nation's leaders.

439. (B) While the 1950s are often thought of as times of social conformity, groups such as the beatniks emerged. The Beat Generation was defined by authors such as Alan Ginsberg, who introduced poems such as *Howl*, and Jack Kerouac, who authored *On the Road*. In their works, as well as in their lifestyles, they rejected social conformity and consumerism in favor of spontaneity, drugs, sexual freedom, and often spirituality through Eastern religion. The

1960s also saw the emergence of a counterculture, which became known as the hippies. Like the beatniks of the 1950s, hippies rejected social conformity and often were part of the drug culture of the time. Some also adopted policies of social dissonance, rejecting the Vietnam War. An offshoot of the 1960s counterculture was the Youth International Party (YIPPIES), founded by Abbie Hoffman in 1968. This group challenged social conformity and politics through large-scale theatrical public events that mocked the Establishment.

440. (A) While the 1950s are often described as a time of cultural and social conformity, it was in fact a period of cultural divergence. Many people experienced a religious reawakening, as illustrated by the rise and popularity of televangelists such as Oral Roberts and increased overall church attendance. At the same time, the decade witnessed the emergence of a new youth culture that popularized the rock-and-roll music of performers including Elvis Presley, Chuck Berry, and Buddy Holly.

441. (C) Beginning in Long Island in 1947, William J. Levitt introduced the first mass-produced housing development, which became known as Levittown. His system of constructing homes was in some ways similar to the method Henry Ford used to produce cars, focusing on standardization. Levitt's first Long Island development consisted of nearly 11,000 standardized, prefabricated homes, and his model was copied widely throughout the nation, helping fuel the growth of suburban America. Further promoting suburban sprawl was the Federal Housing Administration, established during the New Deal. It provided government-insured loans to homebuyers and was used by numerous American in the postwar era. The interstate highway system introduced under the Eisenhower administration, as well as the increased number of automobiles in the United States, also allowed for the expansion of suburbs by providing efficient means for people to commute to their jobs from greater distances.

Chapter 17

442. (B) As noted in the excerpt above, the Supreme Court argued that, under the Fourteenth Amendment, individuals were being deprived of equal protection through the segregation of schools. The clause states, "All persons born or naturalized in the United States, and subject to the jurisdiction thereof, are citizens of the United States and of the State wherein they reside. No State shall make or enforce any law which shall abridge the privileges or immunities of citizens of the United States; nor shall any State deprive any person of life, liberty, or property, without due process of law; nor deny to any person within its jurisdiction the equal protection of the laws." The court also stated that students were being denied the due process that was also established by the amendment.

443. (A) In 1954 the U.S. Supreme Court issued its decision in *Brown v. Board of Education*, effectively overturning the constitutionality of "separate but equal" established in the 1896 *Plessy v. Ferguson* decision. The NAACP lawyer Thurgood Marshall successfully proved that segregated educational institutions were inherently unequal, and the Supreme Court ordered school districts to integrate their schools with all "deliberate speed." The 1964 Civil Rights Act further ended discrimination in the United States by outlawing racial discrimination by employers as well as unions. In 1952 the Supreme Court's Youngstown decision limited the power of the president to seize private property. The case was based on an attempt made by the president to seize a steel production facility that was threatening to strike during the Korean War. The 1947 Taft–Hartley Act limited the power of unions by outlawing closed shops and required anticommunist oaths to be taken by union officials.

444. (A) The Southern Manifesto was issued in 1956 by white Southern leaders, pledging to fight desegregation in the wake of the *Brown v. Board of Education* decision. To ensure that African American students could attend the schools despite local government attempts to stop integration, President Dwight Eisenhower responded by deploying the 101st Airborne Division to Arkansas and put the Arkansas National Guard under federal control.

445. (C) The excerpt above was an initial draft of a speech given during the Washington March in the August of 1963. When the draft was circulated prior to the speeches delivery both, the Attorney General, Robert F. Kennedy, as well as march organizers, were concerned that the language was too inflammatory towards the federal government. A. Philip Randolph, who was the head of the march directly met with Lewis, stating the speech could endanger the entire event and the movement, convincing Lewis to tone down his rhetoric. A. Philip Randolph was a long-time veteran of the Civil Rights movement, as well as the American Labor movement. In 1925, he established Brotherhood of Sleeping Car Porters, the first African-American labor union. During the Second World War, he convinced President Roosevelt to ban discrimination in the defense industries through an executive order. Later during the Korean War, he helped convince President Truman to desegregate the military.

446. (A) When SNCC was initially established, it was interracial, inviting both black and white members to join and participate. Furthermore, the group used nonviolent protest as the major tool in attempting to bring about an end of discrimination against African Americans. However, by the end of the 1960s, under the leadership of people such as Stokely Carmichael, the organization became more militant and adopted the notion of black power. Carmichael himself also pushed to exclude white activists from SNCC.

447. (C) Unlike SCC, which became more militant overtime, the Congress of Racial Equality (CORE), founded in 1942, and the Southern Christian Leadership Conference (SCLC), founded by Dr. Martin Luther King Jr. and others in 1957 both advocated challenging discrimination within the United States through nonviolent means. The founders of CORE and the SCLC were inspired by the nonviolent or passive resistance adopted by Mohandas Gandhi in India. CORE established Freedom Rides, in which African-American and white volunteers traveled through the South, challenging Jim Crow laws. The SCLC's first major action was the Montgomery bus boycott in 1957. Both movements worked together through the 1950s and 1960s to fight against segregation and for racial equality. In 1963 the two groups organized the March on Washington, where King delivered his now immortal "I Have a Dream" speech. The massive march eventually led to the passage of the 1964 Civil Rights Act and the 1965 National Voting Rights Act.

448. (D) The ratification of the Twenty-Fourth Amendment in 1964 officially made poll taxes unconstitutional. Poll taxes had been used by several Southern states to keep poor African Americans from voting. This constitutional amendment, along with the 1965 Voting Rights Act, politically empowered many African Americans, creating a new voting population in the South. The Civil Rights Act of 1964 outlawed discrimination in jobs, education, and public accommodations, as well as supported early attempts to help African Americans register to vote.

449. (D) The 1960s were a time of political activism in many areas of American life. One example was the publication of *Silent Spring* by Rachel Carson, a leader in the environmental movement. Carson's book helped bring about the banning of the pesticide DDT, which had a deep and deadly impact on the environment by contaminating water supplies and killing off or endangering many species of fish and birds, including the bald eagle, which almost became extinct. Her book also prompted President Johnson to include environmental reforms in his Great Society program. Carson was not, however, involved in the efforts of Japanese-American citizens who had been forced into internment camps and later fought to be compensated for losses they had suffered. The Japanese American Citizens League began to push for legislation for monetary compensation for losses during the Second World War, which they finally settled in 1965. Author Betty Friedan reawakened the women's rights movement with the publication of her book *The Feminine Mystique* in 1963. In 1966, Friedan went on to help form the National Organization for Women (NOW), which campaigned for equal rights for women. César Chávez created the United Farm Workers (UFW) during the 1960s to improve the labor conditions and treatment of migrant workers. Dennis Banks, along with George Mitchell, established the American Indian Movement (AIM) in 1968 to fight for treaty rights as well as better conditions and opportunities for the Native American people.

450. (B) While Malcolm X is often depicted as more militant; he followed many of the philosophical beliefs also held by W. E. B. Dubois. In this passage he echoes the necessity of African Americans pursuing political power for themselves immediately, as Dubois did in his work *The Souls of Black Folk*. At the same time Malcom X also advocated Black Nationalism, which reflected the ideals of Marcus Garvey in the 1920s. Black Nationalism called for a separate identity and racial unity within African-American communities. This notion was not necessarily supported by Dubois.

451. (D) In many ways, Martin Luther King Jr. and Malcolm X illustrated a split within the African-American population during the 1960s. While King fought for desegregation and racial equality, Malcolm X advocated Black Nationalism, which called for a separate identity and racial unity within African-American communities. This reflected the ideals expressed by Marcus Garvey, a major influence on Malcolm X, during the 1920s. Later, Malcolm X's calls for Black Nationalism would be adopted by Stokely Carmichael, a leader of the Student Nonviolent Coordinating Committee who modified these views into a movement that became known as black power, which also called for establishing a sense of pride and independence within African-American communities.

452. (A) During the summer of 1964 and in March 1965, civil rights organizations launched movements to bring attention to the lack of voting rights in African-American communities in the South. The 1964 event known as Freedom Summer saw over 3,000 African-American and white volunteers register voters in Mississippi. In 1965, Martin Luther King Jr., recognizing that many black residents of Alabama were still being denied the right to vote, organized a march to raise awareness. Alabama law-enforcement officials, however, used violent means to break up the march. News agencies captured images of the brutal tactics being employed against the peaceful protestors, raising sympathies among many Northern whites. These two events helped push the passage of the 1965 Voting Rights Act, which eliminated barriers to voting such as literacy tests and allowed federal officials to register voters if the local government refused. The 1964 Civil Rights Act, which banned discriminatory practices in employment, education, and public accommodations, was passed partly in response to the 1963 March on Washington. The black power movement and the Black Panthers illustrated the formation of a more militant arm of the civil rights movement that emerged after 1966. Stokely Carmichael popularized the notion of black power through his organization, the Student Nonviolent Coordinating Committee. The Black Panthers were founded by Bobby Seale and Huey Newton. Both organizations reflected Malcolm X's call for black pride within independent black communities. The Southern Manifesto was issued in 1956 by white Southern leaders, pledging to fight desegregation in the wake of the *Brown v. Board of Education* decision.

453. (B) The Fair Labor Standards Act of 1938 was part of the Second New Deal of the Great Depression. The act allowed for the creation of a federal minimum Wage. Under the Kennedy administration, the Equal Pay Act was added to this measure in the June of 1963. The Equal Pay Act mandated that all employees doing the same work in the same work place deserved equal compensation. The Trade Expansion Act of 1962 gave the president increased power to cut tariffs. This allowed the president to reduce protectionist trade policies and further encourage free trade. Kennedy also signed the Limited Nuclear Test Ban Treaty along with the United Kingdom and the Soviet Union. The treaty banned nuclear weapons tests underwater, in the air, or in space.

454. (C) During Kennedy's campaign, he cited the slow growth of the American economy on the later years of the Eisenhower administration as need to get the economy "moving again." During the 1960 election, Kennedy secured 303 electoral votes; however, he only won by fewer than 119,000 popular votes over his chief Republican rival Richard Nixon. This led to accusations of voter fraud and denied him a strong mandate for leadership in the early part of his presidency. Furthermore, like the earlier presidential candidate Alfred Smith, Kennedy's membership in the Catholic faith served as a major hurdle, illustrating a continued anti-Catholic sentiment amongst many in the United States. Kennedy had to give a speech in the September of 1960 to the Protestant Greater Houston Ministerial Association where he stated, "I believe in an America where the separation of church and state is absolute, where no Catholic prelate would tell the president (should he be Catholic) how to act," to assure his loyalty to the Constitution over the Catholic Church.

455. (D) On November 22, 1963, President Kennedy was shot by Lee Harvey Oswald while visiting Dallas, Texas. He died later that day, and Lyndon Johnson, Kennedy's vice president, assumed the office. Johnson then introduced his Great Society Program, which continued many of the initiatives of the New Frontier and also great expanded on many such as efforts to combat poverty, civil rights, and education.

456. (B) The major escalation of American troops in Vietnam began after an American destroyer, the *Maddox*, was allegedly attacked 30 miles south of Vietnam in the Gulf of Tonkin. Congress responded in 1964 by passing the Gulf of Tonkin Resolution, which gave the president nearly complete control of American military actions in Vietnam without officially declaring war. While the Vietnam conflict officially began for the United States with the 1964 Gulf of Tonkin Resolution, American involvement had begun much earlier when the French withdrew from the region in 1954 and the United States became involved to keep the Viet Cong from leading a communist revolution in southern Vietnam. The My Lai Massacre refers to a mass killing of unarmed citizens in South Vietnam by the U.S. Army, including a soldier named William Calley, who was later sentenced to three years in prison. The Pentagon Papers, a military report on American military actions in Vietnam, were leaked to American newspapers in 1971. They exposed that the military had expanded the war by bombing the neighboring countries of Cambodia and Laos and by launching coastal raids on North Vietnam. This caused a further decline in support for the war and hurt the Nixon administration.

457. (C) When President Kennedy took office, he attempted to keep communism from spreading into southern Vietnam. He did this by sending several thousand military advisors and other military assistance to prop up the government led by Ngo Dinh Diem against the communist northern Viet Cong, led by Ho Chi Minh. After the 1964 Second Gulf of Tonkin incident, in which the American destroyer *Maddox* was allegedly attacked by Viet Cong torpedo boats, Congress gave President Johnson the authority to send more troops into the region, officially starting the Vietnam War. In 1970, President Nixon began a bombing campaign in Cambodia, a neighboring country to Vietnam, to disrupt Viet Cong supply routes known as the Ho Chi Minh Trail.

458. (C) In 1968, during the Vietnamese New Year celebration, North Vietnam and Viet Cong forces launched a massive offensive attack known as the Tet Offensive. It included numerous surprise attacks on South Vietnamese cities and American bases, including the capital city of Saigon. The My Lai Massacre was the brutal killing of several hundred Vietnamese citizens by American soldiers. Operation Rolling Thunder refers to aerial bombing campaign of North Vietnam introduced by the Johnson administration. The operation continued from 1965 to 1968. The Ho Chi Minh Trail was the supply route of the Viet Cong that stretched through Cambodia. To disrupt this supply route, Nixon ordered the carpet bombing of the region and a short-lived invasion of the region by American troops. Domestically, these actions increased antiwar sentiments within the United States. In Cambodia, the instability caused by Nixon's actions, as well as the war in general, allowed for the emergence of the Khmer Rouge, led by Pol Pot, which maintained control of the country from 1975 to 1979 by use of extreme force and genocide.

459. (D) Even though American troops withdrew from Vietnam by the end of March 1973, the fighting between North and South Vietnam continued until April 1975, when the Viet Cong, the army of North Vietnam, captured Saigon, the capital of South Vietnam. At this time, they were able to take control of the entire southern nation. President Nixon did perform heavy bombing of Cambodia, hoping to disrupt the Ho Chi Minh Trail in 1970, but Congress ended this operation by June 1970. In 1954, a conference held in Geneva divided Vietnam at the 17th Parallel, creating the state of North Vietnam, led by Ho Chi Minh, and the southern state of South Vietnam, initially led by Bao Dai. Dai was quickly overthrown by the fiercely anti-communist Ngo Dinh Diem.

460. (A) In January 1973, the United States, North Vietnam, and the Viet Cong met in Paris and negotiated a peace settlement. The United States agreed to remove its military force from the region, and all parties agreed to stop military action in Cambodia and Laos, release all prisoners of war, and recognize the 17th Parallel as the border between North and South Vietnam. No agreements were made on the holding of free elections, and North Vietnam eventually defeated South Vietnam.

461. (B) Article I of the U.S. Constitution states that only Congress has the power to declare war, yet the president is the commander in chief of the nation's military forces. In response to the nation's disillusionment with the conduct of the Vietnam War, Congress passed the 1973 War Powers Act over the veto of President Nixon. The act limited the president's use of the nation's armed forces by requiring the president to notify Congress of any overseas troop deployment and to provide justification for the action. It also stated that troops could not be deployed for more than sixty days without congressional approval, and it allowed Congress to force the president to recall troops if the legislators felt it were necessary.

462. (B) The War Powers Act was first used when President Ford attempted to supply military aid to South Vietnam in 1975. The nation as a whole, like Congress, did not want to become militarily involved in the region again, so Congress used the War Powers Act to deny the president's request. As a result, South Vietnam fell to the North Vietnamese in April 1975.

463. (D) Even though President Johnson believed the United States could simultaneously fight in the Vietnam War and continue his ambitious Great Society domestic policy, the heavy costs of Vietnam drained money from Johnson's domestic programs and undermined the Great Society. The Great Society did have a wide-reaching impact, which included Medicare programs, the Elementary and Secondary Education Act, the creation of the Department of Housing and Urban Development, and clean-air and clean-water regulations, while at the same time cutting taxes. After Martin Luther King Jr. was killed in 1968, race riots broke out in numerous American cities. Johnson created the National Advisory Commission on Civil Disorders, also known as the Kerner Commission, to investigate the causes. The commission found that the nation was deeply divided along racial lines. Johnson responded by pushing for the passage of the 1968 Civil Rights Act, which barred discrimination in the sale or rental of housing. In a program started by Kennedy, Johnson's administration successfully completed a manned lunar shuttle landing on July 20, 1969, through the Apollo program. NASA itself was established on July 29, 1958 under the Eisenhower administration.

464. (C) Medicaid and Medicare were passed through Congress in 1965. Medicaid was designed to provide low-cost health insurance coverage to low-income American families who could not afford to provide themselves with private health insurance. Medicare was designed to provide hospital and affordable medical insurance to Americans over the age of 65. Head Start was part of the Great Society's War on Poverty. It was a preschool program for low-income families that provided healthcare for children, as well as nutrition and social services. Volunteers in Service to America, or VISTA, was a federal program designed to send volunteers into low-income communities to offer assistance.

465. (B) During the time of the Great Society, poverty rates did decline. From the mid-1960s into the early 1970s, the number of Americans living in poverty declined by half. Furthermore, initially, Johnson's programs were relatively popular amongst the American people. In 1964 Johnson's popularity surpassed that of his predecessor, John Kennedy.

However, as time went on, many critics began to emerge. Some criticism was very similar to that of the opponents of the New Deal. Individuals, such as future president Ronald Reagan, argued that the federal government was taking on too much authority and taking away powers that belonged to the state. Others argued that the programs illustrated creeping socialism into America's capitalist system. Ultimately, however, as the fighting in Vietnam escalated, resources for the Great Society were depleted, ultimately ending the Great Society, though many programs such as Medicare and Medicaid were continued.

Chapter 18

466. (D) During his 1968 campaign, Nixon continually called for law and order. In doing so he rejected many of the calls of the antiwar movement and civil rights protests that were taking place across the nation. Instead he focused on what he called the silent majority. In the passage above he notes, "It is another voice. It is the quiet voice in the tumult and the shouting. It is the voice of the great majority of Americans, the forgotten Americans—the non-shouters; the non-demonstrators." While personally not well liked by many, Nixon held respect by many who previously supported President Eisenhower, as Nixon served as his vice president. Furthermore, his message appealed to many American conservatives, as he looked to move away from many of the policies of the two previous Democratic presidents that were deemed radical and an overexpansion of the federal government. Finally, his message was part of his Southern Strategy, which sought to gain the support of white Southerners, who traditionally voted Democratic but had become uneasy with the party over the issue of civil rights.

467. (C) After receiving less than 12 percent of the African-American vote in 1968, Nixon felt he had little to gain by advancing civil rights, so he began to relax desegregation laws. Instead, he focused on gaining the support of the former Southern Democrats who felt alienated by the Great Society and civil rights programs of the Johnson administration. John Mitchell, Nixon's attorney general, attempted to prevent the extension of provisions found in the 1965 Voting Rights Act. Nixon also allowed the restoration of funding to school districts that were still segregated. Furthermore, he tried to interfere with the *Swann v. Charlotte-Mecklenburg* Supreme Court decision, which called for the use of busing to help end school segregation. He also loosened restrictions in earlier fair-housing laws.

468. (B) President Nixon attempted to slow the growth of the federal government under President Johnson's Great Society; however, the Democratic majority in congress thwarted many of these efforts. One of Nixon's early initiatives was the Family Assistance Plan, which was intended to end welfare by providing a guaranteed income to working families. The Democrats, however, defeated this effort. He did, however, shift many federal programs to the state and local level through the use of block grants. This allowed local governments to address what they saw as local needs directly. Republicans hoped this would check the growth of the federal government and give greater responsibilities to the states.

469. (B) To restore lands they had lost to Israel during the Six Days' War, Middle Eastern states created an oil embargo to pressure Western nations that supported Israel in 1973. Henry Kissinger managed to negotiate an end of the embargo, but the Organization of Petroleum Exporting Counties (OPEC)—which included Venezuela,

Saudi Arabia, Kuwait, Iraq, and Iran—drastically increased the price of oil. This caused the cost of gasoline to double and pushed inflation above 10 percent in the United States. The incident became a dark mark on Nixon's foreign policy record, unlike the opening of talks with China and the Soviet Union through détente, as well as the signing of SALT I with Russia in 1972. The Camp David Accord was a foreign policy success of the Carter administration: negotiation of a peace deal ending the war between Egypt and Israel.

470. (A) President Nixon, with his secretary of state, Henry Kissinger, adopted a policy of détente, or the relaxing of tensions with the nation's two biggest rivals, China and the Soviet Union. Under détente, he and Kissinger (one of his most trusted advisors) bypassed Congress and pursued often-secret dialogue with the two nations, changing the direction of American postwar policies. Détente was in many ways an extension of Kissinger's *realpolitik*, or practical politics. This new approach to foreign affairs allowed for the first presidential visit to the People's Republic of China and the ending of the embargo with that nation and the lifting of travel restrictions. It also allowed for Nixon to travel to the Soviet Union in 1972. At this meeting, Nixon and Premier Leonid Brezhnev worked together and finally agreed to sign the Strategic Arms Limitation Treaty (SALT I). This agreement froze the number of intercontinental ballistic missiles and restricted the development of antiballistic missile defense systems.

471. (C) SALT stands for Strategic Arms Limitation Treaty, and the two agreements served to slow the arms race between the United States and the Soviet Union, the world's two superpowers. SALT I was signed by President Nixon and Soviet Premier Brezhnev in 1972, freezing the number of intercontinental ballistic missiles at the 1972 levels, limiting the number of atomic weapons that could be launched from submarines, and limiting the development of antiballistic missile defense systems. SALT II was signed by President Carter and Premier Brezhnev. This agreement set a limit on the number of nuclear devices that either nation could possess. The agreement was never ratified by Congress and deteriorated after the Soviet invasion of Afghanistan in 1979.

472. (B) Shortly after taking office in 1974, President Ford issued a presidential pardon to Richard Nixon, ending all investigations into the Watergate Scandal. While this action marred the rest of Ford's term, he felt it was necessary to allow the nation's healing process to begin. The presidential pardon was only the first challenge Ford faced as president. When he assumed office, the nation faced increasing unemployment and inflation, a combination that was termed stagflation. Ford called for voluntary restraints and asked supporters to wear buttons that said WIN, which stood for Whip Inflation Now. This did little to help the problem, as unemployment increased along with the federal deficit. Ford had mixed success with his foreign policy. When he asked Congress to supply military aid to South Vietnam, legislators used the 1973 War Powers Act to deny his request. However, he did sign the Helsinki Accords, in which the United States, the Soviet Union, Canada, and roughly thirty other nations agreed to economic cooperation, respect for territorial boundaries, and promotion of human rights. He also continued SALT negotiations with the Soviet Union.

473. (B) In June 1972, four members of the Committee to Re-elect the President (CREEP), led by James McCord, broke into the Democratic Party headquarters located in the Watergate Hotel in Washington, D.C. Their mission was to steal Democratic election files and install wiretapping devices to better monitor the Democratic Party's actions during the 1972 election campaign. The men were discovered, and President Nixon denied involvement; but as investigations continued, Nixon's involvement became more apparent. Eventually, when it was discovered that Nixon had used the CIA to block an FBI investigation of the case, Nixon was forced to resign, which he did on August 8, 1974.

474. (C) In the wake of government distrust following the Watergate Scandal, Jimmy Carter was able to win the 1976 presidential race by presenting himself as a political outsider. Carter had graduated from the U.S. Naval Academy and served as an engineering officer, and he later went on to serve as the governor of Georgia. He became known for rejecting many of the formal and ceremonial practices of the presidential office. This, however, generated criticism from those who thought he was downplaying the dignity of his office. After his election, however, he found that being a political outsider had its disadvantages. He and his inexperienced advisors had difficulty promoting his agenda. He did find some success in deregulating certain parts of American industry such as the railroads and lifting price controls on oil and natural gas. This further alienated him from fellow members of the Democratic Party who supported these regulations. His attempt to raise taxes on gasoline sales further hurt his popular support. He felt that convincing people to use less energy and drive less would make the nation less vulnerable to OPEC's price increases, which had plagued the nation since 1973. Despite opposition, he did manage to pass the 1978 Energy Act, which imposed higher taxes on cars that inefficiently used gas, called for alternative energy sources, deregulated prices on domestic oil and natural gas, and offered tax incentives for homeowners who pursued energy efficiency in their homes. The Moral Majority, a conservative Christian political organization, played a major role in the 1980 election, helping to elect Carter's Republican challenger, Ronald Reagan.

475. (D) One successful action of the Carter administration was ending the war between Egypt and Israel with the signing of the Camp David Accords in 1978. The Middle East had become unstable as the Arab nations and Israel had engaged in several conflicts between 1967 and 1973. In 1978, Carter was able to get the Egyptian leader, Anwar el-Sadat, and the Israeli leader, Menachem Begin, to sign the Camp David Accord, a treaty that would lay the groundwork for peace. Under the treaty, Israel agreed to withdraw from the Sinai Peninsula, and in return, Egypt formally recognized Israel as a sovereign nation. The Helsinki Accord was signed by Ford in 1975. It was an agreement between nations calling for economic cooperation, protection of human rights, and respect for territorial boundaries. The Geneva Accords were created in 1967 as an attempt to solve the Israeli–Palestinian conflict.

476. (B) Jimmy Carter's inability to solve the Iran hostage crisis in 1980 helped the Republican presidential challenger win the election in 1980. For decades prior to the incident, the United States had backed the shah of Iran, Mohammad Reza Shah Pahlavi. However, in 1979, a fundamentalist Islamic revolution erupted in the nation. The shah fled the nation and was replaced by the religious leader Ayatollah Khomeini, who was strongly anti-Western and planned to make Iran into a conservative state. Carter allowed the deposed shah to seek refuge in the United States. This caused Iranian revolutionaries to seize the American embassy in Iran and take 52 Americans hostage. Carter took several steps to free the hostages, including freezing Iranian assets in the United States and launching a failed military rescue mission. Unlike the Iran hostage crisis, the Camp David Accords illustrated a success of Carter: negotiation of a peace deal between Israel and Egypt. SALT I was signed by President Nixon with the Soviet leader Brezhnev to limit the production of nuclear weapons. The Iran–Contra Affair was a scandal during the Reagan administration. The president's office was caught in 1986 selling arms to Iran despite an embargo on weapons sales to that nation. The First Persian Gulf War took place in 1991 during the administration of President George H. W. Bush in response to Iraq's invasion of Kuwait.

477. (D) Ronald Reagan's election in 1980 marked a resurgence of the conservative movement that wanted to lower taxes and reduce the size of the federal government. Reagan and fellow conservatives were critical of the New Deal and Great Society programs, believing they led to an overexpansion of the federal government and increased the tax burden. In doing so, Reagan began to cut funding to many government programs such as urban development and the federal assistance programs for the poor through the 1981 Budget Reconciliation Act. This act cut funding to education, welfare, and other social assistance programs. Reagan did, however, increase the size of the military budget by nearly $12 billion. Conservatives such as Reagan rejected Keynesian economics, which believed economic growth resulted from the government providing jobs and financial assistance to workers, and adopted an economic theory known as supply-side economics. According to supply-side economics, also known as trickle-down economics, economic growth is best achieved by deregulation and government tax cuts to business and investment. This would allow companies to expand, increase production, and then hire more workers. While the nation did make some economic gains under the Reagan administration, the gap between the rich and poor greatly increased, the conditions of America's urban centers drastically declined, and the national deficit soared, reaching over $3 trillion in 1990.

478. (A) Reagan believed that the federal government had grown too large and felt that it needed to be reduced. This led to a decrease in federal programs to lower-income citizens as well as a reduction to aid in many inner cities, increasing urban blight. During this time the gap between America's rich and poor greatly increased. Furthermore, he supported supply-side or trickle-down economics, which called for tax cuts to stimulate economic growth.

479. (B) Like the Republicans of the 1920s, Reagan also fought to eliminate government regulation of business and industry. The savings and loan scandal was caused in part by the lack of regulation, which allowed the industry to make risky investments, eventually losing $2.6 billion in depositors' savings.

480. (A) Though in his inaugural address Reagan stated, "For decades we have piled deficit upon deficit," which would lead to, "social, cultural, political, and economic upheavals," during his presidency, his budgets increased the debt by $1.8 trillion. Several factors led to this increase in debt. First, when Reagan entered office he had to respond to a recession which lasted from July 1981 to November 1982 and was caused by high interest rates. In addition, high unemployment rates plagued his time in the White House. For most of his time as president, unemployment was above

6 percent and peaked at nearly 10 percent in 1982. Furthermore, Reagan's tax cuts greatly reduced government income. Top income tax rates were reduced from 70 percent at the start of his presidency to 28 percent by the end of his term. Meanwhile, spending on the military, as well as programs such as Medicaid and Medicare, increased. As a result, the deficit spiked to levels previously seen only in times of war.

481. (B) In 1981, Ronald Reagan appointed Sandra Day O'Conner to the Supreme Court, making her the first woman to serve in the nation's highest court. Reagan also appointed the conservative Antonin Scalia to the Supreme Court in 1986, as well as Anthony Kennedy in 1988. In 1986, Reagan appointed Justice William Rehnquist to be Chief Justice. These appointments helped establish a strongly conservative court that in many ways mirrored Reagan's political beliefs and catered to his political support in the conservative movement as well as in the religiously conservative Moral Majority. Ruth Joan Bader Ginsburg was the second female appointed to the Supreme Court. She was appointed by President Clinton in 1993. Sonia Sotomayor was selected for the Supreme Court by President Barack Obama in 2009, making her the third woman to serve. Frances Perkins was the first female to serve in the president's cabinet. She served as secretary of labor under Franklin Roosevelt.

482. (D) In November 1986, it was discovered that senior officials in President Reagan's administration were secretly selling weapons to Iran despite a congressional embargo. The officials hoped the arms sales would aid in the release of hostages and provide funds to aid rebels in Nicaragua against the Sandinista government. The savings and loan (S&L) crisis involved the failure of more than 700 financial institutions in part caused by the climate created by the deregulation policies approved by the Reagan administration. Nearly $160 billion in federal funds were used to avoid collapses in the financial sector, leading to a large increase in the national deficit. In the HUD scandal, members of the Department of Housing and Urban Development gave large contracts to political supporters of the Reagan administration. In the Inslaw Affair, officials in the Department of Justice under Reagan were accused of committing software piracy and deliberately driving the Inslaw information technology company into bankruptcy. The Whitewater Scandal plagued the Clinton administration. Clinton was accused of unethical investment practices in a failed real estate investment venture.

483. (C) Perestroika and glasnost were the basis of the policy initiated by Soviet Premier Mikhail Gorbachev during his tenure from 1985 to 1991. *Perestroika* refers to restructuring, and *glasnost* refers to openness. This policy illustrated Gorbachev's push to reform the Soviet's government practices and provide greater transparency. The result, however, was that the communist nations, which for years had run single-party police states, lost their grip, and the Eastern European regimes began to collapse, marking the end of the Cold War. In 1989, Poland held its first free elections; during the same year, the Berlin Wall fell, and Germany reunited. Ultimately, the Soviet Union also collapsed after a failed coup in 1991.

484. (C) After the collapse of the Soviet Union, at the conclusion of the Cold War, the United States tried to assist Russia in the transition to democracy and establish a free market economy. American leaders supported Boris Yeltsin, the newly elected president of Russia. They also offered Russia an aid package worth over $2.5 billion to assist with these developments.

485. (C) After Iraq invaded the independent nation of Kuwait in 1990, the United States and its allies attacked Iraq to liberate the tiny, oil-rich state. President Bush hoped that the liberation of Kuwait and the defeat of the Iraqi-led invasion would lead to a revolution within Iraq that would result in the overthrow of Saddam Hussein. Yet Bush did not support supplying Iraqi rebels with military aid, and the later uprisings were quickly crushed by Saddam's forces. Saddam Hussein remained in power until he was overthrown by the United States during the Second Gulf War, led by Bush's son, President George W. Bush, in 2003.

486. (C) Though Manuel Noriega had worked as an operative for the CIA as early as the 1960s, in 1983 he took control of the Panamanian military and became a military dictator. Furthermore, he was highly involved in the drug trade and in 1988; the United States government indicted him on drug trafficking charges. After several members of the US military were attacked and killed, President Bush launched Operation Just Cause in the December of 1989, to remove Noriega from power. In June 1989, the Chinese government used a strong military response to suppress a pro-democracy demonstration in Beijing's Tiananmen Square. While Congress called for a severe response to the Chinese government's actions, Bush illustrated a conservative and pragmatic response to the event by sending diplomats to China to repair and maintain peaceful terms between the two nations. With the unification of Germany following the fall of the Berlin Wall in 1989, there was a concern whether the unified Germany would join NATO despite protests from Russia. In this situation, President Bush negotiated that Germany would join NATO, but NATO troops would not be stationed there. The Strategic Arms Reduction Treaty, or START, was a designed to decrease the nuclear arsenals of the United States and Soviet Union. It was signed by President Bush and Premier Gorbachev in July 1991.

487. (A) In 1992, Bill Clinton won the presidency in a three-way race against the incumbent president George H. W. Bush and independent candidate Ross Perot. As he began his term in 1993, he focused his domestic program on reforming the nation's healthcare system by providing over 37 million uninsured Americans with healthcare coverage. He called for the creation of a government-supervised healthcare system, which would provide affordable coverage to all Americans. Insurance companies and medical companies lobbied heavily against the measure, and after nearly a year of debate, the plan ultimately failed.

488. (D) During the midterm elections in 1994, House Republicans under the leadership of Speaker of the House Newt Gingrich launched what they called the "Contract with America." In the contract, the Republican candidates promised a balanced budget within seven years by drastically cutting public services. Most of their plans failed, as their intended cuts were rejected by both parties in the Senate, as well as rejected by Clinton through vetoes. Ultimately, the battle between House Republicans and the president led to a brief shutdown of government in 1995. The Republicans' attacks on public services and social spending measures raised Clinton's popularity in the polls while causing their own to decline. The Star Wars program, a nickname for the Strategic Defense Initiative, was a costly nuclear defense developed by the Reagan administration, which added to further increases in military spending during his two terms.

489. (B) President Bill Clinton was the second president in U.S. history to be impeached. The first was Andrew Johnson, in February 1868. The Radical Republicans in the House of Representatives charged Johnson with violating the Tenure of Office Act of 1867. Clinton was charged with perjury and obstruction of justice in an investigation concerning allegations of sexual harassment in a suit brought by Paula Jones, a former Arkansas state worker. While Johnson avoided removal by a single vote, 55 Senators voted against Clinton's removal.

490. (C) The *Bush v. Gore* decision settled the recount dispute in Florida during the 2000 presidential election. The ruling was issued on December 12, 2000, and stated that the previously halted recount would be suspended and the previous vote certification made by the Florida Secretary of State would stand. This gave George W. Bush Florida's 25 electoral votes and helped him secure the presidency.

491. (B) During the 2000 presidential election, many Florida voters used punched card ballots that improperly punched holes leaving hanging pieces of paper from the ballots often referred to as a "hanging chad." These votes were not counted by the tabulating machines. In the highly contested presidential race in Florida, these improperly completed ballots led to calls for recounts. Previously, in the 1992 war in Bosnia and Herzegovina, President Clinton proposed using military forces to bomb Serbian supply lines. In 1993, the First Battle of Mogadishu took place, where the United States military launched an operation against militants loyal to strongman Mohamed Farrah Aidid. The operation, beginning on October 3, 1993, was initially supposed to last only an hour, but stretched into an overnight standoff. The military action was a reaction to Aidid supporters shooting down a Black Hawk helicopter, killing three crew members near the New Port in Mogadishu a week prior. In December of 1995, the United States experienced a 21-day government shutdown when President Bill Clinton and the Republican-controlled Congress fell into disagreement over a government spending bill.

492. (C) In both the 1824 election and the election of 2000, the candidate who received the largest percentage of the popular vote lost the overall presidential election. During the 1824 election, the House of Representatives decided the election in favor of John Quincy Adams over Andrew Jackson. In the 2000 election, the final decision fell into the hands of the Supreme Court. On the election night of 2000, the race became too close to call, and neither candidate received enough electoral votes to win the presidency, though Democratic candidate and former vice president Al Gore won in the popular vote over the Republican candidate, George W. Bush. Eventually, Florida emerged as a battleground. After the two candidates waged legal battles for nearly a month, the Supreme Court decided the election with its decision in the *Bush v. Gore* case, which ended the vote recounts in Florida, awarding the presidency to Bush.

493. (C) Like the burning of Washington, D.C., during the War of 1812 and the attack on Pearl Harbor, which brought the United States into the Second World War, the events of September 11, 2001, helped inspire a feeling of national unity. Congress established a bipartisan resolution in response to the attacks and worked together, along with the executive branch, to develop both domestic and foreign policy responses to the event.

494. (C) The Oklahoma City Federal Building bombing took place on April 19, 1995, and was carried out by Timothy McVeigh, who was a sympathizer of the American militia movement. The bombing of the Alfred P. Murrah Federal Building in Oklahoma City killed 168 people and injured nearly 700 others. It was considered the largest terrorist attack on American soil until the Al Qaeda attacks of September 11, 2001.

495. (A) The USA PATRIOT Act, or Uniting and Strengthening America by Providing Appropriate Tools Required to Intercept and Obstruct Terrorism Act of 2001, was signed into law by President George W. Bush on October 26, 2001. The law was created in direct response to the Al Qaeda terrorist attacks on the World Trade Center and the Pentagon on September 11, 2001. The law was designed to reduce restrictions on law enforcement and intelligence agencies' ability to gather intelligence concerning future terrorist threats. The law was deemed controversial because it contradicted earlier legislation such as FISA, the Foreign Intelligence Surveillance Act of 1978, which was signed into law by President Carter. FISA was created specifically to limit intelligence agencies' ability to use surveillance on American citizens in the wake of the Watergate Scandal under President Nixon. The McCain–Feingold Act, or Bipartisan Campaign Reform Act of 2002, was a bipartisan attempt to regulate the financing of political campaigns. Portions of the law were struck down as unconstitutional in 2010 with the Supreme Court decision in the case *Citizens United v. Federal Election Commission*. The Brady Bill, or the Brady Handgun Violence Prevention Act, was signed into law by President Bill Clinton in 1994. The law required federal background checks on people wishing to purchase a firearm.

496. (B) Due to a financial crisis that lasted from 2007 to 2008 and U.S. sub-prime mortgage crisis of that began in 2007 and lasted into 2009, the United States found itself in what became known as the Great Recession. The Great Recession led to the collapse of the financial sector in the world economy. Domestically, certain banks in the United States were bailed out by the government.

497. (C) During the Clinton administration, a 1993 deficit reduction plan was created to accomplish smaller budget deficits each year; at the same time, the United States experienced a strong economic growth. Under these conditions, the Clinton administration and congressional Republicans developed a budget agreement in 1997 that allowed the federal government to experience the first budget surplus since the 1960s.

498. (A) Between 2001 and 2003 the administration of George W. Bush passed a series of tax cuts that included the Economic Growth and Tax Relief Reconciliation Act of 2001 (EGTRRA) and the Jobs and Growth Tax Relief Reconciliation Act of 2003 (JGTRRA). Many critics believed that these actions undid the surplus that was created by the Clinton administration in its budget compromise with the Republican-led congress. The Troubled Asset Relief Program or (TARP) was a program created by the Presidency of George W. Bush and continued by the Obama administration to address the sub-prime mortgage crisis. In this program the government purchases what were called toxic assets to strengthen its financial sector. The Affordable Care Act was signed into law on March 23, 2010. This act became a signature policy of the Obama administration and was the largest reform and expansion of the healthcare system in the United States since the passage of Medicare and Medicaid.

499. **(B)** Following the events of September 11th, the United States sent its military forces into Afghanistan and Iraq. While there was strong evidence that Afghanistan offered a safe haven for members of Al Qaeda and their leader, Osama bin Laden, the case for war in Iraq became extremely controversial. Later in his presidency, Obama was faced with additional problems with the Middle East, which included the Arab Spring, which started in Tunisia in the December of 2010. The event was marked by both violent and nonviolent protests and uprisings that spread through the region. One nation that was particularly impacted by the Arab Spring was Syria, which moved into a full civil war starting in the March of 2011 and continues to this day.

500. **(C)** The Obama administration successfully launched a Navy SEAL raid into Pakistan on May 2, 2011, where the founder of Al Qaeda was captured and killed. Previously, Saddam Hussein was captured and publicly executed on charges of crimes against humanity by the Iraqi Special Tribunal. The execution took place on December 30, 2006, during the Bush administration. Though the Obama administration attempted to deescalate U.S. involvement in both Iraq and Afghanistan, U.S. troops continued to be deployed in those regions well after the end of his presidency. Furthermore, President Obama was not successful in closing the prison at Guantanamo Bay.

BIBLIOGRAPHY

Alderman, Ellen, and Caroline Kennedy. *In Our Defense: The Bill of Rights in Action.* New York: Avon, 1991.

Ayers, Edward L. *American Passages: A History of the United States.* Vol. 1: To 1877. Fort Worth: Harcourt College, 2000.

Cayton, Andrew R. L., and Elisabeth I. Perry. *America: Pathways to the Present.* Boston: Pearson/Prentice Hall, 2007.

Davidson, James West. *Nation of Nations: A Concise Narrative of the American Republic.* New York: McGraw-Hill, 1996.

Ellis, Elisabeth Gaynor, and Anthony Esler. *World History: Connections to Today.* Upper Saddle River, NJ: Prentice Hall, 1997.

Hall, Kermit, David Scott Clark, James W. Ely, Joel B. Grossman, and N. Hull. *The Oxford Guide to American Law.* Oxford: Oxford University Press, 2002.

Jordan, Winthrop D., Miriam Greenblatt, and John S. Bowes. *The Americans: A History.* Evanston, IL: McDougal Littell/Houghton Mifflin, 1996.

Kennedy, David M., Lizabeth Cohen, and Thomas Andrew Bailey. *The American Pageant: A History of the American People.* Boston: Wadsworth Cengage Learning, 2010.

LaFeber, Walter. *America, Russia, and the Cold War, 1945–1996.* New York: McGraw-Hill, 1997.

O'Neill, William L. *A Democracy at War: America's Fight at Home and Abroad in World War II.* Cambridge, MA: Harvard University Press, 1995.

Stokesbury, James L. *A Short History of World War I.* New York: Morrow, 1981.

Tindall, George Brown, and David E. Shi. *America: A Narrative History.* New York: W. W. Norton, 1993.